COPING WITH CRISIS

FUJI CONFERENCE SERIES VI

COPING WITH CRISIS
International Financial Institutions in the Interwar Period

Edited by

MAKOTO KASUYA

OXFORD
UNIVERSITY PRESS

OXFORD

UNIVERSITY PRESS

Great Clarendon Street, Oxford OX2 6DP

Oxford University Press is a department of the University of Oxford.
It furthers the University's objective of excellence in research, scholarship,
and education by publishing worldwide in

Oxford New York

Auckland Bangkok Buenos Aires Cape Town Chennai
Dar es Salaam Delhi Hong Kong Istanbul Karachi Kolkata
Kuala Lumpur Madrid Melbourne Mexico City Mumbai Nairobi
São Paulo Shanghai Taipei Tokyo Toronto

Oxford is a registered trade mark of Oxford University Press
in the UK and in certain other countries

Published in the United States
by Oxford University Press Inc., New York

© The various contributors 2003

The moral rights of the author have been asserted
Database right Oxford University Press (maker)

First published 2003

British Library Cataloguing in Publication Data

Data available

Library of Congress Cataloging in Publication Data

International Conference on Business History (26th : 2000 : Fuji, Japan)
Coping with crisis : International financial institutions in the interwar period
edited by Makoto Kasuya.
p. cm.
1. Financial institutions, International—History—20th century—Congresses.   2. Banks
and banking, International—History—20th century—Congresses.   I. Kasuya, Makoto.
II. Title.
HG3881 .I5754   2000   332.1'09'042–dc21   2002035557
ISBN 0–19–925931–3

1 3 5 7 9 10 8 6 4 2

Typeset by Newgen Imaging Systems (P) Ltd., Chennai, India
Printed in Great Britain
on acid-free paper by
T.J. International Ltd., Padstow, Cornwall

ACKNOWLEDGEMENTS

All the papers in this book were presented at the twenty-sixth International Conference on Business History, held from the eighth to the eleventh of September 2000 at the foot of Mt Fuji. The Conference, held every January for the twenty-five years from 1974 to 1998 with the generous financial assistance of the Taniguchi Foundation, became known throughout the world as the 'Fuji Conference'. The Foundation was dissolved after the death of its head, Mr Yuichiro Taniguchi, but because of a generous donation it left to the Business History Society of Japan, the Society decided to keep holding the Conference once every two or three years on the basis of the donation.

The organizing committee of the Conference, chaired by Professor Etsuo Abe, decided to entrust Makoto Kasuya with the work of organizing the twenty-sixth Conference around the theme of 'Business History of Financial Institutions'. As the Japanese economy had experienced financial crises in the second half of the 1990s, Kasuya decided it would be good to investigate how financial institutions reacted during financial crises in the interwar period. The topic of financial institutions had never before been taken up at any of the previous twenty-five International Conferences.

Financial assistance was received from the Nomura Foundation for Social Science to invite a presenter to the twenty-sixth Conference. Kasuya and the entire organizing committee would like to express their sincere appreciation for the assistance given by both the Taniguchi Foundation and the Nomura Foundation for Social Science.

In addition to nine authors (Wixforth did not attend), twelve distinguished scholars were present at the Conference as commentators and guests. They were: Etsuo Abe, Yoshiko Hiraki, Masako Kurohane, Yurio Mukai, Kiyoshi Nikami, Junko Nishikawa, Shizuya Nishimura, Yuji Nishimuta, Toshio Suzuki, Kazuhiko Yago, Hiroaki Yamazaki, and Takau Yoneyama. The papers in this book were revised in accordance with points raised and suggestions made during the Conference. The editor would like to thank all those who attended for their active participation and valuable contributions.

International conferences require much administrative and secretarial support, and such support was provided by Tetsuro Hattori, Eijiro Igari, and Fumiko Takeda. Without their tireless efforts, the Conference would not have been as effective as it was. Two scholars, Azumi Ann Takata and Tohru Yoshikawa, acted as interpreters at the Conference and helped ensure smooth communication among the participants. Edmund R. Skrzypczak served as copy editor for the present volume; his diligent support and expert advice greatly facilitated the publication of this book. Last but not least, the editor would like to express his gratitude to the many business historians, not mentioned above, who helped him in many ways.

M. K.

CONTENTS

PART III. INSURANCE AND SECURITIES

LIST OF FIGURES

LIST OF TABLES

LIST OF ABBREVIATIONS

C
CEF   Constructions Électriques de France
CFCT   Compagnie Française des Câbles Télégraphiques
CFP   Compagnie Française des Pétroles
CNEP   Comptoir National d'Escompte de Paris
CNF   Chantiers Navals Français
CSF   Compagnie Générale de Télégraphie Sans Fil

D
DLI   Daiichi Mutual Life Insurance Co.

E
EEC   English Electric Company

F
FDIC   Federal Deposit Insurance Corporation

I
IBJ   Industrial Bank of Japan

J
JBHI   Japan Business History Institute
JLICA   Japan Life Insurance Companies Association

K
KCS   Kanegafuchi Cotton Spinning Company

L
LICA   Life Insurance Control Association
LICCA   Life Insurance Central Control Association

M
MCI   Ministry of Commerce and Industry
MHA   Ministry of Home Affairs
MITI   Ministry of International Trade and Industry
MOF   Ministry of Finance
MRISEH   Mitsui Research Institute for Social and Economic History

N
NSC   Nomura Securities Co.
NYSE   New York Stock Exchange

O
OCC   Office of the Comptroller of the Currency
OTC   Over-the-Counter

R
RFC   Reconstruction Finance Corporation

S
SEC   Securities and Exchange Commission

T
TSE   Tokyo Stock Exchange

NOTES ON CONTRIBUTORS

MAE BAKER is a Senior Lecturer in Finance and Accounting at Leeds University Business School.

ERIC BUSSIÈRE is a Professor of History at the University of Paris IV—Sorbonne.

YOUSSEF CASSIS is a Professor of History at the University of Grenoble II and a Visiting Research Fellow in the Business History Unit at the London School of Economics.

MICHAEL COLLINS is a Professor at Leeds University Business School.

MAKOTO KASUYA is an Associate Professor of Business History in the Faculty of Economics, the University of Tokyo.

SHINJI OGURA is a Professor in the Faculty of Commerce and Economics, Chiba University of Commerce.

EDWIN J. PERKINS is an Emeritus Professor of History of the University of Southern California.

MARIKO TATSUKI is a Professor in the Faculty of Humanities, Keisen University.

EUGENE N. WHITE is a Professor in the Department of Economics, Rutgers University.

HARALD WIXFORTH is a Research Fellow at the Hannal-Arendt Institute.

1

Introduction

MAKOTO KASUYA

Issues in Finance during the Interwar Period

In November 1997 Hokkaido Takushoku Bank, one of the top twenty Japanese city banks, and Yamaichi Securities, one of the four major Japanese securities firms, both declared bankruptcy. Since then, failures of large commercial banks and life insurance companies have become commonplace in Japan. Many critics blame this phenomenon on the burst of the 'economic bubble' of the late 1980s and early 1990s and the intense competition resulting from financial deregulation. Deregulation of the financial sector began in the 1970s in the United States and became a worldwide phenomenon with the 1986 'Big Bang' reforms in the United Kingdom. With the development of computer technology, the traditional boundaries that have existed between banking, securities, and insurance have become blurred. Now financial institutions compete not only within traditionally defined industry sectors but also against financial institutions in other sectors. Companies in different industries are beginning to form cooperative groups, or to merge into single organizations on a worldwide scale. Given these conditions, the strategic moves of financial institutions have become particularly important to assure their survival and growth.

From a historical perspective, the thorough regulation of the finance sector in many countries began in response to various financial crises of the interwar period, particularly the problems associated with the worldwide depression of the 1930s. Prior to the First World War, little government regulation existed, such that the regulatory conditions surrounding financial institutions at that time were somewhat similar to what they are at the present day. The gold standard, however, was one important institutional element that no longer exists today. As nations returned to the gold standard after the First World War and their economies stabilized, the capital needs of private companies increased. This increased demand for financial services led to the growth of financial institutions. Since there were virtually no regulations separating the various financial activities, banks and securities firms often competed against each other in providing underwriting services, while cooperating in the distribution of securities. Thus, different types of financial institutions simultaneously competed against each other and complemented each other, depending on the type of transactions involved.

With the Great Depression, failures of financial institutions increased dramatically, and governments introduced regulations in an attempt to stabilize the financial sector. The interwar period was a time of great change for financial institutions. How did financial institutions respond to the changing business climate? To what extent did the management of financial institutions understand these changes, and what strategies did they implement in response to these changes? More specifically, what decisions did managers make, and how did organizations change structurally and functionally? The purpose of this book is to consider these questions through a comparative examination of the United Kingdom, Germany, the United States, France, and Japan.

Financial Architecture

In order to make this comparison meaningful, it is necessary to take into consideration what the nature of competition was among the various financial institutions within each country. This is important, since, even today, considerable differences exist among nations in the division of labour between banks and securities firms. Broadly speaking, the concept of financial architecture refers to the division of labour among different financial institutions. To understand how different financial architectures arose, we begin with a consideration of the reasons behind the differences in the nature of competition.

The fundamental purpose of financial institutions is to act as intermediaries for savings and investments. As an intermediary between those with surplus funds looking for investment opportunities and those with capital requirements looking for investors, financial institutions serve to reduce the costs of transactions and the risks of investment for potential investors. Financial institutions are able to do so by providing monitoring and risk diversification, which are difficult for investors to achieve individually. Financial institutions screen borrowers when they apply for loans, then monitor them until funds are recovered completely. Screening and monitoring both involve economies of scale; thus, financial institutions can reduce the social cost of information gathering. Second, by pooling the funds of many investors together, intermediaries can invest in many more opportunities than a single investor can. By diversifying their portfolio, financial institutions can reduce the risk borne by individual depositors. Moreover, since a bank's capital is pooled with depositors' funds in investment and repayment of deposits has priority to that of the bank's capital, the bank can reduce depositors' risk. By simultaneously making loans and providing a variety of deposit products, banks also increase the liquidity of depositors. In addition to brokering money, banks play a central role in the diffusion of transactions by using notes and cheques that reduce the costs of settlements. These are the *raison d'être* of financial institutions.

Financial institutions can be divided into two groups: banks that sell their own debt as products, or indirect securities (e.g. deposits and bank debentures) to ultimate lenders (usually households) and buy primary securities (e.g. corporate bonds and bills) issued by ultimate borrowers (usually firms); and securities firms that broker the sale of primary securities.[1] Banks may be further divided into those that issue primarily long-term debt and those that issue primarily short-term debt. In addition, insurance companies perform some financial functions through issuing insurance policies. Various functions of these financial institutions are not necessarily specific to a particular type of institution, and financial architecture refers to how different types of financial institutions are allocated rights to enter different activities. Furthermore, financial architecture differs by nation and over time, and is governed by legal and regulatory differences, borrower reputations, and the time horizon of investors.

The first differentiating factor is the difference in regulatory structures set by law and regulation.[2] Regulations prohibiting banks from setting up branches or owning stocks, for example, have a significant influence on the division of labour among financial institutions. The nature of the central bank, as an institution, has a similar impact. For instance, the nature of private financial institutions will differ considerably depending on whether the central bank has a large network of branches that lend funds directly to private firms, or whether the central bank functions as a bankers' bank. Even if the central bank does not lend directly to private firms, it may provide funds transfers through a large network of branches. Provision of such services, in turn, affects the development of private networks for funds transference and settlement as well as the composition of the money market.[3]

The second factor is the nature of borrowers and the extent to which they rely on different types of financial products. When the borrowers have strong reputations, they can issue securities in addition to borrowing from banks. Governments and major corporations fall into this category. Less-established medium and small enterprises have greater difficulty in issuing securities and are more reliant on bank loans. The strength of borrowers' reputations, from the central government to small business, has a strong impact on the financial architecture. Furthermore, organizations that are highly creditworthy are able to obtain funds not only domestically but also from foreign financial institutions and securities markets. Of course, inter-national transactions involve foreign exchange risks and require the col-lection of information on foreign economic conditions, increasing the likelihood that domestic and international transactions will be handled by different organizations. Thus, the extent to which borrowers have access to foreign markets also affects the financial architecture. Moreover, a flow of funds into one nation implies a flow of funds out of another nation; thus, international transactions can be potentially handled by financial institu-tions of either the exporting nation or of the importing nation. International competition between financial institutions of different countries for these transactions, as well as the level of international activity in general, affects the financial architecture.[4]

The third factor is differences in the time horizon of funds for both bor-rowers and lenders. The composition of financial institutions varies con-siderably depending on whether the supply of funds is long-term or short-term and whether the demand for funds is long-term or short-term. Since the nature of screening for risk differs depending on the term of the loan, financial institutions cannot readily diversify their mixture of long- and short-term loans. The time horizon of funds depends, in part, on the sophistication of the nation's financial market; the more developed the market is, the more likely it is that long-term funds, for example, those invested overseas, will exist.

With regard to the supply of long-term funds, the role played by stocks and bonds has been more important historically than loans from banks. The role of banks in the provision of long-term funds can be sorted by the degree to which banking and securities activities are separated. On the one extreme, the two activities can be almost completely separable, as in the case of the United Kingdom, while on the other, there was the universal bank model of Germany, where banks engaged in both activities.[5] In those countries where banking and securities activities were separated, how-ever, deposit banks were able to issue corporate bonds, and this provided a way to liquidate outstanding loans. The extent of bank participation in underwriting, selling, and holding bonds varied considerably by nation and over time. In addition, as insurance companies and savings banks became holders of stocks and bonds, the methods by which securities were distributed became quite different from those distribution systems based primarily on individual ownership.

Changes in Financial Architecture during the Interwar Period

There were five major factors that led to changes in financial architecture during the interwar period.

The first factor was the impact of inflation. During and after the First World War, major European countries, including France and Germany, experienced significant inflation, whereas other countries did not. While the real value of financial assets declined due to inflation, the impact of this decline on financial institutions varied.

The second factor was economies of scale and the resulting consolidation of financial institutions. With mergers of banks and the failure of many small and medium banks, the banking industry in many countries became increasingly oligopolistic in most countries except the United States. Bank mergers increased the number of bank branches per bank, and this led to the emergence of banks with national networks of branches.

Third, governments had issued large amounts of bonds during the First World War for war-related expenditures. These government bonds, many of which were in the hands of private citizens, became the foundation for a broadened securities sector. In addition to railroads, utility companies—such as those providing electricity, gas, telegraph, and telephone services—began to issue stocks and bonds in large quantities. As large industrial enterprises became the norm in many countries, the stocks and bonds of these companies also entered the market. Moreover, as the markets for these securities became more organized, the trading of stocks and bonds increased.

Fourth, the variety of financial institutions increased with the accumulation of financial assets. As per capita income increased, accumulation of financial assets progressed, even among the lower-income classes. An increasing number of middle- and low-income households began to deposit their funds in savings banks, which were often governmental or quasi-governmental in nature, rather than in commercial banks. As families began to accumulate financial assets, however, they chose from a wider variety of financial products. The percentage of families that owned securities—such as stocks, government bonds, and corporate bonds—as well as various forms of insurance increased over the period. Savings banks, insurance companies, securities brokerages, and investment banks developed under these conditions.

Fifth, the regulation of financial institutions increased worldwide with the Great Depression. The introduction of new regulations changed the conditions under which financial institutions competed, and this in turn led to significant changes in financial architecture.

Financial Regulations Introduced during
the Interwar Period

Financial regulations were tightened in all countries during the interwar period, though the extent of the regulations differed from country to country. In this section, we briefly survey how and why these regulations were introduced.

It might be said that financial regulations were implemented in an attempt to maintain public trust in money. Historically, governments have always enforced strict control over the issuance of coinage. Once banks began to issue notes, however, maintaining the public trust became essential. In the United States, the National Banking Act of 1864 contained very strict regulations on the issuance of currency by banks. On the other hand, in the United Kingdom, although regulations governing banknotes were strict, rules applying to commercial bank activities (such as loans and cheques) were virtually nonexistent. However, with the enactment of the Bank Charter Act of 1844, the circulation of banknotes other than those of the Bank of England diminished. Because the Bank of England was under the strict control of such acts, regulations actually played an important role in maintaining public confidence in banknotes.

Over time, as notes and cheques became common instruments for payments and debt settlements, people began to treat bank deposits as readily available money. With the rise in average household income over the period, the number of households with bank deposits increased. Given these conditions, the regulation of deposit banks became necessary for maintaining public trust in money and protecting depositors, and some governments began to institute bank regulations. In many countries, however, much of the bank regulations of the time were implemented in direct response to the sharp rise in bank failures before and during the Great Depression. Accordingly, in both the United States and Germany, where the impact of the Great Depression on the status of banks was the greatest, the regulations were the strictest. On the other hand, in the United Kingdom and France, where the effects of the Great Depression were comparatively less seriously felt, governments implemented little or virtually no additional regulation. In Japan, stricter regulation had been implemented in 1928, just prior to the Great Depression.

Bank regulations introduced during this period can be broadly divided into three types. The first was the protection of deposits through the reduction of risk factors. This type of regulation applied to the ratio of capital to total assets, the concentration of loans, and deposit reserves within banks. Deposit insurance, as a measure for protecting deposits, might also be included in this group, even though it does not necessarily directly improve the financial health of banks.

The second type of regulation sought to protect deposits by limiting competition. These limitations increased the profitability of financial institutions and provided them with financial stability. This type of regulation included regulations on interest rates and the establishment of bank branches. The establishment of new financial institutions or branches required governmental approval, such that the regulatory agency could limit competition through the approval or disapproval process.

The third type of regulation sought to control the range of activities that various types of financial institutions were allowed to perform. The most typical regulation of this type prohibited banks from conducting securities-related activities. When economies of scope are possible through the combining of banking and securities activities, however, it is somewhat difficult to defend such regulations as a means of protecting deposits.

Of course, not all these types of regulation were implemented in all nations. Of the three types just described, the third type had the most direct impact on financial architecture. The most complete implementation of this type of regulation took place only in the United States. With respect to the second type, regulation of interest rates affected the share of deposits held by various financial institutions. For instance, if the interest rates for commercial banks were regulated but those for savings banks were not, the commercial banks' share of deposits would decline. On the other hand, if interest rates of all financial institutions were regulated, the relative strengths of various types of financial institutions tended to be stabilized. Moreover, if interest rates were regulated tightly, such regulation also acted to influence the securities market.

During the 1930s, as nations went off the gold standard, regulatory agencies gained greater power in imposing financial policies. As a result, governments also had more latitude in setting interest rate targets, and regulatory agencies intensified the regulation of interest rates, which had previously been managed through self-regulation among banks through the operation of a cartel. In the United Kingdom, where the banking sector was concentrated in a few firms, the role of the cartel was relatively large, while the role of the regulating agency was more informal in nature. As deregulation of the financial sector began in the 1970s, the second and third types of regulations were gradually removed. Some of the regulations of the first type, however, such as the ratio of capital to total assets, have instead been strengthened in order to foster market discipline.

Financial Architecture in Five Countries

In this section, we examine briefly the changes in financial architecture during the interwar period in five countries: the United Kingdom,

Germany, the United States, France, and Japan. For each country we begin with an examination of the division of labour among different types of financial institutions, the clientele that each type served, and the changes in their relative strengths during this period. Second, we consider changes in government regulation of the financial sector and how these changes affected the financial architecture in each country. Last, we consider the impact of changes in macroeconomic conditions, particularly the effects of inflation.

The United Kingdom[6]

The financial market of the city of London was segmented, such that British commercial banks did not undertake securities activities. From the turn of the century, commercial banks gradually moved into the foreign exchange and the acceptance business. Some British commercial banks set up overseas subsidiaries during this period. Merger activity, which continued until 1918, consolidated the commercial banking industry into five major banks: Barclays Bank, Lloyds Bank, National Provincial Bank, Westminster Bank, and Midland Bank. The government then restricted further mergers between banks.

While these five banks already had a wide network of branches at the beginning of this period, each sought to widen its network further. The London clearing banks determined the interest rates for deposits and loans on the basis of the Bank of England's discount rate, and thus they did not compete on interest rates. In terms of asset allocation, commercial banks increased the purchase of government bonds and treasury bills during the interwar period. In terms of their relationship with industry, there was a longstanding debate on whether the primary factor behind the lack of lending activity at the time was the banks' supply of funds or the industry's demand for funds.[7] The supply side argument is that British commercial banks concentrated on short-term financing, preferring to stay away from management issues within industrial firms. On the other hand, those on the demand side argue that it is unreasonable to assume that financial institutions completely ignored opportunities for profit making. The mechanism for supplying funds to industrial firms was adequate since the securities market was active. Proponents of this argument thus conclude that the demand for long-term loans on the part of industrial firms was weak.

The British financial system was quite stable during the Great Depression, with virtually no bank failures. This absence of bank failures can be attributed to the easier consolidation of the banking industry, the concentration of bank activities to short-term commercial activities, and the high proportion of government bonds and treasury bills in bank assets. It could be said that the managerial strategy of British banks contributed to the stability of banks through the Great Depression.

Discount houses earned their profits by borrowing at call or at short notice from commercial banks and by purchasing commercial bills and treasury bills. During the interwar years, treasury bills became the central part of their investment portfolios, with some investment also in government bonds. By the 1930s, however, with the implementation of a low-interest-rate policy, the interest rate on treasury bills fell. The call rate remained stable because it was determined by mutual agreement among clearing banks. As the treasury bill interest rate fell below the call rate, the discount houses became less profitable. In 1935, the Bank of England interceded and the commercial banks and discount houses agreed to lower the call rate and not to compete against each other in the purchasing of treasury bills. Consequently, the control of the Bank of England over the short-term money market increased.

Merchant banks specialized in issuing securities, especially foreign securities, and accepting foreign trade bills. For a number of reasons, however, the issuance of foreign bonds and the acceptance of foreign trade bills both diminished during the interwar period. First, the role of the US dollar as an international currency rose; consequently, the international role of pound sterling diminished. Second, the government tightened informal controls on the flotation of foreign bonds in London. Finally, trading activity in general fell with the Great Depression. In response to these changes, merchant banks expanded into other activities, such as the issuance of securities for domestic firms and the trading of stocks and foreign currency for arbitrage. Both foreign and colonial banks also played an important role in international finance.

While building societies, the Post Office Savings Bank, trustee savings banks, and insurance companies all rapidly increased their business during the interwar period, commercial banks did not increase their deposits by very much. One main reason for the difference in the growth rates was that the commercial banks maintained a common low interest rate on deposits and a relatively uncompetitive high rate on loans. Also, as average household incomes rose, households began to invest in a wider variety of financial products.[8] During the building boom of the interwar period, building societies provided funds to households through mortgages.

Germany[9]

German commercial banks could be divided into large metropolitan banks, regional banks, and private bankers. All of these banks were universal banks, which provided short-term banking, capital market operations, broker services, and property management. The proportion of securities in their total assets was not very high. The large Berlin banks lent to industrial firms and recovered their loans by assisting the industrial firms in the issuance of securities. They monitored the industrial firms by holding their shares and exercising their trust voting rights (*Depotstimmrecht*), and by sending their directors to firms' auditors' meetings (*Aufsichtsräte*).

After the stabilization of the Deutsche mark in 1924, the large Berlin banks began to face competition from foreign banks. Competition arose because of the high interest rates in Germany and the consequent slump in the capital market, which, in turn, pushed the German industrial firms into floating bonds in the United Kingdom and the United States. Moreover, large industrial firms set up their own investment companies and in-house banks, and the relationship between the large Berlin banks and large industrial firms weakened. During the 1920s the dispatch of bank directors to industrial firms' *Aufsichtsräte* increased; since industrial firms accepted auditors from multiple banks, this did not necessarily mean that the influence of individual banks over industrial firms increased.

The large Berlin banks improved their branch network by acquiring regional banks, and large banks merged amongst themselves. The result was the formation of the Danatbank in 1921, and the Deutsche Bank und Discontogesellschaft in 1929. But these larger institutions were not necessarily stronger. By the late 1920s the ratio of capital to total assets of the large Berlin banks had fallen from their pre-First World War levels as a result of inflation. The increase in deposits over the period came mainly from overseas, while the proportion of liquid assets had also fallen. These conditions made the banks especially vulnerable to the withdrawal of foreign funds.

With the onset of the Great Depression, foreign funds were withdrawn and the large Berlin banks faced a crisis. The Danat Bank failed in 1931. The government brought the crisis under control by declaring all banks closed and by temporarily purchasing, together with a subsidiary of the Reichsbank, most of the shares of the large Berlin banks. After the bank crisis, the government tightened banking regulations. It introduced restrictions on large loans, new liquidity rules and reserve requirements, a government approval process for the establishment of new banks, and government control over the setting of interest rates. Despite these regulations, during the 1930s deposits at the large Berlin banks increased little. Industrial firms obtained financing from other sources, while their relationship with the large Berlin banks continued to weaken.

In addition to foreign banks, savings banks also competed with the large Berlin banks. Although savings banks were disadvantaged during the period of inflation because their deposits were primarily long-term in nature, they increased their share of deposits after the stabilization of the

Deutsche mark. This growth in the share of deposits at savings banks was due, in part, to the interest rate cartel of the commercial banks. In 1928 commercial banks and savings banks agreed to form a cartel. This is why the interest rate regulation of the 1930s included savings banks as well. Earlier, in 1908, savings banks had been granted permission to engage in funds transfer services, and by 1921 the government had removed most of the specific regulations concerning their operation. Prior to the First World War savings banks had established special institutions (*Girozentrale*) to centrally manage their funds transfer services, and the functions of these institutions were strengthened during the interwar period. The *Girozentrale* performed interregional settlement as well as lending to public bodies. In 1931 savings banks were given full legal personhood. By the 1930s savings banks had come to operate as regional universal banks largely catering to a broad middle-class clientele, and this status brought the saving banks under the tightened governmental regulation and oversight of the period.

Cooperative banks were local universal banks that mainly serviced farmers, independent craftsmen, and shopkeepers. Like the savings banks, these banks also operated special centralized institutions, the role of which also increased during the interwar period. In addition to these savings and cooperative bank institutions, many state banks also took deposits and made loans to industry.

Furthermore, the Reichsbank itself discounted notes of large industrial enterprises directly, as well as providing funds to agriculture and industry through its subsidiaries. The Reichsbank also performed a wide range of funds transfer and settlement services.

The United States[10]

The American commercial banks were under the dual system of federal and state charters. Besides commercial banks, trust companies (which were regulated by states) also conducted commercial banking activities. Federally chartered banks were under strict regulations, including those that limited large loans, required reserves for note issue and deposits, and discouraged real estate loans. Federally chartered banks were required to participate in the Federal Reserve System, but participation was voluntary for state-chartered banks and trust companies. Member banks maintained an interest-free reserve with their Federal Reserve Banks. The Reserve Banks provided clearing and collection services for their members, although this did not eliminate a separate system of private clearinghouses.

Generally speaking, state-chartered banks were not as tightly regulated as federally chartered banks. In some states, banks had been permitted to open branch offices; in 1927, federally chartered banks were permitted to open branches within the same city as the main offices, in states where state-chartered banks were allowed branches. Since branches were limited, the United States had an extremely large number of independent banks. Although the numbers were declining slowly, the United States had over 23,000 banks in 1929. Many local and regional banks were linked to New York banks through correspondence agreements. These smaller banks often sent their excess deposits to their big city correspondents, and they, in turn, put these funds to work in the securities market in the form of call loans.

Investment banks originated, underwrote, and distributed securities. Although federally chartered banks were prohibited from performing securities activities, they established investment bank subsidiaries in the early twentieth century, which, in effect, enabled them to perform such activities. Investment banks differed in their range of activities and specialization. For example, J. P. Morgan concentrated on originating and underwriting bonds, while National City Company provided a comprehensive service ranging from origination to retail sales.[11] During the 1920s numerous corporations began to issue securities in large numbers. At the same time, more foreign securities were issued in New York, which became an international financial market. Issues of common stocks increased dramatically toward the end of the 1920s, and the volume of stock trading soared.

With the stock market crash in October 1929 and the Great Depression that followed, bank failures skyrocketed. In 1933 banks were closed temporarily after the declaration of a bank holiday. In response to the financial crisis, the federal government tightened the regulation of financial institutions. Banking and securities operations were separated, interest rates were controlled, and the Federal Deposit Insurance Corporation was established. Although federally chartered banks were allowed to establish branches like state-chartered banks, branches across state lines were prohibited. Disclosure requirements for securities at the time of issuance were strengthened. This led to an increase in private issues and term loans. However, the transparency of the securities market increased with positive effects over the long run.

During the 1920s and 1930s insurance companies increased their funds at a faster pace than bank deposits, and their role as an institutional investor in the securities markets increased. In addition, the volume of mortgages increased. On the other hand, the amount of funds invested in mutual savings banks and savings and loans associations was not significant, and these institutions' share of deposits relative to banks did not change during this period.

France[12]

French banks can be divided into five groups: the four major deposit banks (Crédit Lyonnais, Société Générale, Comptoir National d'Escompte de Paris, Crédit Industriel et Commercial), investment banks or *banques d'affaires* (Paribas, Banque de l'Union Parisienne), metropolitan universal banks,[13] regional universal banks, and local universal banks. Inflation from the end of the First World War to the stabilization of the French franc in 1926 caused a massive flight of funds, and only with the stabilization of the currency did the funds return to France. However, with the onset of the worldwide depression, bank deposits decreased as capital again fled the country.

Deposit banks had established branches nationwide prior to the First World War and continued to improve their branch networks during the interwar period. Rather than acquiring local banks, they chose to open their own branches. Rediscounting of notes to Banque de France became negligible. Deposit banks invested their funds primarily in short-term investments. Instead of dealing with industrial firms, they began to establish subsidiaries that provided medium-term loans to industrial firms. At the same time, large industrial firms, such as electric power companies, established their own financial subsidiaries for raising funds. Thus, deposit banks did not have a close relationship with industrial enterprises. Because of these investment policies, French deposit banks did not face a serious crisis during the Great Depression; however, by the middle of the 1930s, deposits had begun to decline. This decline was partly due to the transfer of funds overseas. Universal banks provided long-term financing to business firms. Some universal banks increased the scale of their operation through mergers, but many of them failed during the Great Depression in the face of the large withdrawal of deposits.

The international activities of investment banks declined after the First World War. During the inflationary period, securities underwriting by the investment banks decreased, while savings and loans activities increased. The issuance of securities expanded again after the stabilization of the currency. Because Paribas liquidated its loans by issuing corporate securities for its indebted clients, it survived the Great Depression. On the other hand, Banque de l'Union Parisienne, whose activities were more concentrated in savings and loans, had to be rescued by the Banque de France. Investment banks competed against deposit banks in underwriting bonds. Since investment banks did not have branches, they depended on deposit banks and country banks for retail distribution of securities. On the other hand, deposit banks did not underwrite stocks, but sold stocks underwritten by investment banks. While deposit banks and investment banks simultaneously competed against each other in underwriting bonds, they complemented each other with respect to the retail distribution of stocks and bonds.

Savings banks and postal savings banks increased their deposits during the 1930s. These banks deposited their funds into Caisse des Dépôts et Consignations, which provided them with confidence backed by the national government. This enabled them to offer relatively high interest rates in comparison with other types of banks, and it allowed them to increase their deposits.

Banque de France had an extensive network of branches throughout the nation, through which they lent funds directly to industrial firms. It also provided funds transfer services, which played a large role in funds settlement.

Japan[14]

Japanese commercial banks can be divided into city banks, regional banks, and local banks. City banks, with main offices in Tokyo or Osaka, conducted their business primarily with large industrial enterprises, underwrote corporate bonds, and provided foreign exchange services. In contrast, regional banks operated only within a single region and did not conduct business with large firms. The establishment of new banks, the opening of bank branches, and mergers required governmental approval. During the 1920s the government actively recommended bank mergers. However, it did not welcome the expansion of city banks into the periphery through the acquisition of local banks. Rather, it promoted the merger of local banks in the same area to form larger entities. With the establishment of a minimum capital requirement in the Bank Law of 1927, 617 commercial banks (out of 1,283 in existence in 1928) were forced to increase their capital or to merge. Since the government rarely approved capitalization increases, these banks were forced to merge. Consequently, the number of commercial banks had fallen to 683 by 1932.

In addition, there were government-related banks such as the Yokohama Specie Bank, which specialized in financing foreign trade, and the Industrial Bank of Japan, which specialized in providing long-term financing through bond issues. The roles of these organizations increased as government control of the finance sector tightened.

When new companies were established, founders usually sought share subscribers through kinship, regional, and other ties rather than through selling shares on the open market. Additional shares from capitalization increases were usually assigned to existing shareholders. Occasionally, when share prices were high, securities firms underwrote a stock issue, but for the most part securities firms participated in new share issues only through the handling of subscription requests.

The portfolio of financial assets increased in variety during the 1920s in Japan, as in other countries. Funds committed to life insurance and in trust companies increased at a faster pace than those of commercial banks. Life insurance companies invested mostly in securities and loans. During the 1920s most of the securities were corporate bonds; investment in stocks increased gradually in the 1930s. Thus, as institutional investors life insurance companies played a large role in the development of the Japanese securities market. The designated joint operating trust, of which funds were used mainly for the purchase of bills and bonds, was the main product of the trust companies. They competed against term deposits offered by commercial banks, and they succeeded in increasing their share of funds through offering high rates of return.

The depression of 1920 resulted in the fall of securities and real estate values. Japanese banks were left with a large amount of bad debt, and many failed. In 1927 a large-scale run on banks began with the failure of the Bank of Taiwan. The government responded by declaring a three-week moratorium on the payment of debts. This crisis resulted in a dramatic shift of deposits from medium and small banks to large city banks, large trust companies, and postal savings. Funds deposited in postal savings accounts grew at twice the pace of commercial banks between 1925 and 1935. Private savings banks, which were required by law to invest only in relatively safe products such as government bonds, increased their deposits. In the rural areas, agricultural cooperatives also increased their deposits. The government's bank merger policy was a response to the medium and small banks that lost out in this fund shift.

During the 1930s the government tightened control over foreign exchange. Moreover, the Bank of Japan increased its influence in the period of economic recovery following upon the Great Depression. It guided interest rates lower by purchasing government bonds directly from the government. The Bank of Japan supported an interest rate cartel of commercial banks. With the interest rates guided lower, the value of loan collateral rose and the financial stability of banks improved.

The Organization of This Book

The purpose of this book is to analyse, in an international comparison, the behaviour of financial institutions, their managers' strategies, and their implementation, given the financial architecture in each of five countries.[15]

First we take up the management of commercial banks. Industrial firms developed large-scale operations and professional managerial structures during this period. Did banks develop similar organizational structures? In Chapter 2 Cassis considers to what extent the large deposit banks in the United Kingdom, France, and Germany had developed professional managerial structures and how bank managers rose to their positions. He concludes that banks in these countries were in the process of transition from individual private bankers to organizations with professional management.

Next we take up commercial banks in the United Kingdom, the United States, and Japan. In Chapter 3 Collins and Baker demonstrate that British commercial banks were not heavily involved in lending to industrial firms and limited their activities to holding government bonds and treasury bills and lending short-term funds. As a result, the British banking system was relatively stable for most of this period. In the United States, banking regulation put in place during the New Deal prohibited banks from securities operations. Commercial banks responded by increasing long-term loans. White shows in Chapter 4 that, although this increased the maturity mismatch, interest rate stability in the immediate postwar period limited any problems from increased exposure to risk. In Chapter 5 Ogura examines Mitsui Bank, one of the major commercial banks of prewar Japan. He shows the transformation of Mitsui Bank operations during the interwar period from active securities operations and short-term loans to limited securities operations as a result of government regulations and expansion of syndicated loans.

We next consider universal banks. In Chapter 6, Bussière examines the case of Paribas, a French *banque d'affaires*, or investment bank. In response to the decline of its international business and the securities market in France after the First World War, Paribas expanded its deposit and loan activities, developed close ties with industrial firms, and moved into universal banking. With the rejuvenation of the securities market after the stabilization of the French franc, however, Paribas reduced its loans by selling them off through securities issuance; this policy enabled Paribas to survive through the Depression. Bussière concludes that Paribas's subsequent move away from universal banking made its survival possible. Wixforth considers large banks in Germany in the 1920s in Chapter 7. German banks were financially weakened during this period by the reduction of the capital-to-asset ratio as a result of inflation, increased independence of industrial firms from banks, and competition from foreign banks. As Wixforth makes clear, this lack of financial strength made survival during the Depression difficult.

Finally, we take up insurance companies and securities firms. In Chapter 8 Tatsuki shows that large Japanese life insurance companies benefited from increasing government control over the economy and decreasing managerial independence. She also argues that Japanese life insurance companies continued to play a substantial role in the capital market well into the 1930s. In Chapter 9 Perkins examines the career of Charles Merrill, the founder of the stock brokerage firm, Merrill Lynch. Charles Merrill succeeded in developing a new business in selling growth stocks to middle-class customers. Merrill underwrote securities for many retail chain stores, including groceries and consumer nondurables. However, Merrill himself sold off almost all his stock holdings during the later stage of the bull market of the 1920s and was in semi-retirement during the 1930s. But Merrill returned to the brokerage business in 1940 after some years managing chain stores in the retail sector. Following the retail chain store model, he started a securities business with a national network of branches, targeting the upper middle class. Finally, Kasuya considers the development of Yamaichi Securities, one of the major Japanese securities firms, in Chapter 10. Although Yamaichi Securities gradually developed its underwriting activities, first selling corporate bonds underwritten by commercial banks, it was eventually pushed out of the underwriting business by pressures from bank cartels. When wartime controls limited stock placement to life insurance companies, Yamaichi Securities was stripped of growth opportunities.

Acknowledgement

I would like to thank Michael Collins, Ayako Ishizuka, Toshio Suzuki, Edwin J. Perkins, Eugene N. White, Stefan Worrall, and Kazuhiko Yago for providing me with helpful comments that improved this chapter greatly, and to Azumi Ann Takata for translating and editing this chapter's earlier version.

NOTES

1. John Gurley and Edward Shaw, *Money in a Theory of Finance* (Washington, DC: the Brookings Institution, 1960).
2. Of course, financial architecture can also be affected by whether regulations are written laws and rules, which are made public, or government decisions made on a case-by-case basis. In this case, differences in legal culture, which defines what constitutes government regulation, lead to differences in financial architecture.

3. There are instances, such as in the United Kingdom, when customs within the industry are maintained without formal regulations. Such customs can be interpreted as a form of cartel.

4. Of course the nature of lenders may also affect financial architecture. For example, as individuals buy insurance (especially life insurance) and become covered by pension plans, institutional investors such as life insurance companies and pension funds develop, and this changes the financial architecture.

5. There are, of course, long-standing debates as to the effectiveness of the German-style universal bank model in the economic development of late-developing economies, or in the rationalization of industry.

6. Michael Collins, *Money and Banking in the UK: A History* (London: Croom Helm, 1988); Stanley Chapman, *The Rise of Merchant Banking* (London: George Allen and Unwin, 1984); Stefanie Diaper, 'Merchant Banking in the Inter-War Period: The Case of Kleinwort Sons, & Co.', *Business History* 28/4 (1986), 55–76.

7. Michael Collins, *Banks and Industrial Finance in Britain, 1800–1939* (Cambridge: Cambridge University Press, 1995).

8. Forrest Capie, 'Commercial Banking in Britain between the Wars', in Charles H. Feinstein (ed.), *Banking, Currency, and Finance in Europe between the Wars* (Oxford: Clarendon Press, 1995), 407.

9. Gerd Hardach, 'Banking and Industry in Germany in the Interwar Period 1919–1939', *Journal of European Economic History* 13/2 (1984), 203–34; Theo Balderston, 'German Banking between the War: The Crisis of the Credit Banks', *Business History Review* 65/3 (Autumn 1991), 554–605; Gerd Hardach, 'Banking in Germany, 1918–1939', in C. H. Feinstein (ed.), *Banking, Currency, and Finance*, 269–95.

10. Vincent P. Carosso, *Investment Banking in America: A History* (Cambridge, Mass.: Harvard University Press, 1970); Eugene N. White, *The Regulation and Reform of the American Banking System, 1900–1929* (Princeton, NJ: Princeton University Press, 1983).

11. Harold van B. Cleveland and Thomas F. Huertas, *Citibank, 1812–1970* (Cambridge, Mass.: Harvard University Press, 1985).

12. Jean Bouvier, 'The French Banks, Inflation and the Economic Crisis, 1919–1939', *Journal of European Economic History* 13/2 (1984), 29–80; Michel Lescure, 'Banking in France in the Inter-War Period', in C. H. Feinstein (ed.), *Banking, Currency, and Finance*, 315–36.

13. Two of these banks, Crédit Commercial de France and Banque Nationale de Crédit, increased their deposits. During the interwar period, these two banks were grouped together with the four major deposit banks as the six major deposit banks.

14. Raymond W. Goldsmith, *The Financial Development of Japan, 1868–1977* (New Haven, Conn.: Yale University Press, 1983); Norio Tamaki, *Japanese Banking: A History, 1859–1959* (Cambridge: Cambridge University Press, 1995).

15. As for the application of the methodology of business history to financial institutions, see also Alfred D. Chandler, Jr., 'Editor's Introduction', in Cleveland and Huertas, *Citibank*.

PART I

COMMERCIAL BANKING

2

European Bankers in the Interwar Years

YOUSSEF CASSIS

Introduction

Compared with the history of industrial enterprises, the business history of financial institutions is still in its infancy. This is surprising, given that many banks originated as private undertakings and have remained so in most industrialized countries (the postwar nationalization, and later privatization, of the French commercial banks and insurance companies being one of the most conspicuous exceptions). Financial institutions, particularly banks, have also come to feature among the largest companies, especially before 1914 but also in more recent years. Comparisons with industrial undertakings are fraught with danger, but in 1907 the largest German company, measured by share capital, was the Deutsche Bank and the largest French company the Crédit Lyonnais. French banks maintained their position in the interwar years, though with a reduced margin, while German banks lost ground to the largest industrial concerns.[1] In 1999, 80 of Europe's 500 largest companies measured by market capitalization were banks, more than any other sector (telecommunication services came second with 43), and another 34 were insurance companies.[2] As business enterprises, financial institutions had partners and then, increasingly, shareholders, directors, and managers. In their development, senior managements have continually been confronted with strategic choices arising from growing or falling profits, mergers, acquisitions, and so on.

There are, therefore, very good reasons to approach banks within the framework of business history. It must also be admitted, however, that banks have characteristics that set them apart from other business enterprises. In the first place, the state, especially in the twentieth century, has given particular regard to the financial sector. One clear illustration is the attitude of any government towards a foreign takeover bid of a major commercial bank (as opposed to a smaller, specialized type of bank such as an investment bank): opposition has generally been the rule, though no such move has been attempted since the introduction of a single European currency. One of the reasons for such sensitivity on the part of the state is the central role played by banks within the economy. Whatever their degree of diversification, the sphere of influence of industrial companies is necessarily more circumscribed than that of a major bank. Through its innumerable customers coming from all economic sectors, a bank acquires a close knowledge of the entire industrial and commercial spectrum. Another difference is that by definition a bank works with the financial resources of others. The safety of deposits has come to be a major concern for the authorities who have to resolve the problem of their degree of responsibility for ensuring that (more than in the case of any other business enterprise) banks may not fail, or that at least their depositors have some security. Historians themselves have not considered banks to be like other businesses. Following Alfred Chandler's monumental work, the major debate in business history in the last two or three decades has centred on the strategy and structure of large companies. Until very recently, however, banks have on the whole been excluded from these discussions and the studies that they have generated.[3] Instead, banking has generally been approached simply as the execution of an economic function, that is, as intermediation between lenders and borrowers, especially in terms of how efficiently this has been performed, rather than as a business. Nevertheless, over the last twenty years or so, the business history of financial institutions has developed as a genre in its own right, mainly (though not exclusively) through company monographs.[4] Although there has been no serious attempt at theorizing the development, as opposed to the functions, of financial institutions, certain types of financial activities have been approached through the collective experience of a number of institutions.[5]

The time is thus ripe for a major advance in the business history of financial institutions. Such an approach, however, will have to take account of the idiosyncrasies of the banking business. This chapter will attempt to contribute to the debate by considering the people at the helm: European bankers in the interwar years. Who were they? What was the competence of this particular business group; its ability to make the right strategic choices; its degree of professionalization; its relationships with other elite groups? In order to answer these questions, this chapter will first consider the banking scene in the interwar years, in particular the diversity of institutions making up the banking population, with an emphasis on the larger and most influential firms. A socioeconomic profile of Europe's leading bankers (senior executives of the big banks) will be drawn in a second part, paying particular attention to family background, education and training, career patterns, and economic and financial interests. The issues of business culture, business strategy, and business achievements will be discussed in a third part, in an attempt to ascertain the extent to which bankers have been able to shape the environment within which they were operating. A concluding part will deal with the characteristics of bankers as businessmen and the degree of European convergence and divergence.

The Banking Scene in the Interwar Years

In all European countries, the rise of large joint-stock banks and increased banking concentration have been the dominant features of banking history from the 1880s to the 1930s. Before the First World War, a neat parallel can be observed among the three major European economies of Britain, France, and Germany. By 1913, five banks of roughly equal size (with total assets exceeding £100 million) had emerged at the top of their country's banking system. Three were British (Lloyds Bank, London City and Midland Bank, and London County and Westminster Bank), one French (Crédit Lyonnais), and one German (Deutsche Bank). Six others stood a little behind, with total assets between £40 million and £60 million: Barclays Bank and National Provincial Bank in Britain; Société Générale and Comptoir National d'Escompte de Paris (CNEP) in France; Dresdner Bank and Disconto-Gesellschaft in Germany. These banks were still in the forefront after the First World War. Indeed, most of them are still in existence today. There were, however, significant changes in their relative size, with English banks becoming far larger than their Continental counterparts (Table 2.1).

Table 2.1. *The leading banks in Britain, France, and Germany, 1929, measured by total assets and paid-up capital (£1,000)*

	Total assets	Paid-up capital
Lloyds Bank	431,138	15,810
Midland Bank	408,315	13,343
Barclays Bank	385,539	15,858
Westminster Bank	332,592	9,320
National Provincial Bank	306,695	9,479
Deutsche Bank	145,965	7,500
Danat Bank	131,101	3,000
Dresdner Bank	125,631	5,000
Commerzbank	93,826	3,750
Disconto-Gesellschaft	85,183	6,750
Crédit Lyonnais	111,531	3,624
Société Générale	108,431	5,000
CNEP	82,243	3,200
Paribas	36,410	2,400

Source: Banking Almanac.

The change was partly due to domestic developments in one of the three countries, namely, the wave of mergers in English banking. In 1918 five mergers took place, involving the ten largest banks in the country, and resulted in the formation of five huge banks that immediately came to be known as the 'Big Five'. But the change also resulted from the difficulties encountered by German and French banks. Even though they expanded by taking over provincial banks in the early 1920s, the big German banks were weakened by the devastation of war and hyperinflation: in 1924, the commercial banks' capital was valued at 30 per cent of its prewar gold value, their assets at only 21 per cent. French banks also suffered from the devaluation of the franc in the 1920s and the absence of significant mergers. Another convenient measure of size is provided by workforce. If one takes 10,000 employees as the lower limit to qualify for big business status,[6] then banks had undoubtedly become large companies by 1929 (Table 2.2), requiring complex managerial structures.[7] Only one bank, Crédit Lyonnais, employed more than 10,000 people before 1914 and only one other (Deutsche Bank) more than 5,000. The fact that Crédit Lyonnais remained the largest European bank, measured by workforce, in the late 1920s, emphasizes the distorting effects of currency depreciation on international comparisons of size of companies.

Table 2.2. *The leading banks in Britain, France, and Germany, 1929, measured by workforce and number of branches (national networks only)*

	Workforce	Number of branches
Barclays Bank	13,470	2,198
Midland Bank	13,192	2,100
Lloyds Bank	12,640	—
Westminster Bank	9,000[a]	—
National Provincial	8,000[a]	—
Crédit Lyonnais	23,276	1,251
Société Générale	—	1,371
CNEP	10,000	523
Deutsche Bank	14,337	489[b]
Dresdner Bank	9,484[c]	—
Disconto-Gesellschaft	9,600	—
Danat Bank	7,500[c]	—

[a] 1935.
[b] 1930, after the merger with Disconto-Gesellschaft.
[c] 1925.

Sources: Various yearbooks and directories; company monographs.

Other differences were more deeply rooted in the three countries' banking history. In Germany, and to a lesser extent in France, the big banks only formed the tip of the iceberg. Underneath, the banking population remained very dense, whether in terms of number of banks, level of concentration, or division of labour within the banking system. There were more than 26,000 banks in Germany in 1929. Admittedly, more than 21,499 were co-operative banks and more than 3,000 savings banks. But there were still 1,100 private banks and nearly 300 regional joint-stock banks. The figures are less precise for France, but if one excludes savings and similar types of banks, there were probably around 1,500 banks in 1929, most of them local private banks, though only 276 published a balance sheet in that year.[8] Only in Britain had the number of banks fallen dramatically, with only seventeen banks left in England and Wales in the early 1930s. However, this figure only applies to banks defined in the English sense of the word, that is, deposit banks, and does not include merchant banks, overseas banks, savings banks, and building societies.

Levels of concentration are notoriously difficult to compare between countries. Statistics are not available for all countries, and those available are based on heterogeneous banking populations. British figures are usually based on deposit banks, and French figures on banks publishing their balance sheets, while German figures cover the entire banking system. Nevertheless, some general trends can be perceived. In Germany in 1929 the Berlin big banks controlled 23 per cent of the banks' total assets, an exceptionally high share, only to be found in the mid- to late-1920s: from the early century through to the 1960s, it stood at around 12 per cent. However, if only commercial banks are taken into account, the share of big metropolitan banks rose from 39 per cent in 1913 to 70 per cent in 1930 and 77 per cent in 1938.[9] In France, the four largest banks controlled 45 per cent of the deposits of the commercial and investment banks that published their balance sheets in 1937. However, their share falls to 25 per cent if the publicly owned financial institutions (especially the savings banks and the Caisse des Dépôts et Consignations) are taken into account.[10] Concentration levels were higher in Britain. By the eve of the First World War, a dozen banks based in London with a network of branches throughout the country controlled some two-thirds of the clearing banks' deposits. With the formation of the 'Big Five' in 1918, their share rose to 80 per cent. But it would fall to about 50 per cent if the accepting houses, discount houses, finance houses, savings banks, and building societies were taken into account.[11] The position of the big banks must thus be put into perspective even at the peak of their development during the period under review.

Finally, the depression of the 1930s was another factor of differentiation between European banks and bankers. It is true that everywhere the rise of the big commercial banks, which had gathered pace in the 1920s, came to a halt, with savings banks, mortgage banks, co-operative banks, and so on gaining ground against commercial banks. There were, however, varying degrees of intensity. The shift was most dramatic in France. By the late 1930s the share of deposits held by the publicly owned institutions, in the first place the savings banks, far outstripped those held by the commercial banks. Deposits held by the former rose from 67 to 113 billion francs between 1930 and 1937, while those held by the latter actually fell from 87 to 67 billion francs.[12] In Germany, the share of the saving banks in the total assets of the banking system rose from 31 per cent in 1929 to 45 per cent in 1938, while those of the commercial banks fell from 33 to 15 per cent, the remaining being in the hands of other specialized institutions such as co-operative banks and mortgage banks.[13] On the other hand, savings banks and building societies never reached such a dominant position in Britain, even though their assets grew faster than those of the clearing banks: by 1933, they represented 37 per cent of those of clearing banks, up from 17 per cent in 1920.[14] The experience of the banking crisis of the 1930s was not the same in the three countries. The English banks were hardly affected by the crisis and it is during these years that they gained their reputation for stability. French banks encountered more difficulties, including some large banks such as the Banque de l'Union Parisienne, a *banque d'affaires* that was rescued by the government, and the Banque Nationale de Crédit, a deposit bank that was liquidated in 1932 and reconstructed the following year under the new name of Banque Nationale pour le Commerce et l'Industrie (BNCI). The crisis mostly affected local and regional banks, however, with some 670 banks filing a petition for bankruptcy between 1930 and 1937.[15] As is well known, the banking crisis was most severe in Germany. The Danat Bank, one of the big five Berlin banks, closed its doors on 13 July 1931, and the government had to intervene directly through a rescue package that included an imposed merger of the Danat Bank and the Dresdner Bank, which was also badly weakened; the purging of the big banks' management; and the quasi-nationalization of the big German banks (which, however, were denationalized during the Third Reich).[16]

Europe's Leading Bankers

Bankers as a socio-professional group are by now fairly well known for the period prior to the First World War. Recent works on banking elites in Paris and Berlin[17] have been added to my own study of City bankers,[18] as well as others dealing with smaller European countries,[19] to provide a comprehensive cross-border view of this most significant business group. Much less is known about European bankers in the interwar years. Some of the leading protagonists are of course well-known figures, but no collective biography has so far been written. It is to be hoped that major research in this direction will be undertaken in the near future. In the meantime, this chapter is a first, modest attempt at filling this gap. It is based on a small sample of twenty-seven men consisting of those effectively in charge of their country's leading banks in 1929. The chairman and managing director[20] of the following banks have been selected: the 'Big Five' clearing banks in Britain (Midland Bank, Lloyds Bank, Barclays Bank, Westminster Bank, and National Provincial Bank); the three major Parisian *établissements de crédit* (Crédit Lyonnais, Société Générale, and Comptoir National d'Escompte de Paris) as well as France's leading *banque d'affaires* (Banque de Paris et des Pays-Bas, or Paribas); and the five largest Berlin *Kreditbanken* (Deutsche Bank, Dresdner Bank, Darmstädter un National Bank, Disconto-Gesellschaft, and Commerz- und Privat-Bank).

This is only a section of the British, French, and German banking communities in the interwar years. However, the small size of the sample is somewhat compensated for by the prominence of those included. In addition, 1929 provides a convenient vantage point from which to observe the entire period, as several executives stayed in office throughout the 1920s and 1930s. The record (twenty-four years) undoubtedly belongs to Reginald McKenna (1863–1943), chairman of the Midland Bank between 1919 and 1943, closely followed by Beaumont Pease, later Lord Wardington (1869–1950) and the Baron Georges Brincard (1871–1953), respectively, chairmen of Lloyds Bank and the Crédit Lyonnais between 1922 and 1945 (twenty-three years). Interestingly, they were assisted throughout their chairmanship by fairly stable management teams. At the Midland Bank, Frederick Hyde (1870–1939) was appointed joint managing director in 1919 and sole managing director ten years later until his retirement because of ill health in 1937. At Lloyds Bank, George Abell (1875–1946) and Francis Beane (1872–1959) had been part of a team of general managers since 1923 before becoming chief general managers in 1929; they remained in office until 1935 and 1938, respectively. At the Crédit Lyonnais, Edouard Escarra (1880–1973) and Robert Masson (1875–1956) served as general managers between 1926 and 1945. Other executives whose period of office covered most of the interwar period include Frederick Goodenough (1866–1934), chairman of Barclays between 1917 and 1934, and Paul Boyer (1863–1939), chairman of the CNEP between 1926 and 1939, both having previously been general managers. Horace Finaly (1871–1945) was general manager, and the real boss, of the Banque de Paris et des Pays-Bas between 1919 and 1937, while Charles Lidbury (1880–1978), held the same position at the Westminster Bank between 1927 and 1946. A continuity in the leading personnel can thus be observed in all but two (Société Générale and National Provincial Bank) of the major French and British banks. The situation was different in Germany. The leadership of the Deutsche Bank,

Dresdner Bank, Danat Bank, and Disconto-Gesellschaft underwent considerable change in the early 1930s, at both executive and supervisory board
levels. This was mainly, though not exclusively, a consequence of the dis-
missals following the banking crisis of 1931, the anti-Semitic policy of the
Third Reich and, to a lesser extent, the mergers involving these four banks.[21]

Not surprisingly, banking leaders in the interwar years were not, so to
speak, 'new' men. With an average age of sixty-three in 1929, most of them
had already reached a senior position, though not necessarily the highest
level of responsibility, before the war. There were, however, some differences within the group. In the first place, German bankers were on the
whole older than their French and British counterparts: sixty-six as against
sixty-one and sixty, respectively. Second, chairmen, at sixty-seven, were
older than managing directors, who averaged fifty-seven. French and
(especially) German chairmen were older than their British counterparts,
the respective ages being sixty-eight, seventy-one, and sixty-two. This was
partly due to varying conceptions of the role of a bank chairman.
In Germany, chairmen of supervisory boards were, as a rule, not involved in
the running of the firm. In Britain and France, they could assume, depending on the banks, either an executive role (e.g. at Barclays or the Crédit
Lyonnais) or an honorary position (Westminster, Paribas), or something in
between (Midland, Lloyds, CNEP). The doyen was Gaston Griolet, eighty-
seven in his penultimate year as chairman of the Banque de Paris et des
Pays-Bas; he had been elected in 1915, already aged seventy-three. Other
elder statesmen included Max von Schinckel (Disconto-Gesellschaft), aged
eighty; Max Steinthal (Deutsche Bank), aged seventy-nine; and Jakob
Riesser (Danat Bank), aged seventy-six. Interestingly, the youngest chairman, Fritz Andreae (Dresdner Bank), aged fifty-three, was also German.
Managing directors were a mixture of young (primarily in France, where
the average age was fifty-four) and old (primarily in Germany, where
the average age was sixty-one).[22] Three were still under fifty and could
be seen as representatives of a new generation: Jakob Goldschmidt (Danat
Bank), aged forty-seven; Charles Lidbury (Westminster Bank), aged forty-
eight; and Alexandre Célier (CNEP), aged forty-nine. Representatives of the
older generation included Arthur Salmonsohn (Disconto-Gesellschaft),
aged seventy; and Henry Nathan (Dresdner Bank), aged sixty-seven. Age
was thus also a consequence of the generation effect, with some bankers
clearly reaching the end of their professional career in the late 1920s.

How well were these men prepared for their task? Answering this question requires looking at social origins, education and training, and career
patterns. Leading European bankers were mostly recruited among the
privileged classes (landowners, businessmen, senior civil servants, professionals), in accordance with what is known about the social origins of the
business elite of industrialized countries.[23] Overall sons of businessmen
were in a majority (fourteen out of twenty-seven, with another three sons

of small businessmen). However, there were marked differences between the three countries. In Germany, *all* those in the sample had a business family background (including one shopkeeper). In France, by contrast, this was only the case of three out of eight (again including one small businessman), while Britain was in between with half being businessmen's sons. In both Britain and France, the rest consisted of professionals and civil servants. Despite the small size of the sample, these differences clearly reflect the pre-1914 status of business elites in the three countries. The German business elite (*Wirtschaftsbürgertum*) remained isolated from the rest of the bourgeoisie as well as from the aristocracy, while a greater degree of mobility within the elite—the passage from one elite group to another—could already be observed in France and, to a lesser degree, in Britain.[24] In that respect, French senior executives represented a more 'modern' type of business elite than was found elsewhere in Europe.

The relevance of social origins to the study of businessmen's competence mainly concerns the extent to which top jobs were obtained through the privilege of birth. Could the chairmen and chief executives of Europe's largest banks still inherit their position from their father? The phenomenon had not entirely disappeared in the interwar years, though it had clearly become marginal, as most banking leaders of the period could be described as salaried managers. Inheritance could take different forms. Direct inheritance occurred more often in German banks. The Disconto-Gesellschaft is a case in point: Arthur Salomonsohn and his cousin Georg Solmssen (1869–57), a highly influential member of the executive board, were respectively the nephew and son of Adolph Salomonsohn, a former managing director.[25] In France, the Baron Georges Brincard, chairman of the Crédit Lyonnais, was the son-in-law of the bank's founder and long-serving chairman Henri Germain, though there was a seventeen-year gap between the latter's death in 1905 and the former's accession to the top in 1922. Brincard's right hand, the bank's general manager Robert Masson, was the son of a former senior manager and later director of the Crédit Lyonnais. Indirect inheritance is not always easy to detect. Beaumont Pease and Rupert Beckett (1870–1950), chairmen of Lloyds Bank and Westminster Bank, respectively, were both scions of private banking dynasties who joined the board after the takeover of the family firm and eventually became chairmen. André Homberg (1867–1948), who joined the Société Générale in 1919 as general manager and was its chairman between 1922 and 1932, was the nephew of Joseph Octave Homberg (1840–1907), a manager of the bank between 1880 and 1890.[26] Family connections also played a role. Fritz Andrea's rise within the German corporate elite, including his chairmanship of the Dresdner Bank, owed a great deal to the fact that he had married the daughter of Emil Rathenau, founder of the Allgemeine Elektricitäts-Gesellschaft (AEG), and became a key component of the family's powerful network of relationships.[27]

While these cases point to strong remnants of nineteenth-century family capitalism, it should not be forgotten that family relationships have never ceased to play a role in the transfer of power within large companies, even in the most modern version of managerial capitalism. The more important question concerns the suitability of these men, whether inheritors or managers, for a top banking job. Education and training could be seen as a first indicator of their abilities. On this count, French bankers received the highest score: seven out of eight (88 per cent) were university-educated, twice the proportion of their English counterparts (four out of nine), and almost three times that of their German counterparts (only three out of ten). The figures for Germany might appear surprising given the usual assumptions about the educational level of German businessmen.[28] However, German banks relied on a strong tradition of learning on the job, with less emphasis on formal education than in France and even Britain, where, conversely, bankers were more educated than industrialists. Significantly, an apprenticeship, before or after a full secondary education, was a course chosen by bankers from different generations (e.g. Max Steinthal, born in 1850, Henry Nathan, born in 1862, and Jakob Goldschmidt, born in 1882). The tradition has in fact persisted well into the 1990s, though to a far lesser degree. The figures for France are much less surprising, as French business leaders have consistently had the highest level of education in Europe. The *grandes écoles*, the bedrock of the education of French elites, were not particularly prominent for this generation of bankers. One reason is that the Ecole Polytechnique, an engineering school, was not the obvious choice for a would-be banker, even though two of them (Georges Brincard and André Homberg) did follow this course. Another is that the Ecole Nationale d'Administration (ENA) was only established after the Second World War. Nevertheless, the education of French banking leaders appears to have been well suited to their future professional activities. Law studies were obviously popular and were often combined with a commercial and financial training. This mainly applied to the former *inspecteurs des finances* (controllers of state finance) who left the civil service to run a major bank.[29] In England, education reflected to a large extent the deep-seated division between 'gentlemen' and 'players': the five chairmen were all educated at a public school, followed (in the case of three of them) by Oxford or Cambridge, while three of the four managers were trained on the job. There were two minor variations on this theme: one general manager (George Abell, of Lloyds Bank) was educated at a public school (Repton), while one chairman (Frederick Goodenough, of Barclays) attended the University of Zurich, in Switzerland, after Charterhouse.

The importance of education in the shaping of a successful businessman remains a contentious issue. Attempts at correlating education with business performance have so far remained inconclusive. The professional experience gained before reaching a senior position is of at least equal importance. From this viewpoint, it should be noted that the vast majority of banking leaders (nineteen out of twenty-seven, or 70 per cent) entered their firm at board or senior management level. In other words, they did not learn their trade in-house, but in other institutions. These institutions were essentially of three sorts: a private firm, another corporation, or the state sector. During the first-half of the twentieth century, the traditional route to a top position in a major company varied among the three countries: a partnership in a private firm was most common for British business leaders, senior managerial responsibilities within the corporate sector for German business leaders, and a stint in the civil service for French business leaders.[30] Nevertheless, this pattern applied only partially to bankers.

In the first place, the corporate route was firmly established (about half the cases) in all three countries.[31] For a minority, this meant joining their bank in a junior position and climbing every step of the ladder. George Abell, for example, joined Lloyds Bank in 1893, aged eighteen, and became joint chief general manager thirty-six years later.[32] Frederick Hyde had a similar career at the Midland Bank. Robert Masson was a little older, twenty-one, and a graduate from HEC (Hautes Etudes Commerciales, one of the French *grandes écoles*) when he joined the Crédit Lyonnais in 1897, becoming general manager in 1926. A few others, such as Horace Finaly at the Banque de Paris et des Pays-Bas or Henry Nathan at the Dresdner Bank, joined the bank in their late twenties or early thirties in a junior managerial capacity. Some reached the top of a leading bank through the amalgamation movement, being already at the head of a smaller institution. Herbert Hambling (1857–1932), for example, joined the London and South Western Bank aged eighteen, becoming general manager in 1911; however, his hour of glory came after the war, when he became vice-chairman of Barclays Bank following the merger of the two banks in 1918. Similarly, Max von Schinckel (he was ennobled in 1917), managing director of the Norddeutsche Bank, in Hamburg, joined the *Vorstand* of the Disconto-Gesellschaft following the takeover of his bank in 1895. The corporate ladder could even lead to the bank's chairmanship, though more often in Germany (Max von Schinckel at the Disconto-Gesellschaft, Max Steinthal at the Deutsche Bank) and in France (André Homberg at the Société Générale, Paul Boyer at the CNEP, Georges Brincard at the Crédit Lyonnais) than in England, where the only case was Frederick Goodenough, at Barclays.

Second, the partnership in a private firm was as common in Germany as in Britain. The business *notable* chairing a major company had not disappeared in the interwar years: Harry Goschen, chairman of National Provincial Bank, was a partner in the City merchant bank Goschen & Cunliffe; Fritz Andreae, chairman of Dresdner Bank, was a partner in the Berlin private bank Hardy & Co.; Heinrich Witthoeft, chairman of Commerzbank, was a partner in the Hamburg merchant firm Arnold Otto Meyer. At the same time, the trade-off between a partnership in a private

firm and a senior appointment in a large joint-stock company was starting
to emerge. Such a move could follow the takeover of a prestigious private
family bank, as in the cases of Beaumont Pease at Lloyds Bank and Rupert
Beckett at Westminster Bank; or it could mean leaving the former for the
latter, as in the case of Oscar Wassermann at the Deutsche Bank and Jakob
Goldschmidt at the National Bank für Deutschland, later to become the
Danat Bank. Finally, the recruitment of senior executives from the civil
service did occur more often in France (André Homberg and Joseph Simon
at the Société Générale and Alexandre Célier at the CNEP) than elsewhere,
though one should not disregard the unique case of Reginald McKenna,
a former Chancellor of the Exchequer, who left politics to become chairman of the Midland Bank.

Business Culture, Business Strategy, Business Achievements

The banking profession was thus a mixture of old and new. While modern
careers were being put in place, the organization of a banker's working life
remained in many respects antiquated. The distinction between employment and retirement, for example, had not yet been clearly established,
hence the group's age structure referred to above. On average leading
bankers stayed at the helm for seventeen years, with 60 per cent leaving
aged seventy or over. Some would have stayed longer. Georges Brincard
had to relinquish the chairmanship of the Crédit Lyonnais in 1946 at the
age of seventy-five following the bank's nationalization, not because of his
advancing years.[33] Horace Finaly was forced to resign as general manager
of Paribas in June 1937 because of his conflict with the chairman, Emile
Moreau, not because he had reached the age of sixty-six.[34] For a good third,
death (at an average age of seventy-five), rather than retirement, was the
reason for ceasing to work.
    The hierarchical structure of the profession was also evolving. In
Germany, salaried managers had been fully integrated into the business
elites since the late nineteenth century. The members of the *Vorstand* were
in charge of defining the firm's long-term strategy as well as its day-to-day
running. They enjoyed a social and professional status equal to that of the
members of the supervisory board, they represented their bank on the
boards of other companies, and several were seriously rich, though not as
much as the partners of the leading private banks.[35] In France, the gap separating directors and managers was quickly being bridged with the emergence of a new elite of professional bankers at the head of the big deposit
banks. The phenomenon was particularly striking at the Crédit Lyonnais

where, by 1913, eleven of its sixteen directors (69 per cent) were staff-promoted; the proportion was also high at the CNEP (54 per cent), and still significant at the Société Générale (43 per cent).[36] Most of these 'internal' directors were executive directors, combining a seat on the board with an active managerial role.[37] In 1929, the chairmen of the three major deposit banks were all former general managers. At Paribas, directors continued to be primarily recruited among business and political *notables*; and though senior managers were effectively running the show under the leadership of their 'general', Horace Finaly, their decisions had ultimately to be sanctioned by the board.[38] In any case, the status of French salaried managers had always been enhanced by their high level of education. This, as we have seen, was not the case in Britain, where a new type of professional banker was slower to emerge. Staff-promoted managing directors remained in a minority on the boards of the big banks. Still, their status and power should not be underestimated. It was a remarkable fate for Frederick Goodenough, a salaried manager, to become the second chairman of Barclays Bank in 1917, a bank still very much in the hands of the founding families of private bankers. Social cleavages were also being progressively eroded. Charles Lidbury, a self-made man who started at thirteen, was elected a director of the Westminster Bank while chief general manager, and to a degree he admired and emulated the lifestyle of his fellow directors.[39]

At the same time, the old banking aristocracy was far from having been displaced. In a banking world dominated by giant companies, private bankers continued to enjoy a privileged status. This did not derive from their business activities, which, even in Britain, were increasingly confined to a few lucrative niches. It was a matter of overall influence within the profession. The most prominent private bankers displayed a high capacity of adaptation and were able to retain commanding positions as directors, and sometimes chairmen, of large banks and other financial institutions—a phenomenon particularly pronounced in, but in no way confined to, England.[40] Moreover, at the highest echelons of the profession, especially in the realm of international finance, the game continued to be played according to the unwritten rules and code of conduct of the financial aristocracy. Financial diplomacy took on a new dimension in the aftermath of the First World War. With their experience of international affairs and their network of relationships, private bankers were, for the last time, in a position to play a political role incommensurate with their economic weight. The most important German figures during the Peace Conference and the discussion on the reparations question were two private bankers, Max Warburg and Carl Melchior, both partners of M. M. Warburg & Co., ahead of the directors of the Deutsche Bank.[41] A few banking houses were still in a position to offer their government financial assistance in time of crisis, as did Lazard Frères during the speculation against the franc in 1924.[42]

Central bank co-operation in the 1920s was in many respects a re-creation of the old-fashioned world of the *haute banque*, with its club-like atmosphere and the emphasis on personal relationships. The dominant figure of the period, Montagu Norman, Governor of the Bank of England from 1920 to 1944, was a most accomplished product of the nineteenth-century world of London private banks.[43] The close collaboration of the Bank of England with prominent private banking houses in Britain and America, in particular in the schemes for the financial reconstruction of central Europe, added to the weight of private bankers in international finance.[44] So did the fact that several key directors of the Bank of England were partners in leading merchant banks such as Morgan Grenfell, Schroders, or Lazards. Members of the Parisian *haute banque* were also well represented at the Banque de France, making up a third of the *régents*. But the *gouverneur* traditionally came from the higher ranks of the Treasury and international affairs were in the hands of senior officials such as Charles Rist or Pierre Quesnay in the late 1920s. Private bankers' representation was weaker in the Reichsbank, though leading names such as Max von Warburg and Alfred von Oppenheim sat in its general council.

Discussing the strategic options developed by Europe's leading bankers would go far beyond the scope of this chapter. One aspect of the question will be briefly addressed: the banks' response to competition. Before the war, large commercial banks established a dominant position by pursuing three types of strategies: amalgamations with other banks, alliances through interest groups, and internal growth.[45] The merger and acquisition model is best exemplified by Britain. The growth of the big banks was the result of an intense amalgamation movement that started in the mid-nineteenth century, gathered pace in the 1890s following the Baring Crisis of 1890, kept its momentum until the First World War, and culminated with the megamergers of 1918. The interest group model is most commonly associated with Germany. Before the First World War, the big banks established 'communities of interest' (*Interessengemeinschaften*), based on cross-shareholding and pooled profits, with a number of provincial banks. Finally, internal growth was the dominant factor in the consolidation of French banking: leading banks established a national network of branches without taking over local banks. The situation changed in the interwar years. In Britain, the amalgamation movement came to an end in 1918, following the Colwyn Committee's inquiry into the matter, and the agreement that the banks would submit any proposed amalgamation for Treasury and Board of Trade approval. In Germany, by contrast, the big banks followed the British model of merger and acquisition. In the inflationary climate of the 1920s, they took over the provincial banks with which they were already linked through a 'community of interest'. Megamergers followed a few years later, in 1929 between Deutsche Bank and Disconto-Gesellschaft, and in 1931 between Dresdner Bank and

Danat Bank. In France, the big banks did not alter their amalgamation policy. Nevertheless, they came against strong competition from the regional banks. In fact, the share of deposits held by the big banks fell from 59 per cent in 1913 to 37 per cent in 1937, mostly to the advantage of large regional banks such as the Crédit du Nord and the Société Nancéenne de Crédit. More than the big banks, they engaged in a dynamic merger and acquisition policy, absorbing local private banks and establishing a wide network of branches and a solid customer base in their main area of operations.

To what extent were savings banks seen as competitors by the commercial banks? This clearly depended on national conditions. They were undoubtedly perceived as such in France. In an internal note from 1952, Olivier Moreau-Néré, who was to become chairman of the Crédit Lyonnais between 1955 and 1961, clearly stated that 'competition to get sight deposits is harder than ever ... The savings banks in particular have been a very serious competitor, the more so as the limit for the savings book has constantly been raised and has far exceeded the level of price increases ... In addition, the Caisses de Crédit Agricole, which have grown substantially, have been a source of very strong competition, because they aimed at customers who in the past had given us great satisfaction'.[46] As a result, the Crédit Lyonnais increased the number of its branches (from 400 in 1920 to 1327 in 1940) and set about working more closely with industrial customers rather than mainly relying on its traditional clientele, landlords and other capitalists, whose economic position had weakened since 1914. In England, by contrast, savings and building societies, whatever their progress, were in no way seen as a threat by the clearing banks and there was no apparent strategy on their part to compete for this fast-growing mass market in bank deposits. This was a reflection of the former's still limited market share and the persisting class divide between the customers of the two types of institutions. As for German banks, they were confronted with the more pressing problem of adapting to a new order, with state power now paramount and their economic role increasingly marginal as a result of state intervention and industrial self-finance. In any case, neither in Britain nor in Germany were savings banks included in the cartel agreements reached by the commercial banks. In fact, savings banks and other mutual banks lived apart from the world of commercial banking for most of the twentieth century and only recently reached the top of the banking system; in 1995, eight of the top thirty European banks (27 per cent) originated from the world of savings and co-operative banks and included such major banks as the Crédit Agricole in France, Abbey National in Britain, Westdeutsche Landesbank and Hypobank in Germany, Banca Nazionale del Lavoro in Italy, and Rabobank in the Netherlands.

Despite their aggrandizement, and the criticisms to which they were subjected by public opinion, the big banks do not appear to have increased their 'power', or influence over other economic sectors, in particular industry. British banks did not take entrepreneurial initiatives, whether in the City or in the British economy as a whole, and remained strictly within the limits of deposit banking, while from the 1930s, their assets were dominated by government debt. Important exceptions were the overseas ventures of some of the clearers: Barclays Bank, under Frederick Goodenough, established Barclays Bank D.C.O. in 1925 following the acquisition of the Colonial Bank, the Anglo-Egyptian Bank, and the National Bank of South Africa; and Lloyds Bank had a majority control in the Bank of London and South America, formed in 1923 by the merger of two old established British banks operating in the area, the London and River Plate Bank and the London and Brazilian Bank.[47] In the late 1920s, German bankers held more seats on the supervisory boards of other companies than at any time in the country's corporate history; the record holder was Jakob Goldschmidt, with over 100 seats! This was the decade when 'organized capitalism' was intensified by the effects of war and inflation. Rationalization, mergers, ententes, cartels, 'communities of interest' all reached new heights, reflected in the number of overlapping directorships between major companies. Yet bankers' economic 'leadership' did not intensify during the period. If anything, there were fears of being left behind in terms of size by the newly formed giant industrial concerns such as IG Farben and Vereinigte Stahlwerke; indeed, this was one of the arguments brought up to justify the merger between Deutsche Bank and Disconto-Gesellschaft. In industry, decisions were made by industrialists, including those with global strategic implications such as the restructuring of an entire industry. Bankers played only a marginal role in the great merger of the iron and steel industry leading to the foundation of the Vereinigte Stahlwerke in 1926; and even though they favoured such a consolidation, in no way did they initiate it.[48]

In the end, the only real measure of businessmen's achievement is the performance of their enterprise. How well did bankers do during this period? Assessing the performance of European banks in the interwar years is another formidable task going far beyond the scope of this chapter. In the absence of any kind of comparative indication on the matter,[49] however, an attempt at measuring profits and profitability at the end of the 1920s (the only years when broadly similar conditions prevailed in the three countries) is well worth trying, even on the basis of published figures. Published profits provide at the very least a meaningful order of magnitude, and even if 'untrue', they do reflect the image a company wishes to project. Results are presented in Table 2.3.[50]

In absolute terms, profits are to a large extent a matter of size, so it is not surprising to find that the highest profits were generated by the English banks. They were followed by the German banks, and finally by the French banks (whose figures might be underestimated given the devaluation of the franc). Profitability—defined here as return on shareholders'

Table 2.3. *Profits and profitability of the leading English, French, and German banks, 1927–9*

	Profits (£1,000)	Return on equity (%)
Midland Bank	2,626	10.8
Lloyds Bank	2,515	10.1
Barclays Bank	2,296	8.6
Westminster Bank	2,147	11.2
National Provincial Bank	2,131	10.8
Deutsche Bank	1,425	11.2
Disconto-Gesellschaft	769	8.2
Danat Bank	746	12.4
Dresdner Bank	632	9.5
Commerzbank	543	10.5
Crédit Lyonnais	503	8.6
Société Générale	444	7.7
CNEP	427	10.1
Paribas	403	11.3

Source: Author's calculations from the *Stock Exchange Yearbook, Handbuch der deutschen Aktiengesellschaften*, and *Cote Desfossé*.

equity—provides a good indication of how efficiently the funds belonging to the company's owners have been used by those in charge of the company's affairs. Three remarks will be briefly made in this context. The first concerns the relative performance of individual banks. From a national perspective, German banks were the most profitable, though by a small margin—10.3 per cent, as against 9.9 per cent for the English banks and 9.2 per cent for the French banks. The most profitable bank was the Danat Bank, the only bank of the sample that had to suspend payment during the 1931 banking crisis. Still, its rate of profit was not inordinately high: 12.4 per cent as against 10.1 to 11.3 per cent for a wide range of highly stable banks, including four of the five English clearers. Only five banks had a rate of return lower than 10 per cent, for reasons that remain to be explained. The second remark concerns banks' performance by comparison with other major companies. German banks, once again, did particularly well: 10.3 per cent as against 7.2 per cent for a sample of leading industrial, commercial, and financial companies. In fact, banking was then the most profitable sector within German big business. By comparison, return on equity was 5.1 per cent in the heavy industries, 9.1 per cent in electricity, 9.4 per cent in chemicals.[51] English and French banks were closer, though slightly lower than the national average (which was significantly higher than in Germany): 9.9 per cent as against 10.6 per cent in Britain, and 9.2 per cent as against 9.8 per cent in France. Finally, it is interesting to note that the French and German banks were more profitable in the late 1920s than in the prewar years: 9.2 per cent as against 8.3 per cent, and 10.3 per cent as against 9.1 per cent, respectively. Conversely, the English 'Big Five' lost in profitability what they had gained in size: 9.9 per cent as against 13.6 per cent in the years 1911–13.

Conclusion

To sum up: the leaders of Europe's top banks in the interwar years largely conformed to the model of the pre-1914 businessman, whether in terms of family background, education and training, entry into the profession, or career development. Moreover, at its upper echelons, the banking community remained imbued with nineteenth-century values. It is all too easy to characterize the interwar period as transitory. In fact, if there was a transition from the nineteenth-century private banker to the twentieth-century professional senior bank executive, its beginning dates back to the 1890s rather than to the 1920s. Yet it would be erroneous to see those bankers as ill prepared to the challenges of the interwar period. The business of banking underwent little change during the first-half of the twentieth century. And from a business point of view bankers proved rather successful, at any rate in the late 1920s, and arguably throughout the entire period as far as French and English bankers were concerned. Figures for profits and profitability need to be complemented by qualitative analysis: Hubert Bonin, for example, considers the CNEP 'a solid bank, a prosperous bank, and a profitable bank [that] went through the interwar years with equanimity despite some temporary frights, easily dispelled thanks to its financial reserves and the plasticity of a management capable of quickly adapting to cyclical constraints'.[52] CNEP was not an isolated case.

What lessons can be drawn from a comparison between European countries? The historian will always be torn between the conflicting temptations of splitting or lumping. A lot has been written about the differences between the British, German, and French banking systems, especially with regard to the relationships between banks and industry. This is not the place to reopen the debate. The consensus is that their impact on economic growth has proved limited. From a business history perspective, a number of clear divergences can be observed in the interwar years: some reflected national traditions, in particular the characteristics of each banking system; others resulted from specific circumstances such as merger waves or economic crises. Yet the general trend in banking development was the same across Europe, and the problems with which bankers were confronted were very much alike. If performance is used as the yardstick for assessing their response, little divergence can be detected when economic conditions were broadly similar in the three countries.

NOTES

1. See Y. Cassis, *Big Business: The European Experience in the Twentieth Century* (Oxford: Oxford University Press, 1997).
2. *Financial Times*, Thursday, 4 May 2000.
3. For a recent attempt at filling this gap, see the session on 'Banks As Firms: The Internal Organization and Structure, 1850 to the Present' organized by Michael Collins and José Luis Garcia Ruiz at the Twelfth International Economic History Congress, Madrid, 1998.
4. For a recent compilation, see the section on 'Banking and Finance', in F. Goodall, T. Gourvish, and S. Tolliday (eds), *International Bibliography of Business History* (London and New York, NY: Routledge, 1997).
5. See, for example, V. Carosso, *Investment Banking in America: A History* (Cambridge, Mass.: Harvard University Press, 1970); S. Chapman, *The Rise of Merchant Banking* (London: George Allen and Unwin, 1984); and G. Jones, *British Multinational Banking 1830–1990* (Oxford: Oxford University Press, 1993).
6. See Cassis, *Big Business*, 6–7.
7. On this question see P. Wardley, 'The Commercial Banking Industry and Its Part in the Emergence and Consolidation of the Corporate Economy in Britain before 1940', *Journal of Industrial History*, 2000.
8. H. Laufenburger, *Les banques françaises* (Paris: Sirey, 1940), 43.
9. G. Hardach, 'Banking in Germany, 1918–1939', in C. Feinstein (ed.), *Banking, Currency, and Finance in Europe between the Wars* (Oxford: Clarendon Press, 1995), 274, 280.
10. J. Bouvier, *Un siècle de banque française: Les contraintes de l'Etat et les incertitudes du marché* (Paris: Hachette littérature, 1973), 125, 147.
11. M. Collins, *Money and Banking in the UK: A History* (London: Croom Helm, 1988).
12. A. Gueslin, 'Banks and State in France from the 1880s to the 1930s: The Impossible Advance of the Banks', in Y. Cassis (ed.), *Finance and Financiers in European History 1880–1960* (Cambridge: Cambridge University Press, 1992), 78.
13. Hardach, 'Banking in Germany', 274.
14. Collins, *Money and Banking*, 215.
15. H. Bonin, *L'argent en France depuis 1880* (Paris: Masson, 1989), 37.
16. See K. E. Born, *Die deutsche Bankenkrise 1931: Finanzen und Politik* (Munich: R. Piper, 1967); H. James, 'The Causes of the German Banking Crisis of 1931', *Economic History Review*, 2nd ser., 37/1 (1984); T. Balderston, 'The Banks and the Gold Standard in the German Financial Crisis of 1931', *Financial History Review*, 1/1 (1994).

17. C. Belot-Ronzon, 'Banquiers de la Belle époque: Les dirigeants des trois grands établissements de crédit en France au tournant du XXème siècle', Unpublished Ph.D. dissertation (University of Paris X-Nanterre, 2000); M. Reitmayer, *Bankiers im Kaiserreich: Sozialprofil und Habitus der deutschen Hochfinanz* (Göttingen: Vandenhoeck & Ruprecht, 1999).

18. Y. Cassis, *City Bankers 1890–1914* (Cambridge: Cambridge University Press, 1994, 1st French edn. 1984).

19. See in particular G. Kurgan-van Hentenryk, *Gouverner la Générale de Belgique: Essai de biographie collective* (Bruxelles: De Boeck Université, 1996), and Y. Cassis and F. Debrunner, 'Les élites bancaires suisses, 1880–1960', *Revue suisse d'histoire*, 40 (1990), 258–73.

20. In the case of the German banks, the chairman of the supervisory board and the official or unofficial leader of the executive board have been selected. Most French and British banks had a single chief executive; in the few cases where there were two (Crédit Lyonnais, Lloyds Bank), only one of them has been included in the sample. Finally, at Barclays, where the position of general manager was fairly junior, the deputy chairman has been selected instead.

21. See C. Kopper, *Zwischen Marktwirtschaft und Dirigismus: Bankenpolitik im 'Dritten Reich' 1933–39* (Bonn: Bouvier, 1995); H. James, 'The Deutsche Bank and the Dictatorship 1933–45', in L. Gall *et al.*, *The Deutsche Bank 1870–1995* (London: Weidenfeld & Nicolson, 1995).

22. The average age of German managing directors would probably be lower if all members of the Vorstand, and not only the number one, were taken into account.

23. Comparative material can be found in H. Kaelble, 'Long-Term Changes in the Recruitment of Business Elites: Germany Compared to the US, Great Britain and France since the Industrial Revolution', *Journal of Social History*, 13/3 (1980); and Y. Cassis (ed.), *Business Elites* (Aldershot: E. Elgar, 1994).

24. See Y. Cassis, 'Businessmen and the Bourgeoisie in Western Europe', and H. Kaelble, 'French *Bourgeoisie* and German *Bürgertum*, 1870–1914', both in J. Kocka and A. Mitchell (eds), *Bourgeois Society in Nineteenth Century Europe* (Oxford/Providence: Berg, 1993).

25. Another board member of the Disconto-Gesellschaft, Ernest Enno Russel (1869–1949), was the son of a former managing director, Emil Russel. At the Dresdner Bank, Herbert Gutmann (1879–?), son of the bank's founder Eugen Gutmann, was also on the executive board without, however, playing the leading role.

26. Belot-Ronzon, 'Banquiers de la Belle époque', 1353.

27. D. Ziegler and I. Köhler, 'Heirats- und Verkehrkreise als Instrumente wirtschaftsbürgerlichen Aufstiegs: die Familie Andrae', *Genealogie*, 1/2 (1997), 385–402.

28. A wider sample, including the leaders of the largest industrial, commercial, and financial companies, reveals that 61 per cent of those active in 1929 were university-educated; see Cassis, *Big Business*, 132–42.

29. On the influence of the *inspecteurs des finances* on French business, see E. Chadeau, *Les inspecteurs des finances au XIXe siècle (1850–1914): Profil social et rôle économique* (Paris: Economica, 1986).

30. Cassis, *Big Business*, 148–56.

31. Five out of nine in Britain, four out of eight in France, five out of ten in Germany.

32. J. R. Winton, *Lloyds Bank 1918–69* (Oxford: Oxford University Press, 1982), 75.

33. J. Rivoire, *Le Crédit Lyonnais: Histoire d'une banque* (Paris: Le Cherche midi, 1989), 131.

34. E. Bussière, *Horace Finaly, banquier 1871–1945* (Paris: Fayard, 1996), 407–12.

35. Y. Cassis, 'Financial Elites in three European Centres: London, Paris, Berlin, 1880s–1930s', *Business History*, 33/3, (July 1991), 53–71 (61–3).

36. Belot-Ronzon, 'Banquiers de la Belle époque', 543.

37. Ibid., 50–2. See also H. Bonin, 'Une grande entreprise bancaire: le Comptoir national d'escompte de Paris dans l'entre-deux-guerres', in Comité pour l'histoire économique et financière de la France, *Etudes et Documents*, IV (1992), 225–382 (358–63).

38. Bussière, *Horace Finaly*, 265–73.

39. G. Jones and M. Ackrill, 'Lidbury, Sir Charles (1880–1978), Clearing Banker', in D. J. Jeremy (ed.), *Dictionary of Business Biography*, 5 vols. (London: Butterworths, 1984–6), iii, 783–5.

40. See Cassis, 'Financial Elites'; P. Arnold, *The Bankers of London* (London: Hogarth Press, 1938); Bonin, 'Une grande entreprise bancaire'; Bussière, *Horace Finaly*; H. Wixforth and D. Ziegler, 'The Niche in the Universal Banking System: The Role and Significance of Private Bankers within German Industry, 1900–1933', *Financial History Review*, 1/2 (1994), 99–119.

41. G. Feldman, 'The Deutsche Bank from World War to World Economic Crisis, 1914–33', in Gall *et al.*, *The Deutsche Bank*, 184–91; E. Rosenbaum and A. J. Sherman, *M. M. Warburg & Co., 1798–1938* (London: C. Hurst, 1979), 121.

42. See S. A. Schuker, *The End of French Supremacy in Europe: The Financial Crisis of 1924 and the Adoption of the Dawes Plan* (Chapel Hill, NC: University of North Carolina Press, 1976); J.-N. Jeanneney, *L'argent caché: Milieux d'affaires et pouvoirs politiques dans la France du XXe siècle* (Paris: Fayard, 1981).

43. See H. Clay, *Lord Norman* (London: Macmillan, 1957). Norman's father was a private banker and both his grandfathers were directors of the Bank of England.

44. See R. S. Sayers, *The Bank of England 1891–1944* (Cambridge: Cambridge University Press, 1976); P. L. Cottrell, 'The Bank of England in Its International Setting, 1918–72', in R. Roberts and D. Kynaston (eds), *The Bank of England: Money, Power, and Influence, 1694–1994* (Oxford: Clarendon Press, 1995).

45. See Y. Cassis, 'Introduction: A Century of Consolidation in European Banking—General Trends', in M. Pohl, T. Tortella, and H. Van der Wee (eds), *A Century of Banking Consolidation in Europe* (Aldershot: Ashgate, 2001).

46. Archives Crédit Lyonnais, 36 AH 7.

47. See Jones, *British Multinational Banking*, 138–57.

48. See H. Wixforth, *Banken und Schwerindustrie in der Weimarer Republik* (Cologne: Böhlau, 1995).

49. For data and analysis on British banks' aggregate profits see F. Capie, 'Structure and Performance in British Banking, 1870–1939', in P. L. Cottrell and D. E. Moggridge (eds), *Money and Power* (London: Macmillan, 1988), 73–102. Analysis of the performance of individual French banks can be found in Bonin, 'Une grande entreprise bancaire', 374–9 and in Bussière, *Horace Finaly*, 347–51.

50. The analysis is based on the net profits published by the banks. In order to iron out possible distortions caused by occasional erratic results, profits and profitability have been compared on the basis of a three-year average (1927–9). For a discussion of the methodological problems raised by this analysis, see Cassis, *Big Business*, 75–8; 86.
51. Cassis, *Big Business*, 87–92.
52. Bonin, 'Une grande entreprise bancaire', 379.

3

British Commercial Bank Support for the Business Sector and the Pressure for Change, 1918–39

MICHAEL COLLINS and MAE BAKER

Introduction

In the interwar period commercial banks in Britain (as elsewhere) came under severe pressure to change their traditional approach to the provision of finance for the business sector. Problems arising from the disruption of the First World War, the Great Depression of 1929–32, and the long-term contraction of overseas markets for British manufacturing goods, led to major structural changes within the country's industrial sector and to large-scale unemployment. Central to the disruption were the chronic difficulties facing the so-called traditional industries that were heavily dependent on export markets—in particular, the coal, textiles, iron and steel, shipbuilding, and heavy engineering sectors. Such problems led to an unprecedented amount of pressure (both economic and political) on the banks to become more actively involved in the affairs of their business clients.

This chapter outlines the nature of that pressure and examines the banks' response, especially with regard to the critical issue of bank provision of finance for the business sector. A main finding is that, despite the large amount of high-profile pressure for change, there was, in fact, little change in the banks' traditional lending practices. This chapter seeks to explore the rationale underlying this conservative, enduring quality of bank lending practice.

The chapter is organized in the following manner: Section 2 outlines the traditional approach of British commercial banks to the provision of corporate finance; Section 3 discusses how aspects of agency theory may offer a rationale to underpin the British banks' version of 'transaction banking'; Section 4 summarizes the position adopted by English banks in the years prior to the First World War; Section 5 examines the pressures arising in the interwar years for the banks to abandon their traditional approach to financing the business sector, and the banks' response to that pressure; Section 6 examines the characteristics of a sample of loans for what it reveals of the type of financing provided by the banks for the business sector; Section 7 concludes by summarizing the evidence.

The Traditional Approach

Since at least the late nineteenth century British commercial bank lending has been confined predominantly to the provision of short-term credit and has involved the banks maintaining an arm's-length approach to the affairs of their business clientele. Indeed, the core business of commercial bank lending to the business sector has been characterized by a strong element of continuity in its focus on short-term loans and minimal involvement with clientele. It is this focus that has, through many years, attracted much criticism. In effect, British banks have been accused of ignorance of, and insensitivity to, the requirements of British business. On the positive side, it is generally accepted that the banks met sufficiently the short-term credit requirements of business firms—essentially requirements to finance operating costs and to iron out variations in cash flows—but criticisms are levelled at the banks' failure to provide longer-term finance, especially for small and medium-sized enterprises.[1]

The debate is sometimes conducted within a comparison of stylized, alternative systems for the provision of corporate finance: a market-based system, and a bank-based system. The former refers to a system wherein businesses seeking external finance raise borrowed funds or capital in large, impersonal, and competitive markets. In countries like the United Kingdom, where such a system has been important historically, the role of commercial banks has been largely supplementary, essentially confined to short-term credit provision. This is in contrast to bank-based systems, where—as the name implies—banks have played the dominant role in the provision of corporate financial requirements. In countries such as Germany and Japan the banks at different times in recent history have forged partnerships with major corporate clients and have become actively involved in the conduct of their clients' businesses. It is this greater involvement and 'commitment' to business clients that is often portrayed as a long-term strength of the bank-based system, as indicative of the banks' informed responsiveness to the financial requirements of the corporate sector.

Awareness of the contrast between German and British banking is of long standing. Thus, in 1917 an influential article by Foxwell criticized the failure of British banks to match their German counterparts in financing industrial development and structural change.[2] More recently, Kennedy has attacked the minimal role played by British financial institutions in financing new technological developments in the decades before the First World War.[3] Those decades are seen by Kennedy as pivotal to Britain's inability to embed a faster rate of economic growth into its long-term development. Such criticisms persist to the present day. Hutton, for instance, has lambasted City of London institutions for their overconcern for short-term returns and their persistent failure to finance adequately long-term investment to enable the country to sustain the sort of economic growth rates enjoyed by other developed economies.[4]

The thrust of the above arguments (and those of many other economic historians, including Elbaum and Lazonick,[5] Best and Humphries,[6] and Crafts[7]) is to claim that there was a significant supply-side constraint in British financial markets. In other words, a claim that British bank practices—with their concentration on short-term credit provision and their minimal involvement in the affairs of their business clients—have, over the course of more than a century, damaged British rates of investment and economic growth.

A major weakness with this argument, however, is that over such a long period of time it would be reasonable to expect profit-seeking institutions and agents to respond positively to unsatisfied demand from the business sector for more longer-term funding. In other words, why should the banks have ignored a profit-making opportunity, especially as commentators such as Kennedy claims that the lost profit potential has been substantial? One possible explanation is that the significant factor may have lain on the demand-side for funds. Perhaps British firms have not sought greater involvement from their bankers but have instead preferred the independence that comes from minimal commitment from creditors? On this line of argument, the limited nature of British bank involvement in corporate finance may have a demand-side explanation rather than a supply-side one.[8] Even so, those who stress supply-side deficiencies have sought to counter this view by invoking nonmarket, or supramarket, explanations. In particular, they claim that British banks and banking practice have been subjected to serious institutional sclerosis. Once banking business practices (such as minimal involvement with the business sector) were established in the nineteenth century, future lending became heavily path-determined, with vested interests and innate conservatism inhibiting the banks' response to the financial needs of the British corporate sector. In other words, institutional sclerosis rendered the banks insensitive to market demand for funds, to the detriment of long-term competitiveness and growth.

The Rationale behind Transaction Banking

This chapter reiterates and develops a somewhat different approach that we have expounded elsewhere.[9] The approach amounts to an attempt to offer an explanation for the historical durability of the traditional type of bank/corporate relations in Britain that is somewhat less critical of the banks than that adopted by many of the commentators summarized above.

The above account of the historical record reveals how durable has been British banking practice with respect to the provision of corporate finance. It is a durability that argues for the power of the economic rationale that lies behind the banks' behaviour. The understanding of that rationale can be found in aspects of modern finance theory—a theory that acknowledges market imperfections and deals with the consequences of information deficiencies and agency relationships. For banks making loans, the fundamental concern is to ensure that the debtor concurs with contractual arrangements and repays the loan in full. Undoubtedly, for the creditor there are costs associated with bankruptcy, asymmetric information, and incomplete contracts, and there always exists the possibility of borrower default.[10] It is for this reason that banks give careful consideration to screening potential borrowers and to monitoring debtors' performance, especially during the duration of loans.

Moral hazard and adverse selection are the twin dangers in making loans. The former can be viewed conveniently as a form of agency cost: the creditor bank acting as principal, the borrower as the agent. In this case the principal hands over control of the sum lent to the borrower for the duration of the loan. Conflicts of interest may arise with, for instance, the borrower tempted to use the loan to finance high risk projects (to maximize returns), whereas the lender seeks to maximize the chances of being repaid in full. The dangers of moral hazard are likely to be greater where shareholders in the borrowing company enjoy limited liability because, in such circumstances, debtors' losses and banks' powers of redress in case of default will be restricted. Also in the case of small and medium-sized enterprises (SMEs), available assets to pay off any bank debt in the case of liquidation may be limited. The danger of adverse selection can arise where information asymmetries make it difficult for the creditor to distinguish satisfactorily between good and bad risks (of either the borrower or the investment project, or both).

Finance theory suggests that banks have devised a variety of strategies to cope with the twin threats of moral hazard and adverse selection. In financial systems dominated by relationship banking, banks invest a great deal of resources in monitoring debtors, in acquiring privileged, detailed information on the performance of client firms, and on commitment.[11] In this context, commitment refers to a relationship that both client and bank perceive as long-term; in which they share information unavailable to other potential lenders (e.g. on the client's investment plans or product development); in which the bank might agree to provide finance in periods of distress; and in which the client might agree to keep the account with the bank during prosperous times.

Partly because of the short-term nature of their deposit liabilities, however, British commercial banks have never exhibited as deep an involvement in clients' affairs as have some German and Japanese banks. Although individual industrial clients in Britain might retain an account at the same bank for a very long period, the banks have been associated with an arm's-length approach to industry, to a lending policy more akin to transaction banking than to relationship banking. In its extreme form, transaction banking occurs where banks treat each loan as a separate transaction and deal with it on its own merits (wealth of borrower, collateral, duration, interest charges, etc.). In such circumstances, no detailed, privileged information is available to the creditor; the banks' procedures pay no particular regard to the long-term client/bank relationship; and clients are largely free to approach other potential lenders for the most competitive terms. In consequence, transaction bankers will lend for shorter periods and hold a much more liquid portfolio than relationship banks and will, thus, be under less pressure to reduce risk by engaging in deeper information gathering and deeper involvement in clients' affairs. The likelihood that the banks do not get involved is, of course, increased if the business firms are reluctant to allow dilution of control by conceding too much information and influence to creditor banks (the demand-side constraint raised earlier).

The transaction bank stereotype is useful in highlighting the distinguishing features of bank lending to industry in a banking system such as has existed in Britain over a very long time. Within transaction banking of this sort, control theories offer some insight into how creditors might try to offset the dangers inherent in client default. Thus, bankers will engage in the careful screening of would-be borrowers (assessing the applicants' net worth, establishing the purpose of the loan, and so on); they will filter applications to exclude high risk/low quality; they will show a strong preference for short-maturity loans subject to frequent review; and they will impose collateral and other requirements that will enable the easy and low-cost recovery of debt in case of client default. As will be shown, all these characteristics were prominent in British bank lending in the early part of the twentieth century.

Bank Lending Practices before the First World War

Extensive research has been carried out on surviving internal records of the English commercial banks in the four decades or so before 1914 with the overall objective of establishing the extent and nature of the commercial banks' involvement in the finance of the domestic business sector.[12] This has involved the analysis of transactions on over 3,000 industrial accounts at seventeen different banks (with the archives of the present-day Lloyds Bank and HSBC containing most of the information).

The first aim has been to identify the general characteristics of loans made by the banks to the business sector. The results here confirm that the bulk of commercial bank support for industry in the period 1880–1914 was in the form of short-term credits.[13] In fact, fewer than 5 per cent of the sample business loans were granted formally for longer than twelve months. Even allowing for the renewal of overdrafts, the actual duration of loans averaged no more than nineteen months and, in all, three-quarters of loans were of under two years' duration in the years just before the First World War. Moreover, it was found that bank overdrafts were used mainly to provide industrial concerns with a ready means of meeting cash flow and working capital requirements. In fact, 83 per cent of the sample loans to private firms were for these two purposes, and 72 per cent of the loans to limited liability companies. The financing of firms' fixed capital requirements accounted for 11–20 per cent (depending on period) of all sample loans, but even here relatively short-period loans were the norm. In addition, there was no evidence of commercial banks holding equity shares in industrial client firms.

Another finding of the study is that, whereas two-thirds of industrial loans were unsecured in the early 1880s, this practice declined over time and by 1914 it was common for the banks to take collateral against industrial loans, with three-quarters of loans being secured by 1914. This strong trend towards the greater provision of collateral was associated with changes in company law that led firms in the period to opt for much wider adoption of the corporate structure and of limited liability on share holdings. In other words, when sole owners and private partnerships with unlimited liability predominated amongst the banks' business borrowers, unsecured loans were common; but the widespread adoption of limited liability by firms raised the risks to creditors in case of liquidation, so that, in response, the banks tightened the terms of their loan contracts and imposed collateral requirements. Finally, the study of internal archives also shows that the value of such loan collateral almost always covered the full value of the loan outstanding.

The second line of investigation on the pre-1914 period identified 319 episodes of client distress and examined the response of the banks.[14]

This analysis shows that the English commercial banks did not engage in any deep involvement in clients' affairs, even in periods of client distress. In other words, they persisted with an arm's-length approach even in extremis. The investigation shows that the banks almost always continued to provide financial support for industrial firms during these difficult periods. There is also no evidence that the banks tried to exploit their stronger bargaining position during periods of client distress by raising interest charges on the account at the expense of distressed clients, despite the higher risks of default on such distressed accounts. In this sense, the English commercial banks continued to support their industrial clients during periods of distress—they displayed this degree of commitment. However, the reasons for the banks' ability and willingness to continue support lay in the effectiveness of their screening and control procedures. They were able to minimize loss to shareholders through the effective screening of both clients and loan applications (in order to minimize risk), by confining their business to loans of short formal duration that ensured frequent reviews, and by stipulating adequate collateral requirements. As a result, bank losses were very low even on these troublesome accounts. In fact, the banks' procedures were adequate to confine losses to fewer than 2 per cent of the total sample of 3,010 industrial loans, and on only 0.2 per cent of those loans was there complete loss for the banks of the sum loaned. Even in the distress cases, losses occurred on fewer than one-quarter of these high-risk accounts, and even then prior collateral stipulations confined those cases in which there was total loss of the banks' loans to under 3 per cent of the distressed cases. A major finding, therefore, is that normal commercial bank practices regarding the short duration of loans, collateral arrangements, and the initial screening of business applications enabled the banks to retain highly liquid loan portfolios and to minimize loss.

Overall, the findings from the archive-based study are consistent with the general findings of studies by Cottrell,[15] Newton,[16] and Watson,[17] though the emphasis is somewhat different. The other studies, in their various ways, tend to stress evidence of the banks supporting business firms. The latest results do not deny this, but they do emphasize that the great bulk of business loans were short-term, that they were used to cover fluctuations in cash flow and working capital costs, and that they involved minimal engagement by the banks in their clients' business.

Pressures for Change and Bank Reactions

In the interwar period British banks came under severe pressure to change this traditional approach to business finance provision. The pressure was both economic and political. On the economic front, from the collapse of the immediate postwar boom in 1921 a historically high unemployment rate characterized British economic fortunes for the following two decades. During the 1920s unemployment averaged just under 13 per cent of the insured labour force; in the 1930s the average was 16.5 per cent. A major feature was the great variation in sectoral and regional unemployment, with some geographically concentrated sectors such as Lancashire cotton, South Wales coalfields, and coastal shipbuilding areas all enduring unprecedentedly high and chronic rates of bankruptcy and unemployment. This contrasted with other regions of the country where industries prospered, especially in the South East of England and the West Midlands, where a number of rapidly expanding consumer goods and light engineering industries (motor vehicles, electrical goods, etc.) were located. Some figures will illustrate the extent of these disparities.[18] Thus, the rates of insured unemployment in coal mining and shipbuilding in 1929 were 19 and 25.3 per cent, respectively; and in 1937 the corresponding rates were 22.8 and 33.3 per cent. In contrast, the rate of unemployment in the 'cars and aircraft' and 'gas, water, and electricity' sectors were 7.1 and 6.1 per cent in 1929, and 5 and 8.3 per cent in 1937. Geographically, the North East had unemployment rates of 13.7 per cent in 1929 and of 11.1 per cent in 1937, as compared to those of the South East of 5.6 and 6.7 per cent. In Wales the corresponding rates were 19.3 per cent in 1929 and 23.3 per cent in 1937.

The common element for the high unemployment sectors and regions was a heavy reliance on export markets. It was the long-term contraction in British exports that broke the continuity with pre-1914 experience, and it is this that underpinned the severe structural problem of the period. As a ratio to GDP, exports declined sharply from 24 per cent in 1913 to 21 per cent in 1929, and then to 15 per cent in 1937 (all dates business cycle peaks). During the 1930s, exports (in constant price terms) averaged just two-thirds of prewar levels. The consequence was chronic, mass unemployment for export-oriented sectors. Obviously, it is possible that industrial difficulties of such a chronic nature as these may have provoked changes in established bank/industry relationships. Rising corporate indebtedness and pressing cash flow problems may well have drawn the banks more deeply into their customers' affairs, if only to protect already committed resources and to minimize losses.

These economic problems also gave rise to political pressure. As Britain's structural problems persisted over the 1920s and into the 1930s, the banks were exhorted by a growing number of influential contemporaries to use their resources to finance the longer-term regeneration of British industry. In general terms, the argument was that essential industrial 'restructuring'— involving the more rapid adoption of new technology, the application of new production methods and the rationalization of inefficient sectors—could be greatly facilitated if the country's giant financial institutions made available more resources to Britain's entrepreneurs. Henry Clay was one such advocate. He was an economics professor at Manchester, adviser to the Bank of England in the 1930s, a member of the Royal Commission on Unemployment Insurance, a founder member of the National Institute of Economic and Social Research, and, eventually, biographer of Lord Norman, governor of the Bank of England. In other words, Clay was part of the politico-economic establishment, yet he was very critical of the banks. In his *The Post-War Unemployment Problem* published in 1929,[19] he berated the banks for profiteering from the prevailing high interest rates, for helping to keep inefficient firms in business, and for not being adequately involved in the funding of industry. He called upon the banks to show leadership in rationalizing industry, and he advocated government 'propulsion' if they failed to do so. Politically, Clay was mainstream and there were many with more radical plans that helped define the political context within which the banks could contemplate altering their normal practices *vis-à-vis* their business clientele. In the early 1930s the Labour Party Conference endorsed a resolution calling for the public ownership of the country's commercial banks. Disquiet about the banks' role in providing funds for the corporate sector was also a factor in the establishment of the official Macmillan Committee in 1929, with its wide-ranging brief to 'enquire into banking, finance and credit, paying regard to factors both internal and international which govern their operation, and to make recommendations calculated to enable these agencies to promote the development of trade and commerce and the employment of labour'.[20]

In this highly charged atmosphere, the role of the Bank of England was pivotal. The Bank was still a privately owned institution, and its long-serving governor, Montagu Norman, was a jealous guardian of its special responsibilities towards the City.[21] He felt greatly the need to avoid political interference and he was instrumental in launching a number of initiatives from within the financial sector that went some way to address the problems of industry. Thus, the Bank was instrumental in establishing the Bankers' Industrial Development Company in 1930. The company's capital of £6 million was subscribed by the Bank of England, the clearing banks, and other financial institutions. Its proposed business was to vet and finance rationalization plans submitted by industrialists from the export-oriented industries. Another of the Bank's initiatives, the Lancashire Cotton Corporation, was also established (in 1931) with funding from the commercial banks and the Bank itself. Here the aim was to finance the sharp reduction in cotton production capacity. Norman was also involved in establishing a scheme to provide funds for small businesses in the depressed regions and in the promotion of hire-purchase finance for the business sector. In total, these schemes may be judged as fairly conservative compared to some of the political responses that the Great Depression was provoking elsewhere in the world. Nevertheless, they stand out as a major break of tradition for Bank of England involvement in the economy.

How about the commercial banks? Did the mounting economic and political pressure of the time provoke any fundamental change in their provision of corporate finance? There are certainly a number of well-documented cases involving large industrial customers. In these cases, the scale of bad debt and potential losses to individual commercial banks was such as to lead to a greater degree of bank involvement in clients' business affairs, perhaps to an unprecedented extent.

One such high profile case was that of the Royal Mail group, which ran into such deep financial difficulties as to necessitate the major restructuring of the group between 1931 and 1936.[22] The group accounted for about 15 per cent of Britain's total merchant fleet, including the Royal Mail Steam Packet Co., Pacific Steam Navigation Co., Elder Dempster & Co., and White Star. The group also had extensive shipbuilding and steel interests. By the end of the 1920s the group was facing collapse on such a large scale (with £120 million of gross liabilities) that, at one time or other, many of the British commercial banks became involved in the major task of rescheduling the debt while rationalization plans were implemented. The Midland Bank and its affiliates had about £3.5 million of outstanding loans with the Royal Mail group, compared to the bank's total shareholder capital of some £26 million in the first half of the 1930s.[23] In consequence, the bank's most senior staff devoted a great deal of time to the detailed negotiations and arrangements for restructuring the industrial combine.

A similar case was that of Beardmore, a large Scottish steel and engineering conglomerate that was in serious financial difficulties for most of the 1930s.[24] Lloyds Bank, the National Bank of Scotland, and the Royal Bank of Scotland were all large creditors and all three had to work out how to reschedule their client's debt while engaging in detailed negotiations over the business plans to shed capacity and cut costs. One novelty was that the banks converted some of their loans to preference shares (to the extent of £1.4 million). However, they were reluctant participants in the nitty-gritty of the client's business. They were there to protect their own interests; they threatened liquidation when it suited them and kept their commitments to a minimum, although the client's dire financial circumstances and the threat of default obliged them to be more involved than normal.

Greater involvement through necessity, but reluctance and diffidence on the banks' part for industrial involvement, was repeated elsewhere.[25] Tolliday's study of the problems of the steel industry endorses this view.[26] His findings have been summarized in the following manner:

[Tolliday] accepts that the banks became more committed to industry in the sense that they extended their advances to industrial customers in the euphoric boom conditions immediately following the war and that the subsequent problems of Britain's export staples meant that the banks were drawn into a greater consideration of their customers' difficulties in order to protect these loans. However, the response was diffident, relying upon the application of traditional banking values, even in the unusual conditions prevailing.[27]

It is true that in the 1930s a number of City institutions helped to establish a number of new institutions with a view to providing additional sources of finance for industry. For instance, the Charterhouse Industry Development Company was set up in 1934 to enhance the supply of venture capital. This was partly financed by the Midland Bank and Lloyds Bank. But, together with other initiatives of the time, such institutions are generally felt to have made little impact on the provision of corporate finance.[28] In their core activity of providing bank loans to industrial client firms, however, for the most part the banks' response to industry's problems was largely passive—responding, when client difficulties arose, to protect their own shareholders from debtor default and remaining unwilling to make a positive commitment to industrial restructuring. They retained an arm's length approach to their clients' businesses, even in adversity. If anything, losses and threatened losses incurred during this period made the bankers even more cautious.

Sample Evidence Results

In aggregate terms, there is no evidence of the commercial banks diverting more of their resources to the business sector. They remained committed to maintaining a highly liquid balance sheet throughout. Table 3.1 shows changes in the London clearing banks' asset distribution over the interwar period.

Table 3.1. *London clearing banks' asset ratios (%)*

	1924	1926	1929	1932	1937
Cash	12.3	11.9	11.3	10.4	10.5
Money at call and short notice	6.9	7.7	7.9	6.4	6.9
Bills	14.0	13.5	12.6	20.6	13.1
Investments	18.9	15.4	13.8	23.8	26.9
Advances	48.8	52.4	54.6	39.0	42.1
[Absolute amount £m.]	[828]	[905]	[989]	[773]	[948]

Notes: Expressed as a percentage of total deposits, end of year, and cyclical turning points. The district bank excluded throughout.

Source: F. Capie and M. Collins, *The Inter-War British Economy: A Statistical Abstract* (Manchester: Manchester University Press, 1983), 92–9.

This was a very liquid balance sheet. 'Cash' and 'Money at call and short notice' were the most liquid of the banks' assets. 'Cash' consisted of currency and balances at the Bank of England, whereas 'Money at call and short notice', were very short-period loans to London money market institutions. 'Bills' were predominantly Treasury bills, and even 'Investments' were overwhelmingly government securities. 'Advances' were overdrafts and fixed-period loans, and they were the least liquid of the banks' assets. They represented the great bulk of the banks' private sector financing, and they were essentially nonmarketable. As can be seen, advances comprised between 39 and 45 per cent of total bank assets. Significantly, the proportion was lower in the 1930s than in the 1920s—struggling to rise above 40 per cent in the 1930s compared to over 50 per cent in the latter half of the 1920s. Indeed in absolute terms, the total value of bank loans outstanding was down slightly between 1929 and 1937 despite the fairly steady growth in the economy as a whole from 1932 and the continued growth on trend of the banks' total deposit resources. Obviously, in aggregate terms Britain's growth was not being financed by bank loans at that time. Indeed, there is evidence that the commercial banks suffered a sharp loss of market share during those years. Thus, as a proportion of the country's total financial assets, the total assets of UK banks fell from 49.9 per cent in 1924 to 45.7 per cent in 1929, and to 43.3 per cent in 1937 (all dates are business cycle peaks). For the large London-based commercial banks of England and Wales (Barclays, Lloyds, etc.) the decline seems to have been even sharper—from 40.6 per cent of total financial assets in 1924 to 37.1 per cent in 1929, and down to 33 per cent in 1937.[29]

Why was this? Partly, it was a feature of growing financial sophistication. As real incomes rose, there was an increased demand from the public for a greater range of financial assets and financial services than those offered by the commercial banks. However, there were also significant supply constraints. First, the British commercial banks continued to adhere to the established pattern of demarcation in the provision of financial services. So, as they concentrated on the provision of cheque accounts, the supply of short-term loans, and the maintenance of a rapid transmission mechanism, more rapid expansion in other financial services (such as mortgages) meant an inevitable loss of market share. Moreover, the commercial banks continued to exercise oligopoly power based on the high degree of market concentration in both England and Scotland. After the culmination of the bank merger movement from the turn of the previous century, the five largest banks by 1920 accounted for about 80 per cent of domestic deposits in England and Wales.[30] Moreover, they exercised little price competition. The London clearing banks operated a price cartel, and, in the case of advances, they normally operated a minimum interest rate of 4–5 per cent on their best accounts.[31] However, the 1930s was a decade of 'cheap money'. As market interest rates fell, the banks' cartel rate became increasingly uncompetitive and demand for their loans fell.

Those able to do so, found it advisable to borrow elsewhere (such as the debenture market).[32]

Apart from these aggregate figures on the clearing banks' overall lending, it has been possible to conduct a micro-study. The figures in Table 3.2 are an attempt to summarize certain characteristics of a sample of business loans made by the London clearing banks in the period 1920–39.[33]

Table 3.2. *Characteristics of a sample of business loans granted by English commercial banks, 1920–39*

A. *Type of loan facilities (% of sample loans) n = 586*

Overdrafts	49
Loan accounts	19
Bill discounts	19
Credits	9
Other	4

B. *Duration of loans (months) n = 327*

Mean	6.5
Median	6.0
99 percentile	12.0
Maximum	23.9

C. *Purpose of loans (% of sample loans) n = 355*

Trade credit	73
Other trading and working capital	6
Cash flow	7
Fixed capital expenditure	6
Purchase of shares in other businesses	2
Other	6

D. *Type of securities taken as collateral (% of sample loans) n = 367*

None	16
Personal and directors' guarantees	16
Charges on real estate	39
Debentures	9
Equity	10
Claims on produce	1
Other	9

E. *Value of securities as a ratio to the value of loans (excluding loans where no security was taken) n = 255*

Mean ratio	1.1
Median ratio	0.9

Source: Internal archives of London clearing banks.

The number of loans in the samples varies (from 255 to 586) depending on the characteristic identified. As can be seen, overdrafts accounted for almost half of the loans provided, with fixed-term loan accounts and bill discounts each providing another 19 per cent of loans. The great bulk of these loans were for short periods only. The average duration was about six months, and 99 per cent of the loans were granted in the first instance for less than 12 months. The main purpose of these bank loans is obvious from Section C of Table 3.2: trade credit, other trading and working capital, and cash flow requirements together accounted for 86 per cent of all business loans. The financing of firms' fixed capital expenditure features in only 6 per cent of bank loans. These findings are consistent with earlier interwar studies by Ross.[34] To summarize these findings thus far: it seems clear that English banks overwhelmingly concentrated on providing their business customers' short-term credit, trade, and cash flow requirements and on providing bridging arrangements through short-duration loans that were due for repayment fairly quickly, or for early review if renewal was sought by the client. Moreover, the risks to the banks from this short-term credit provision were reduced further by the normal collateral stipulations. As Section D of Table 3.2 shows, the banks took security against loans in all but 16 per cent of cases—with charges on real estate, guarantees, equity, and debentures taken in descending order of popularity. Significantly, in those cases in which security was taken against loans, the value of that security normally covered the full value of the loan. In other words, even if default were to occur in the repayment of these short-duration, low-risk loans, the banks' commitments were usually covered 100 per cent. Even in cases of default, the banks were likely to recover their money if their assessment and valuation of collateral were good. In general terms, these new findings suggest that the commercial banks retained their traditional approach in this core area of their business (the provision of finance to the business sector) despite the perceived pressures on them in the period to break with those traditions.

Conclusion

It has been argued that in the period between the wars, contemporary perceptions of the unusual scale of Britain's economic problems, especially the problems of industry, led to unprecedented pressure on commercial banks to abandon their traditional approach to the provision of corporate finance. As has been shown, this traditional approach effectively confined commercial bank involvement to the provision of short-term credits. The summary presented of recent research findings on the period before 1914 does, indeed, confirm—at least for England and Wales—that the commercial banks maintained an arm's-length approach to their business clients, essentially meeting their working capital and cash flow requirements. Examination of the situation between the wars also shows that, despite pressure to the contrary, bankers generally perceived the problem of reforming Britain's industrial base as a problem for industrialists, not for the banks. For the commercial banks, corporate bad debt in a number of instances did draw bankers further into the business affairs of their clients, but this proved temporary and invoked no fundamental change in the traditional, short-term, arm's-length approach to company finance. Indeed, new results on the profile of a sample of commercial bank loans to the business sector strongly endorse this view. Of course, it is this position of non-involvement with industry that drew criticism onto the heads of the bankers both at the time and subsequently. At its most vitriolic, the criticism has been of the bankers' anti-industry bias and irrational judgement. However, this section has offered some theoretical rationale for the banks' continued loyalty to their traditional approach to lending to the business sector. For the banks, an emphasis on short-term credits, regular reviews, and sufficient collateral minimized both monitoring costs and potential loss from client default. For the wider economy, it also ensured bank stability. In contrast to experience in other countries (both between the wars and subsequently), the transaction banking approach maintained by British commercial banks even in the interwar period, helped assure systemic financial stability and the advantages that flowed from that stability.

NOTES

1. The presumption usually made is that that SMEs find recourse to the new issue market expensive because of the relatively high burden of transaction costs (publicity, legal fees, issuing house fees, etc.) compared to the modest amounts of capital they want to raise. Thus, the importance of bank finance to such firms is that much greater.
2. H. S. Foxwell, 'The Financing of Industry and Trade', *Economic Journal* 27/108 (1917), 502–22.
3. W. P. Kennedy, *Industrial Structure, Capital Markets and the Origins of English Economic Decline* (Cambridge: Cambridge University Press, 1987); W. P. Kennedy, 'Capital Markets and Industrial Structure in the Victorian Economy', in J. J. van Helten and Y. Cassis (eds), *Capitalism in a Mature Economy: Financial Institutions, Capital Exports and English Industry, 1870–1939* (Aldershot: E. Elgar, 1990), 23–51; and W. P. Kennedy, 'Portfolio Behaviour and Economic Development

in Late Nineteenth-Century Great Britain and Germany: Hypothesis and Conjectures', *Research in Economic History, Supplement*, 6 (1991), 93–130.

4. W. Hutton, *The State We're In* (London: Vintage, 1995).

5. B. Elbaum and W. Lazonick, (eds), *The Decline of the British Economy* (Oxford: Clarendon, 1986).

6. M. H. Best and J. Humphreys, 'The City and Industrial Decline', in B. Elbaum and W. Lazonick (eds), *The Decline of the British Economy*, 223–39.

7. N. F. R. Crafts, 'Productivity Growth Reconsidered', *Economic Policy* 15 (1992), 387–414.

8. M. Collins, *Banks and Industrial Finance in Britain 1800–1939* (London: Macmillan Education, 1991; reissued with revisions, Cambridge: Cambridge University Press, 1995); F. Capie and M. Collins, *Have the Banks Failed British Industry?* (London: Institute of Economic Affairs, 1992).

9. M. Baker and M. Collins, 'The Durability of Transaction Banking Practices in the Provision of Finance to the Business Sector by British Banks', *Entreprises et Histoire*, 22 (Oct. 1999), 1–16.

10. D. W. Diamond, 'Financial Intermediation and Delegated Monitoring', *Review of Economic Studies* 51/3 (1984), 393–414; E. F. Fama, 'What's Different about Banks?' *Journal of Monetary Economics* 15/1 (1985), 29–39; C. Mayer, 'New Issues in Corporate Finance', *European Economic Review* 32/5 (1988), 1167–89; E. P. Davis, 'Whither Corporate-Banking Relations?' in K. Hughes (ed.), *The Future of UK Industrial Competitiveness and the Role of Industrial Policy* (London: Policy Studies Institute, 1993); and E. van Damme, 'Banking: A Survey of Recent Micro-Economic Theory', *Oxford Review of Economic Policy* 10/4 (1994), 15–33.

11. T. Hoshi, A. Kashyap, and D. Scharfstein, 'The Role of Banks in Reducing the Costs of Financial Distress in Japan', *Journal of Financial Economics* 27/1 (1990), 67–88; T. Hoshi, A. Kashyap, and D. Scharfstein, 'Corporate Structure, Liquidity, and Investment: Evidence from Japanese Industrial Groups', *Quarterly Journal of Economics* 106/1 (1991), 33–60; E. P. Davis, 'Whither Corporate-Banking Relations?' in K. Hughes (ed.), *The Future of UK Industrial Competitiveness*; J. Edwards and K. Fischer, *Banks, Finance and Investment in Germany* (Cambridge: Cambridge University Press, 1994); O. Sussman, 'Investment and Banking: Some International Comparisons', *Oxford Review of Economic Policy* 10/4 (1994), 79–93.

12. The investigation 'Commercial Banks and Industrial Finance in England and Wales, 1850–1914' was financed by the Economic and Social Research Council [ref. R000 23 2220] and was supervised by Michael Collins and Forrest Capie. Particular gratitude is expressed for the help and encouragement of the HSBC plc, National Westminster Bank plc, Barclays Bank plc, Lloyds Bank plc, and the Royal Bank of Scotland plc. Judith Wale, Phillip Hunt, and Ian Flowers assisted with different aspects of the archival work.

13. F. Capie and M. Collins, 'Banks, Industry and Finance, 1880–1914', *Business History* 41/1 (1999), 37–62.

14. M. Baker and M. Collins, 'English Industrial Distress before 1914 and the Response of the Banks', *European Review of Economic History* 3/1 (1999), 1–24.

15. P. L. Cottrell, *Industrial Finance, 1830–1914: The Finance and Organisation of English Manufacturing Industry* (London: Methuen, 1980).

16. L. Newton, 'Regional Bank-Industry Relations during the Mid-Nineteenth Century: Links between Bankers and Manufacturing in Sheffield, c.1850–c.1885', *Business History* 38/3 (1996), 64–83.
17. K. Watson, 'Banks and Industrial Finance: The Experience of Brewers, 1880–1913', *Economic History Review* 49/1 (1996), 58–81.
18. Unemployment data are from the *Ministry of Labour Gazette*.
19. H. Clay, *The Post-War Unemployment Problem* (London: Macmillan, 1929).
20. (Macmillan) Committee on Finance and Industry, *Report*, cmd. 3897 (London: HMSO, 1931), minute of appointment.
21. R. S. Sayers, *The Bank of England, 1891–1944*, 3 vols. (Cambridge: Cambridge University Press, 1976); S. Bowden and M. Collins, 'The Bank of England, Industrial Regeneration, and Hire Purchase between the Wars', *Economic History Review* 45/1 (1992), 120–36; W. R. Garside and J. I. Greaves, 'The Bank of England and Industrial Intervention in Interwar Britain', *Financial History Review* 3/1 (1996), 69–86.
22. E. Green and M. S. Moss, *A Business of National Importance: The Royal Mail Shipping Group, 1892–1937* (London: Methuen, 1982). For a summary of this and the following cases see M. Collins, *Banks and Industrial Finance in Britain 1800–1939*, 68–75.
23. See A. R. Holmes and E. Green, *Midland: 150 Years of Banking History* (London: B. T. Batsford, 1986), 334.
24. J. R. Hume and M. S. Moss, *Beardmore: The History of a Scottish Industrial Giant* (London: Heinemann, 1979).
25. M. W. Kirby, 'The Lancashire Cotton Industry in the Interwar Years: A Study in Organisation Change', *Business History* 16/1–2 (1974), 145–59; and J. Bamberg, 'The Rationalisation of the British Cotton Industry in the Interwar Years', *Textile History* 19/1 (1988), 83–101.
26. S. Tolliday, *Business, Banking and Politics: The Case of English Steel, 1918–1936* (London: Harvard University Press, 1987).
27. Collins, *Banks and Industrial Finance in Britain 1800–1939*, 73.
28. W. A. Thomas, *The Finance of British Industry, 1918–1976* (London: Methuen, 1978), 121; R. Coopey and D. Clarke, *3i: Fifty Years Investing in Industry* (Oxford: Oxford University Press, 1995), ch. 1; Holmes and Green, *Midland*, 183.
29. Ratios calculated from D. K. Sheppard, *The Growth and Role of UK Financial Institutions, 1880–1962* (London: Methuen, 1971), tables 1.1, (A)1.2 and (A)1.13.
30. M. Collins, 'Organisational Growth of Financial Institutions, 1826–1914', in M. W. Kirby and M. Rose (eds), *Business Enterprise and Industrialisation* (London: Routledge, 1994), 282.
31. (Macmillan) Committee on Finance and Industry, *Report*, cmd. 3897, 32.
32. E. Nevin, *The Mechanism of Cheap Money* (Cardiff: University of Wales Press, 1955), 250–1.
33. The results are derived from a larger project on 'Banks and Industrial Finance in Britain, 1920–71', Economic and Social Research Council [ref. R000 23 6447], 1997–99, which has been supervised by M. Collins, F. Capie, and D. Ross. We are particularly grateful to HSBC plc, National Westminster Bank plc, Barclays Bank plc, Lloyds Bank plc, and the Royal Bank of Scotland plc; and also to Miriam Silverman, who conducted the archival work for this part of the project.

34. D. M. Ross, 'The Clearing Banks and Industry: New Perspectives on the Inter-War Years', in J. J. van Helten and Y. Cassis (eds), *Capitalism in a Mature Economy*, 52–70; D. M. Ross, 'Information, Collateral and English Bank Lending in the 1930s', in Y. Cassis, G. D. Feldman, and U. Olsson (eds), *The Evolution of Financial Institutions and Markets in Twentieth-Century Europe* (Aldershot: Scolar Press, 1995), 273–94; and D. M. Ross, 'Commercial Banking in a Market-Oriented Financial System: Britain between the Wars', *Economic History Review* 49/2 (1996), 314–35.

4

The New Deal and Commercial Banking Lending

EUGENE N. WHITE

Introduction

In the 1990s American banks radically restructured their asset portfolios to better manage risks. They moved away from borrowing short and lending long-term towards more closely matching maturities or hedging risks. One key feature of this transformation was a decline in the importance of banks' 'traditional lending' operations. This traditional lending was not a simple market-driven outcome but was largely shaped by New Deal regulations. In response to the economic collapse of the Great Depression, the New Deal sought to increase bank lending by encouraging banks to forgo their established practice of short-term lending. Although much of the New Deal legislation attempted to make banks into safer, more conservative institutions, its policies towards lending had the result of increasing risk by increasing duration. The effects of this change did not immediately become apparent, but they had long-term consequences for the soundness of the banking industry. The objective of this chapter is to examine the development and implementation of these policies and to measure their initial effects on banks.

Commercial Bank Lending Before the Great Depression

In the wake of the Great Depression, commercial bank lending in the United States shifted dramatically away from an emphasis on pure short-term lending and towards more long-term credits. This transformation, which changed both banking thought and practice, is best understood when compared to the norms of the late nineteenth and early twentieth centuries.

Commercial bank lending was traditionally viewed through the prism of the real bills doctrine. It influenced not only American bankers but also the founders of the Federal Reserve System, guiding Federal Reserve policy through the 1920s. According to the real bills doctrine, banks should offer only short-term loans to finance the production or shipment of goods, which when sold would pay off the loans. These loans were considered to be safe because they financed real short-term commercial transactions. Adherents of the real bills doctrine believed that if banks followed their prescription for lending, loans would be limited to the legitimate needs of business. Banks would have safe assets and maintain liquidity, as loans would be paid off at maturity. In a standard banking text, Kniffin wrote:

> The secret of sound banking is to have a steady stream of money coming in by way of maturing loans, so that the constant stream of obligations falling due daily by reason of the demands of the checking depositors may be met. A demand obligation cannot be met by a time security and only as a bank keeps its funds liquid—that is, flowing in and out—can it meet every demand made on it without hardship.[1]

The real bills doctrine requirement that loans be short-term implied that banks should minimize the maturity mismatch of assets and liabilities. While a bank's earnings were reduced from the term premium on the smaller mismatch, its ability to meet any demand for liquidity or a run on the bank would in theory be improved.

In a world of highly asymmetric information, the real bills doctrine can be interpreted as a simple theory of risk management where collection of information and monitoring were difficult. Reputation, quality of collateral, and brevity of maturity were then the key instruments of risk management when banks offered credit in the form of discounts or loans. Discounts were unsecured loans made on the general credit of the borrower and their quality was often determined by the reputation of the signers and endorsers of the note. Loans were commonly but not always secured by a pledge of collateral, including stocks, bonds, receivables, merchandise, or real estate; hence their quality was determined, in part, by the quality of the collateral.[2] Making discounts and loans required banks to collect information that was not easily marketable or transferable. It was a specialized function that was not replicable by the market.[3] Although there was an active commercial paper market, it was relatively modest in size compared to bank lending. In the 1920s, the outstanding stock of commercial paper declined from $1.2 billion to $265 million, while bank loans grew from $30 to $40 billion.[4] This special function of commercial banks made them the dominant intermediary in the first quarter of the twentieth century, accounting for 63 per cent of all intermediaries assets in 1900 and 1922.[5]

The ability of bankers to acquire information on their customers improved very slowly. The result was that they continued to follow the precepts of the real bills doctrine, focusing on the evaluation of specific transactions, collateral, and the quality of endorsers. Many bankers relied on their general impression of customers' creditworthiness, and they described their approach as the 'character loan' method.[6] If it was determined that a borrower had a good character and record, credit would be offered; if either aspect was flawed, no loan would be forthcoming. This type of lending with low information processing needs did not require a large staff and suited the predominantly small banks. Even larger banks might only employ a cashier who headed daily operations, several tellers and clerks, and perhaps a bookkeeper. Management was largely in the hands of the directors, one of whom was selected as president. The directors verified the cashier's accounts and decided how much to lend and to whom.[7] The directors rarely had a staff to draw up detailed reports on customers and relied on their local knowledge of business and their customers' 'character'.

The first credit department was apparently established by the Importer's and Trader's National of New York in the 1880s.[8] Credit departments would eventually make granting credit more impersonal, examining the financial records, not the character, of prospective borrowers. After the panic of 1893, the idea began to spread, but by 1899 only ten banks in New York had credit departments.[9] Bankers did supplement their own knowledge of business borrowers by subscribing to reports of credit agencies like R. G. Dun and Company. Yet these reports were usually based on estimates of a firm's worth or reports from lawyers and other business people about the character of its proprietors, not on financial statements.[10]

Financial statements played a small role compared to a banker's intimate knowledge of local clients. The absence of uniform accounting standards for business weakened the usefulness of financial statements for decision making. Accountants had little authority to impose standardized accounting practices, as there were few statutory requirements.[11] Without uniform accounting methods, there was no alternative to a banker's qualitative judgement of his customer. Moulton believed that in the late 1870s financial statements were first used for procuring loans, but they were rare even for large banks until the turn of the century.[12] The long-standing problem posed by an absence of accounting standards was highlighted when in 1914 the Federal Reserve Board attempted to guarantee the quality of member banks' paper eligible for discount by requiring that borrowers' statements be certified by public accountants. Strong opposition forced the Federal Reserve to waive this requirement for loans below $2,500, as few banks, except some larger city banks, had loans or discounts that met this standard.[13] Still, bank practices were gradually changing and incorporating more financial and accounting information. Pushed further with inducements from the Federal Reserve, commercial banks' capacity to monitor the changing conditions of their borrowers was improving and would influence the maturities of the loans they offered.

Traditionally, the maturity of loans and discounts was short, although not as short as real bills purists would have desired. The nominal length of most contracts appeared to be short. James concluded that most loans by banks had short-term maturities, typically thirty, sixty, or ninety days, with one year being an upper bound.[14] One survey by the Comptroller of the Currency found that 57 per cent of all bank loans had maturities of less than ninety days.[15] However, lending practices often differed from what appeared on banks' books. Many loans were rolled over, tailoring them to the working capital needs of firms and farmers. One detailed study of a small bank found a portfolio consisting largely of demand loans whose actual maturity averaged nine months.[16] In general, Moulton saw little evidence that loans were liquidated at maturity.[17] He found that country banks granted repeated renewals, extending a loan for years to finance working capital. In commercial centres, bankers estimated that 40–50 per cent of unsecured loans were typically renewed, providing continuous credit. While borrowers often received credit for longer than the initial maturity, the option of the banker to cancel the loan was an important feature of the credit. By keeping this option, the banker retained discipline over the borrower and potential liquidity by demanding repayment.

These lending practices persisted into the 1920s. Jacoby and Saulnier reported that, while bankers continued to offer almost exclusively short-term loans, there was a full expectation on the part of both borrowers and lenders that these would be renewed.[18] One study of Iowa banks for 1914–24 showed that while notes were dated with six-month maturities, actual matur-ities ranged from ten to thirty-two months. Nevertheless, bankers shied away from long-term lending. In the 1920s, bankers often conducted an annual 'clean up' of debt to demonstrate their creditworthiness and that the bank was not financing any permanent capital. Jacoby and Saulnier observed that many businesses continued to extinguish their loans for a particular bank for a short period each year by borrowing from other institutions.

Following the real bills doctrine, the Federal Reserve's discounting rules also were designed to encourage short-term lending. In borrowing from a Federal Reserve bank, a member bank could only discount 'eligible paper', defined as notes, drafts, and bills of exchange arising out of actual commercial transactions. The rules for eligible paper excluded all but short-term paper of the highest quality.[19] Only a fraction of most banks' portfolios were eligible for discount under these criteria.

The expansion in bank lending that accompanied the economic boom of the 1920s was thus based on short-term credits. Figure 4.1 shows the surge

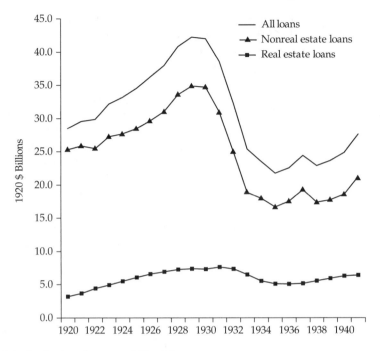

Fig. 4.1. *Real value of commercial bank loans*
Source: US Department of Commerce, *Historical Statistics*: 1021–2.

of bank loans that occurred between 1921 and 1929. Although real estate loans increased in this period, the bulk of the rise was in commercial and industrial lending. Towards the end of the boom, when the stock market began to soar in 1928–9, banks also made more brokers' loans, loans collateralized with stocks and bonds. Apart from real bills strictures and the discounting rules of the Federal Reserve, commercial bankers were hesitant to lend for longer terms before 1914 because most of their deposits were demand deposits.

The National Banking Act of 1864's reserve requirements did not differentiate between demand and time deposits. Among national banks, country banks had a 15 per cent reserve requirement, and reserve and central reserve cities a 25 per cent requirement.[20] State-chartered banks typically had lower reserve requirements. The Federal Reserve Act of 1913 lowered the requirement on demand deposits to 12 and 5 per cent for time deposits for member banks.[21] Responding to states lowering requirements for state-chartered banks, Congress further reduced the requirements for member banks to 7 and 3 per cent in 1917.

This differentiation in reserve requirements altered the composition of bank deposits. In June 1910 commercial banks held $8.3 billion of demand deposits and $3.6 billion of time deposits. By 1920 demand deposits had climbed to $19.6 billion while time deposits increased to $10.5 billion. They moved to near equality by June 1929, with $22.5 billion and $19.6 billion, respectively. This development can also be seen in Fig. 4.2, which depicts the distribution of commercial bank liabilities. Here the share of demand deposits declines while the share of time deposits rises. Given this movement, if the average maturity of the loan portfolio were held constant, this shift from demand deposits to time deposits would have reduced the maturity mismatch, making banks subject to greater risk from interest rate fluctuations and withdrawals of deposits. If, instead, bankers had maintained the same degree of maturity mismatch, they could have easily increased the term of loans and maintained the same degree of risk.

Commercial banks did not, however, become a more important vehicle for the long-term finance of business in the 1920s. They were constrained by regulation from participation and failed to hold on to their business customers. Between 1920 and 1929, commercial banks' share of funds provided to corporations fell from 12 to 2 per cent and to all business from 65 to 56 per cent.[22] This decline in the relative importance of bank loans can be traced to the federal and state regulations that limited branching, loan

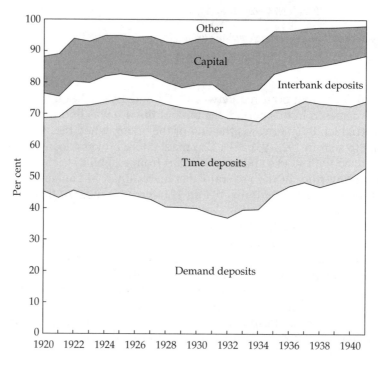

Fig. 4.2. *Distribution of commercial bank liabilities*
Source: US Department of Commerce, *Historical Statistics*: 1021–2.

size, portfolio selection, and other activities. When these rules were imposed in the nineteenth century, they had relatively little effect on banks' ability to supply the credit needs of industry, but they now served as strong constraints.

The limits on branch banking were particularly onerous, as they frustrated banks' efforts to diversify and keep pace with rapidly growing large-scale corporations. The Comptroller of the Currency ruled in 1865 that national banks were limited to one office. This decision was adopted by most states, which banned or severely restricted state-chartered branching. In 1924 only eleven states allowed state-wide branching, and nine permitted some limited form, with very few banks building even a modest branching system. Branching grew slowly; by 1930 there were still only 3,522 branch offices compared to 23,251 banks.[23] These branching constraints kept banks small. Combined with the rule that the maximum loan to any borrower was equal to 10 per cent of capital, many banks could not offer sufficient credit to their larger customers in the form of loans.

Instead, large borrowers seeking long-term credit looked to the capital markets. The market for industrial securities developed rapidly in the last decade of the nineteenth century, but blossomed in the 1920s. Commercial banks that were in danger of losing customers now began to compete on the turf of the investment banks. Many banks were introduced to the securities business by the patriotic campaigns to sell Liberty bonds during the First World War. After the war, customers looked to banks for advice and assistance to find new investments, and banks needed to service their larger customers. Larger banks shifted their corporate finance activities to separate securities affiliates that allowed them to act as full-fledged investment banks and brokerage houses. National City Bank of New York (predecessor of Citibank) and Chase National Bank (predecessor of Chase Manhattan) were two leaders in this field.[24] Numerous depositors enabled banks and their affiliates to distribute securities and gained them participations in underwriting syndicates. By the end of the decade many money centre banks and their affiliates underwrote, distributed, and dealt in most types of securities and may have controlled half of the investment banking business. Thus, investment banks and securities affiliates had become key providers of long-term finance, while commercial banking thus remained wedded to short-term lending.

The New Deal Reshapes Bank Lending

Commercial bank lending was transformed by the Great Depression. Although existing trends improving monitoring and changes in the structure of liabilities may have induced banks to increase the length of loans, New Deal regulations pushed them into offering much longer-term credit than they would have otherwise. Much of the New Deal attempted to eliminate the innovations of the 1920s and halt further change. The structure of the banking system was effectively frozen, branching prohibitions were retained, and the new regulations created a loosely organized cartel where the government imposed barriers to entry and limits on pricing and activities. The federal government felt compelled, however, to innovate and push banks into long-term lending to reverse the collapse of bank loans and the bond and stock markets that deprived business of access to capital. As seen in Fig. 4.1, nonreal estate bank loans fell to half of their peak value of $35 billion in 1929 and failed to recover for the remainder of the 1930s.

One of the driving factors behind the change in the character of bank lending was the federal government's regulation of the securities markets, defined primarily by the Glass–Steagall Act of 1932, the Securities Act of 1933, and the Securities Exchange Act of 1934. A key provision of the Banking Act of 1933 or the Glass–Steagall Act was the separation of commercial and investment banking. A determined proponent of the real bills doctrine, Senator Carter Glass believed that he could put it into effect by separating commercial and investment banking, and he ensured that it was part of the reform legislation.[25] The Glass–Steagall Act achieved a nearly complete divorce of commercial and investment banking. It became unlawful for any person or firm engaged in the business of issuing, underwriting, selling, or distributing securities to engage in the business of receiving deposits. Any affiliation between banks and securities firms and any joint affiliation by shared directors, officers, or employees was prohibited.[26] For commercial banks, security affiliates were eliminated and bond departments were reduced. National City Bank liquidated its affiliate, and First Boston Corporation was formed out of security affiliates of Chase and First National Bank of Boston. Investment houses like Morgan opted for deposit banking, while some partners left to form a new investment bank, Morgan Stanley & Co.[27]

Commercial banks no longer had an indirect hand in the commercial and industrial capital markets. But their business customers did not find it easy or cheap to turn to purely investment banks for assistance in raising funds, as the costs of new issues were substantially increased by the new regulation of the securities markets. Most investment banks were shocked at the regulations imposed on their industry. The new federal legislation was guided by Louis D. Brandeis's philosophy of promoting disclosure to ensure that investors were not misled by insufficient or misleading information. The Securities Act of 1933 and the Securities Exchange Act of 1934 thus aimed at increasing and improving information by establishing tough disclosure rules. The 1933 Act sought to guarantee full and fair disclosure of securities sold in interstate commerce and prevent frauds when new securities were first issued.[28] Except for government issues and certain exempt securities, registration was required for all new publicly offered securities. Specific information on the issuer and the securities was to be kept on file and made available to the public in a prospectus. No sales could be made until twenty days after filing to allow investors time to digest the information. Each underwriter was held liable, and sales could be halted and buyers refunded, if information filed was determined to be false. The Securities Exchange Act of 1934 extended federal disclosure requirements to securities traded on the nation's exchanges. Issuing corporations were obliged to register and file periodic reports. The exchanges were required to register, and their trading systems became the subject of government scrutiny. The act outlawed various practices and regulated short selling and stop-loss orders. Any individual owning more than 10 per cent of a corporation was required to report his holdings. The Securities and Exchange Commission (SEC) was established to administer the new legislation. Composed of five members, the SEC had discretionary authority to set rules and procedures for trading and conduct of exchange members.

The economic collapse of 1929–33 had drastically reduced the new issue market. Participants in the market complained about the new federal regulations for the public offering of new securities. Underwriters worried about changing market conditions during the cooling off period, issuers disliked the public disclosure, and parties signing the registration statement feared the civil liabilities. The result was that the new issue market all but disappeared. New corporate bonds and stocks issues had totalled $4.2 billion in 1925 and $9.4 billion at the peak in 1929 but were under $500 million in 1934. The burdens imposed by the Securities Act of 1933 on issuers and underwriters raised the cost of obtaining credit, with smaller issues bearing a higher cost. In 1938–9 the flotation cost for issues under $1 million was 7.5 per cent, for issues of $1–$5 million 3.4 per cent, for issues of $5–$20 million 2.8 per cent, and for issues over $20 million 2.4 per cent.[29] The higher costs imposed by the Securities Act could be avoided by the private placement of new securities, which climbed from less than 3 per cent of offerings between 1900 and 1933 to 23 per cent by 1939. But privately placed debt was not a perfect substitute, as it is not broadly marketable and the borrower could easily repurchase it.[30]

Commercial banks were pushed to help fill this void in long-term credit. Initially, they had little inclination to do so by history and by the immediate economic conditions. Schooled by experience and the real bills doctrine, bankers viewed themselves as providers of short-term credit. The panics of the Great Depression induced banks to curtail their loans, as seen in Fig. 4.1. At the same time, banks sought increased safety by shifting the composition of their assets towards cash and securities, as depicted in Fig. 4.3. From 58 per cent of bank assets, loans tumbled to under 30 per cent

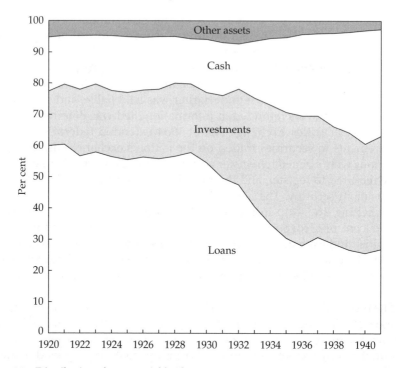

Fig. 4.3. *Distribution of commercial bank assets*
Source: US Department of Commerce, *Historical Statistics*: 1021–2.

by 1935 and remained there for the rest of the decade, while investments climbed from 22 to nearly 40 per cent, and cash from 15 to 30 per cent.

The dramatic reduction in lending during the depression was made feasible in part by the shortness of loan maturities. Borrowers who had used renewable short-term loans to fund capital improvements were devastated. In response to this curtailment of credit, business managers sought to minimize the amount of short-term debt. They were also driven by the fact that this form of debt was treated as 'current liabilities' in accordance with accepted accounting practices and treated as a sign of weakness.[31] Thus, both the demand for and the supply of short-term bank credits declined.

Faced with an unprecedented depression in which the collapse of the banking system played a central role, Congress and regulators sought to encourage banks to lend more and to make longer term loans. Recognizing that banks had few assets that were considered to be eligible paper, Congress gave emergency authorization in the Glass–Steagall Act of 1932 to the Federal Reserve to advance funds to member banks on any good asset. The Banking Act of 1935 gave the Federal Reserve banks permanent authority to lend by rediscount or advance on the security of any sound asset, regardless of maturity.[32] In June 1934 the Federal Reserve banks and the Reconstruction Finance Corporation (RFC) were given industrial loan powers by Congress, allowing them to make loans—including long-term loans—directly to business. They encouraged commercial banks to begin making term loans by taking and offering loan participations. Although the RFC and the Federal Reserve banks offered only a modest amount of credit in the form of term loans, totalling $300 million by 1940, they drew commercial banks into the business and helped to reduce some of the initial risks.[33]

The rules for bank examinations from the Office of the Comptroller of the Currency (OCC), the Federal Reserve banks, and the state supervisory authorities were altered to favour longer-term loans. Before the Great Depression, it was standard practice for bank examiners to classify weak loans as 'slow', 'doubtful', and 'estimated loss'. Traditionally, the standard acceptable maximum maturity on a loan was six months, and many examiners habitually classified any loan over this period as 'slow'. They frequently pressured banks to liquidate such loans and discouraged banks from lending except on short-term notes payable at maturity. In response to the banking crisis, a joint bank examiners' conference was held, including representatives from the OCC, the Federal Reserve System, the FDIC, and the RFC. Chief among their recommendations was a standardization of examination procedures among the government agencies and a revision in the practices of examination to encourage more medium- and long-term lending. These recommendations were approved by the Secretary of the Treasury, the Board of Governors of the Federal Reserve, the FDIC, and the Comptroller on 27 June 1938.[34] The old three-way system of classification of problem loans was revised. Whereas 100 per cent of classified loans were once counted in computing the net capital of a bank, this rule was now eased and set at 50 per cent. The new regulations specifically stated that 'a loan shall not be classified as slow simply because it runs for a long time'. Changes in the rules governing the classification of loans and investments were intended 'to encourage intermediate and long-term loans to business'.

Just in case banks did not realize that they could take advantage of this liberalization of examination rules, Jesse Jones, head of the RFC, moved to encourage banks to lend more freely. He urged them to be more liberal in considering applications, not to wait for new loan applications, and to go out and drum up business. Furthermore, he quietly threatened them by calling attention to the possibility of increased competition from government agencies should banks fail to expand lending. The banks felt the heat, and the President of the American Bankers Association, Orval W. Adams, responded, defending bankers as willing to offer loans and blaming the slow expansion on the depression's reduction in demand for credit.[35]

Many bankers were initially quite apprehensive. The Association of Reserve City Bankers allowed that 'while banks will begin to extend long-term loans, care must be taken that such loans are sound and banks must avoid excessive competition for such business'.[36]

Bankers received additional encouragement to consider long-term loans from the change in the yield curve. For most of the 1920s the yield curve had been flat or negatively sloped. The crisis of the 1930s caused investors to seek less risky short-term assets, and the yield curve acquired a highly positive slope, increasing the potential profit from borrowing short and lending long. In Table 4.1, the term premium jumped approximately to about 2 per cent for government and corporate securities. For bank credit, the slope of the yield curve had been positive in the 1920s, but it, too, became distinctly steeper during the depression. It should be noted that this stimulus was temporary, as spreads declined during the 1940s and the 1950s, while the larger share of term loans in bank portfolios did not.

Bankers received additional assurance to make long-term loans in the form of deposit insurance. The real bills doctrine had cautioned banks to offer short-term credit to keep them in readiness for withdrawals of deposits, including panics. The need for this defence against a panic was greatly reduced by the establishment of deposit insurance. Created by the Banking Act of 1933, the Federal Deposit Insurance Corporation (FDIC) provided limited coverage by the formation of a mutual guarantee fund to pay depositors of failed banks. All Federal Reserve member banks were required to join, and nonmember banks could be admitted upon approval by the FDIC. The mutual guarantee fund to pay depositors of failed banks was created by requiring insured banks to pay a premium calculated as a percentage of their deposits. Under the temporary plan initiated on

Table 4.1. *Term premiums (%)*

	US government securities	Bank credit	Corporate securities
1920–4	0.24	1.50	−0.75
1925–9	−0.33	1.39	−0.29
1930–4	2.11	3.07	2.38
1935–9	2.29	2.38	2.30

Note: The term premium on US government securities is measured as the difference between annual averages for long-term US governments' yields and three-month US Treasuries' yields. For bank credit, it is the difference between commercial business loan rates and rates on 90-day bankers' acceptances; and for corporate securities, it is the difference between the yields on prime long-term corporate bonds and prime 4–6-month commercial paper.

Source: Sidney Homer and Raymond Sylla, *A History of Interest Rates*, 3rd edn (New York, NY: Rutgers University Press, 1996), tables 47–49.

1 January 1934, each depositor was insured up to a limit of $2,500. Within six months, 14,000 commercial banks had joined. The permanent system was established by the Banking Act of 1935, with insurance raised to $5,000, and most commercial banks joined the FDIC. Although coverage was nearly universal and most small depositors were protected, only 43 per cent of all deposits were insured.[37] This insurance should have reduced the concerns of most depositors about the increased risk from longer-term loans and consequently bankers' fear of increased exposure to runs.

While some bankers remained apprehensive, many responded to the opportunities presented by the new rules and the constraints on the capital markets. Edward Brown of the First National Bank of Chicago pointed out the new opportunity for lending, using term loans, now available to banks. Writing in the *Journal of the American Bankers Association*, he counselled:

The alert banker will find the opportunity to suggest such loans to many of his customers, with profits both to his bank and to them. Owing to the novelty of this type of loan, the initial suggestion today generally comes from the banker and not the customer, but as such loans become more common and the knowledge of them increases among the borrowing public, the customer will undoubtedly seek them without any suggestion on the banker's part.[38]

Unlike shorter maturity loans, these new instruments would require additional forms of protection for the bank. He recommended three requirements for any borrower: (1) maintenance of a minimum amount of current assets above all liabilities and a minimum ratio of current assets to current liabilities. If either of these were violated, then the bank should have the option to demand immediate repayment; (2) no mortgage or pledge of any assets during the life of the loan; (3) serial repayment (amortization). Except for the last, all of these required that banks pay more attention to monitoring borrower activity after receiving a loan.

By putting greater weight on accounting and financial information, banks were pushed to make greater use of credit analysis, rather than individuals' reputations or the quality of specific collateral. Banks began to develop specialized personnel and create credit standards for appraising long-term loan risks. Given the longer term of a loan, there was increased moral hazard once the loan was given, and longer-term loan agreements included restrictive covenants governing the use of funds and the conduct of business. Included in these agreements were requirements that banks have access to the firm's records, receive regular certified financial information, and make regular visits and conduct periodic reviews.[39]

The principal financial instrument that lengthened loan maturities was the term loan. Term loans were defined as loans with a maturity of more than one year, including shorter-term credit drawn under revolving or standby credits of longer than one year. Although before the depression many short-term credits were renewed, making them a de facto means of longer term finance, the term loan marked a sharp change in banking philosophy. Some observers initially believed that this 'apparent increase in term lending was really an illusion'.[40] However, the renewal of short-term credits always gave bankers the option of nonrenewal and kept their banks potentially liquid in accordance with real bills doctrine sensibilities. Term loans extinguished this option, and they were thus a new credit instrument.

Even as the total quantity of loans stagnated in the late 1930s, term loans gradually began to increase and become an important component of bank portfolios.[41] Term loans offered by the Federal Reserve banks, the Reconstruction Finance Corporation, and commercial banks are presented in Table 4.2. While the Federal Reserve and RFC may have primed the pump and encouraged banks initially, banks' term loans increased rapidly. In 1933 the quantity of term loans was negligible, but by 1937 total term loans reached a value of $827 million. As a percentage of all nonreal estate loans, term loans rose from 6 to almost 17 per cent of all loans. By 1941 they represented 32 per cent of all industrial and commercial loans, and thereby accounted for most of the increases in commercial bank loans seen in Fig. 4.1.

The term loan innovation was fairly widespread, and one study estimated that 84 per cent of the Federal Reserve's weekly reporting member banks held some term loans in 1939.[42] In a 1941 survey of ninety-nine commercial banks, the maturity of loans ranged from one to ten years, with about one-third having an initial maturity of five years.[43] Of a total of 2,607 loans in this sample with a value of $1.7 billion, only a third by value were secured by collateral, and most were smaller loans. Over half were solely for purchasing plant, machinery, and equipment. Gradual repayment was a feature of most of these loans, with only 7 per cent having one balloon payment at maturity.

Many firms took advantage of this new willingness of banks to lend long-term and used the new type of loans to repay the high interest debt

Table 4.2. *Outstanding term loans*

Year	Federal Reserve banks ($billions)	RFC ($billions)	Commercial banks ($billions)	Commercial bank loans to total nonreal estate loans (%)
1934	14.9	6.6	na	na
1935	41.3	40.0	na	na
1936	32.0	63.6	na	na
1937	27.4	74.8	827	6.0
1938	30.0	107.7	1,083	8.8
1939	24.7	130.6	1,596	13.0
1940	15.5	121.3	2,162	16.6

Sources: Jacoby and Saulnier, *Term Lending*, table 1; US Department of Commerce, *Historical Statistics*, 1021.

Table 4.3. *Federal Reserve member banks maturities of commercial and industrial loans (%)*

Loan maturities	20 November 1946	5 October 1955
Under 6 months	58.3	57.1
6 months to 1 year	7.6	8.8
Over 1 year	34.1	34.1

Source: Federal Reserve Bulletin, 1949 and 1957.

that they had contracted in the late 1920s. Often these loans were very large and a syndicate of banks shared them. The US Steel was unable to carry out a bond issue in 1938 and instead obtained a $50 million three-year loan from twelve banks, including First National Bank of New York, Guaranty Trust, Bankers Trust, J.P. Morgan, Chase National Bank, National City Bank, and Continental Illinois Bank. Similarly, Youngstown Steel obtained a $12.5 million loan, as did oil companies, utilities, and manufacturers who found it hard to issue new securities in the depressed markets. Furthermore, banks and life insurance companies sometimes cooperated to supply a combination of loans and privately placed bonds. In 1941, for example, Chase National Bank headed a syndicate that supplied a seven-year $6 million loan to Safeway Stores, while Metropolitan Life, Equitable Life, and New York Life purchased a $14 million bond issue.[44]

Term lending became a permanent feature of commercial banking, as confirmed by two later surveys conducted by the Federal Reserve of its member banks in 1946 and 1955. As can be seen in Table 4.3, term loans, defined as loans with maturities over one year, accounted for about one-third of all loans. Loans with maturities of six months to one year were only 8 or 9 per cent, with short-term loans representing just under 60 per cent. Given that 75 per cent of commercial bank deposits were demand deposits in 1950,[45] this would imply a greater maturity mismatch than existed before the New Deal and a potential for higher earnings. While this mismatch apparently presented no problems in the 1950s because of the stable economic environment and relatively liquid portfolios of banks, it increased the risk to which banks were exposed when the American economy was hit by multiple macroeconomic shocks in the 1970s.

What the New Deal Wrought

The effects of these changes on banks' exposure to risk are difficult to identify. Ideally one would want to measure the effects of the new policies on

the duration of liabilities and assets. Efforts to expand term loans should
have increased the duration of assets relative to liabilities; this would have
increased the term mismatch and produced higher earnings for banks.
Measuring the effects on earnings is difficult because of the wild swings in
the economy and the New Deal's prohibition of interest on demand
deposits. However, the effects of the new regime on risk can be roughly
assessed by an examination of duration, the average time to repayment.

For the purposes of comparison, two years, 1928 and 1938, were selected
to estimate the changes in duration. In Table 4.4, the current dollar value,
the shares of total assets, and the duration of the components of assets and
liabilities are presented. The duration of assets and liabilities in this period
is largely unknown. For this exercise, some simplifying assumptions were
made. Real estate loans, a relatively small component of commercial bank

Table 4.4. *Changes in duration*

	Total assets	Total loans	Real estate loans	Other loans	Investments	Cash	Other
1928							
$ millions	61.6	34.9	6.2	28.7	14.4	9.2	3.1
Per cent	100.0	56.7	10.1	46.6	23.4	14.9	5.0
Duration (year)	3.5		5.0	0.2	12.4	0.0	0.0
1938							
$ millions	56.2	16.1	3.9	12.2	21.1	16.8	2.2
Per cent	100.0	28.6	6.9	21.7	37.5	29.9	3.9
Duration (year)	4.5		5.0	1.6	10.2	0.0	0.0

	Total liabilities	Demand deposits	Time deposits	Capital	Interbank deposits	Other
1928						
$ millions	61.6	24.9	20.1	7.9	4.3	4.4
Per cent	100.0	40.4	32.6	12.8	7.0	7.1
Duration (year)	0.1	0.0	0.2		0.0	0.0
1938						
$ millions	56.2	26.3	14.9	6.8	6.8	1.4
Per cent	100.0	46.8	26.5	12.1	12.1	2.5
Duration (year)	0.1	0.0	0.2		0.0	0.0

Sources: US Department of Commerce, *Historical Statistics*: 1021–3; Board of Governors of the Federal
Reserve System, *Banking and Monetary Statistics*, table 147; Jacoby and Saulnier, *Term Lending*.

loans were assumed to have a duration of five years, thus allowing for the fact that mortgages in this period were often short balloon loans or medium-term amortized loans.[46] Other loans, which encompasses commercial and industrial loans, were in 1928 assumed to have a ninety-day duration because many writers claimed that this was the standard form of commercial credit. This assumption would also fit the common ninety-day brokers' loans in this category. For 1938, the duration of term loans was approximated by using the initial maturities and payment structures of loans in Jacoby and Saulnier's sample.[47] The share of term loans is assumed to be one-third, the share reached in 1941 and maintained thereafter, rather than the lower value in 1938, to capture the long-term result. The duration of investments was assumed to be equal to the average maturity of outstanding US bonds in 1928 and 1938.[48] Cash has zero duration and the small 'Other' category is also assumed to have zero duration. On the liability side of the balance sheet, demand deposits have a zero duration and other liabilities are assumed to have the same. There is little information on the maturities of time deposits, and these are assumed to have had a duration of ninety days, although this assumption has little effect on the results.

The results of the estimation of duration are revealing. For liabilities, there was little change in duration, which remained at under one-tenth of one year. The only liability that produced a positive duration was time deposits, and these remained a modest element with relatively short maturities. The asset side shows a fairly large change in duration from 3.5 to 4.5 years. This increase occurred because of changes in investments and loans. Securities appear to have had the longest maturities, even though they declined between 1928 and 1938. The rise in the share of securities from 23.4 to 37.5 per cent of assets made the largest contribution to the increase in duration. The effects of the increase in loan duration from 0.2 to 1.6 years was muted by the rapid decline in other loans from 46.6 to 21.7 per cent of assets.

Given the small duration for liabilities, the duration gaps between asset and liability durations (a measure of exposure to interest rate fluctuations) are nearly equal to the asset duration. The duration gap for 1928 was 3.45 years and for 1938, 4.48 years. Thus risk from interest rate changes increased, while the greater gap offered potentially higher earnings. As the decline in the value of assets from a 1 per cent change in interest rates is approximately equal to the change times duration, it would cause a 3.5 per cent decline in asset values in 1928 and a 4.5 per cent decline in 1938.[49] As the magnitude of interest rate swings in this period were often well over 1 per cent in one year, this increase in duration had the potential for creating much greater problems for banks. This result is surprising given that the New Deal generally tried to make banks subject to less risk.

Interest rate risk was an important problem for financial institutions from the period just after the Second World War period to the Savings and Loan debacle and commercial banking crises of the 1980s. During the

Second World War bank portfolios expanded rapidly, filled with government bonds to finance the budget deficit and with term loans to finance industrial expansion. This development did not ease and probably increased duration mismatch. Although the Federal Reserve had pegged interest rates during the war to minimize debt service costs for the Treasury, the failure to end this policy after the war's end is striking.[50] Eichengreen and Garber have argued that the Fed may have feared that a rise in interest rates would cause large capital losses for the banks with portfolios full of long-term government securities. To this problem, they might have added term loans. Continuing the pegging policy after the war allowed banks to reduce their exposure. In March 1951 the Treasury-Federal Reserve Accord finally permitted the Fed to relinquish its support of bond prices. To protect bondholders, the Treasury absorbed part of their losses by a bond conversion that exchanged marketable long-term bonds at par for higher-yield nonmarketable securities.

The stable economic environment of the 1950s and the early 1960s, during which prices and interest rates varied very little, ensured that a term mismatch of assets and liabilities created no significant problem, only higher earnings. Banks and savings and loans were to a considerable degree unprepared for the increased economic volatility of the 1970s, and the abrupt rise in interest rates in 1979 was devastating.[51] The winnowing of the banking industry schooled a new generation of bankers on the dangers of interest rate risk in a volatile environment, and the maturity mismatch appears to have declined in recent years. A survey of new loans for 1996 reported that only 12 per cent had maturities over one year, and over 72 per cent were for one month or less.[52] On the liability side, demand deposits accounted for only 15 per cent of all deposits, or 24 per cent including NOW accounts. In some sense, the banking industry has come full circle back to an approximation of where it was before the Great Depression, with the terms of assets and liabilities more closely matched or hedged.

Back to the Future

Banking remains one of the most heavily regulated industries in the United States. What is assumed to be a practice that was derived from purely market-based decisions was shaped in considerable part by regulations adopted in the wake of the Great Depression. The practice of banks borrowing short-term and lending long-term, with a considerable term mismatch, was thought to be a product of the banking industry's natural development. Its demise, beginning in the 1980s, was believed to be a remarkable innovation and historic shift. However, before the onset of the Great Depression, banks were extremely hesitant to lend long-term. Although the policies of the Federal Reserve and bank examiners certainly encouraged short-term lending, banks hesitated to lend long-term, recognizing the risks. The Great Depression and the New Deal policies, circumscribing the securities markets, left business with few sources of long-term capital. Banks were released from their earlier policy constraint and pressed to offer long-term loans. The result was a major change in bank lending that altered the duration of bank assets, exposing banks to greater interest rate risk with serious consequences for the future.

NOTES

1. William H. Kniffin, Jr., *The Practical Work of a Bank* (New York, NY: Bankers Publishing Company, 1915), 209.
2. Considered poor collateral for commercial banks because it was illiquid, real estate did not fit the real bills doctrine and mortgage loans on real estate were prohibited to national banks until 1913.
3. Sudipto Bhattacharya and Anjan Thakor, 'Contemporary Banking Theory', *Journal of Financial Intermediation* 3/1 (October 1993), 2–50.
4. John A. James, *Money and Capital Markets in Postbellum America* (Princeton, NJ: Princeton University Press, 1978); and Board of Governors of the Federal Reserve System, *Banking and Monetary Statistics 1914–41* (Washington, DC: Board of Governors, 1943).
5. Raymond W. Goldsmith, *Financial Intermediaries in the American Economy since 1900* (Princeton, NJ: Princeton University Press, 1958).
6. Eugene N. White, 'Were Banks Special Intermediaries in the Late Nineteenth Century?' *Federal Reserve Bank of St. Louis Review* 80/3 (May/June 1998), 12–32.
7. Naomi Lamoreaux, *Insider Lending: Banks, Personal Connections and Economic Development in Industrial New England* (New York, NY: Cambridge University Press, 1994).
8. Margaret G. Myers, *The New York Money Market Volume I: Origins and Development* (New York, NY: Columbia University Press, 1931).
9. Ray B. Westerfield, *Banking Principles and Practice* (New York, NY: Ronald Press Co., 1924).
10. Lamoreaux, *Insider Lending*.
11. Richard P. Brief, 'The Origin and Evolution of Nineteenth Century Asset Accounting', *Business History Review* 40/1 (spring 1966), 1–23.
12. H.G. Moulton, 'Commercial Banking and Capital Formation', *Journal of Political Economy* 26/5, 6, 7, 9 (May, June, July, November 1918), 484–508, 638–63, 705–31, 849–81.

13. Henry Parker Willis, *The Federal Reserve System: Legislations, Organization and Operation* (New York, NY: Ronald Press Co., 1923).
14. James, *Money and Capital Markets*.
15. US Comptroller of the Currency, *Annual Reports* (Washington, DC: US Government Printing Office, 1913), 100.
16. Eugene N. White, 'California Banking in the Nineteenth Century: The Art and Method of the Bank of A. Levy', *Business History Review* 75/2 (summer 2001).
17. Moulton, 'Commercial Banking and Capital Formation'.
18. Neil H. Jacoby and Raymond J. Saulnier, *Term Lending to Business* (New York, NY: National Bureau of Economic Research, 1942).
19. Milton Friedman and Anna J. Schwartz, *A Monetary History of the United States, 1867–1960* (Princeton, NJ: Princeton University Press, 1963).
20. See Eugene N. White, *The Regulation and Reform of the American Banking System, 1900–29* (Princeton, NJ: Princeton University Press, 1983) for more details on these reserve requirements.
21. Member banks were composed of all national banks and state-chartered banks that voluntarily joined the system.
22. Eugene N. White, 'Banking and Finance in the Twentieth Century', in Stanley Engerman and Robert Gallman (eds), *Cambridge Economic History of the United States* (Cambridge: Cambridge University Press, 2000), 743–802.
23. Board of Governors, *Banking and Monetary Statistics*; White, *The Regulation and Reform*.
24. W. Nelson Peach, *The Security Affiliates of National Banks* (Baltimore, MD.: Johns Hopkins University Press, 1941); Eugene N. White, 'Before the Glass–Steagall Act: An Analysis of the Investment Banking Activities of National Banks', *Explorations in Economic History* 23/1 (January 1986), 33–55.
25. Charles W. Calomiris and Eugene N. White, 'The Origins of Federal Deposit Insurance', in Claudia Goldin and Gary D. Libecap (eds), *The Regulated Economy: A Historical Approach to Political Economy* (Chicago, IL: Chicago University Press, 1994), 145–87.
26. The divorce was not complete, as banks were permitted to underwrite and deal in US government, state, and municipal securities.
27. White, 'Before the Glass–Steagall Act'.
28. Joel Seligman, *The Transformation of Wall Street: A History of the Securities and Exchange Commission and Modern Corporate Finance* (Boston, MA: Houghton Mifflin, 1982).
29. Securities and Exchange Commission, *Cost of Flotation for Registered Securities, 1938–1939* (Washington, DC: Securities and Exchange Commission, 1941).
30. Jacoby and Saulnier, *Term Lending*.
31. Jacoby and Saulnier, *Term Lending*.
32. Friedman and Schwartz, *A Monetary History*.
33. Jacoby and Saulnier, *Term Lending*.
34. *Commercial and Financial Chronicle*, 2 July 1938, 41–2.
35. *Commercial and Financial Chronicle*, 23 July 1938, 505–6.
36. *Commercial and Financial Chronicle*, 19 July 1939, 2613–14.
37. Over the next half century, the share of deposits protected gradually rose by reason of increases in the maximum insurance per account and depositors spreading their funds among accounts. By the 1990s over 75 per cent of deposits were

insured by the FDIC with an implicit guarantee from the 'too-big-to-fail' doctrine that appeared to completely insure all deposits. See Calomiris and White, 'The Origins'; White, 'The Legacy of Deposit Insurance'.

38. Edward Brown, Address, *Journal of the American Bankers Association* 31/1 (July 1938).
39. Jacoby and Saulnier, *Term Lending*.
40. George S. Moore, *The Banker's Life* (New York, NY: W.W. Norton & Co., 1987).
41. The majority of commercial bank loans to business remained the straight promissory notes payable on demand up to six months maturity. According to one survey in 1942, the most common instrument was the traditional 90-day note. Neil H. Jacoby and Raymond J. Saulnier, *Business Finance and Banking* (New York, NY: National Bureau of Economic Research, 1947).
42. *Federal Reserve Bulletin* (July 1939).
43. Jacoby and Saulnier, *Term Lending*.
44. Tian-Kang Go, *American Commercial Banks in Corporate Finance, 1929–1941: A Study of Banking Concentration* (New York, NY: Garland Publishing, Inc., 2000).
45. US Department of Commerce, *Historical Statistics of the United States: Colonial Times to 1970* (Washington, DC: US Bureau of the Census, 1975), 1022.
46. Eugene N. White, 'Banking and Finance in the Twentieth Century'.
47. Jacoby and Saulnier, *Term Lending*.
48. In 1928 US government bonds accounted for 34 per cent of all investments, while in 1938 their share was 56 per cent. Where a range of years was specified, i.e., 5–10 years, the midpoint was used for the duration. Board of Governors, *Banking and Monetary Statistics*, table 147.
49. Gary Smith, *Financial Assets, Markets and Institutions* (Lexington, MA: D.C. Heath and Company, 1993).
50. Barry Eichengreen and Peter M. Garber, 'Before the Accord: US Monetary-Financial Policy, 1945–1951', in R. Glenn Hubbard (ed.), *Financial Markets and Financial Crises* (Chicago, IL: University of Chicago Press, 1991), 175–205.
51. James R. Barth, *The Great Savings and Loan Debacle* (Washington, DC: Urban Institute, 1991); White, 'Banking and Finance'.
52. *Federal Reserve Bulletin* (May 1996).

5

Mitsui Bank's Lending Policy in Transition in the Interwar Years[1]

SHINJI OGURA

Introduction

In general, Japan's largest commercial banks were little interested in exercising great influence on the managerial policies and fund positions of their customers in the interwar years. As a result, they had little interest in providing long-term loans. Instead, they dealt in short-term loans, the discounting of commercial bills, and foreign bills of exchange.

After the beginning of the 1930s such a situation began to change. The commercial banks were in transition from being the in-house banks of zaibatsu to that of being the main banks for their major customers. In particular, after the hostilities between Japan and China began in 1937, the commercial banks had to meet the demand for long-term funds from their customers in the munitions industry. This was also true for Mitsui Bank, which stuck to a conservative lending policy that had been established before the First World War.

This study will attempt to address three problems: (a) how Mitsui Bank expanded its foreign exchange transactions with major trading companies and developed a securities business; (b) the extent to which these businesses were useful in regulating the bank's average loan period until the breakout of hostilities between Japan and China, while it met the demand for long-term funds from Mitsui-affiliated, electric power and munitions companies; (c) the reasons why, after the end of the 1930s, the bank gave up the long-term loan operations necessary both for the bank and for its customers in the munitions industry.

Background to Mitsui Bank's Sound Loan Policy

In the 1890s the bank underwent modernization reforms carried out by Hikojiro Nakamigawa (1854–1901), under the direction of Kaoru Inoue (1835–1915), the House of Mitsui's main outside adviser (Inoue had been a Meiji Restoration leader and an influential politician in the Meiji government). The economic boom following the Sino-Japanese War of 1894–5 finally ended in 1900 when a depression in the United States and the Boxer Rebellion affected Japan. Unfortunately, some of the companies Nakamigawa had brought under Mitsui control, such as Kanebo, Oji Paper, and Tanaka Seizosho, performed quite poorly during 1900 and 1901, and loans to them put a strain on Mitsui Bank's resources. Moreover, in April 1900 a small daily newspaper, the *Niroku Shimpo*, began carrying articles attacking the bank, particularly, the policies of Nakamigawa. These articles caused runs on deposits in several branches.[2] Although the bank ultimately managed to avoid suspension of payments, the *Niroku Shimpo* articles made it clear that commercial banking was not a good business for Mitsui to be in.

Takashi Masuda (1848–1938), executive director of Mitsui & Co. and a member of the Mitsui General Family Council (Mitsuike Dozokukai), gradually increased his influence within Mitsui by winning the confidence of Kaoru Inoue, and he oversaw Mitsui Bank operations after the articles undermined confidence in Nakamigawa.[3] Though he did not assume the top management position in Mitsui Bank, Masuda began to exercise great influence on its affairs.

First of all, Masuda in 1902 added a Control Department (Kanribu) to the former administrative structure of the Mitsui zaibatsu set up in the 1890s. Then he recommended new management policies for the bank so that after 1902 it would no longer gain control of companies through loans.[4] In effect, Mitsui Bank was demoted to a lower rank in the Mitsui group, and instead Mitsui & Co. became the new nucleus of the group.

After the Russo-Japanese War of 1904–5 Inoue and Masuda took the drastic step of advising the House of Mitsui to withdraw from managing Mitsui Bank, to avoid the risks resulting from the commercial banking business. The main points they made were the following:

1. Mitsui's various businesses had advanced by leaps and bounds during the Russo-Japanese War, making the House of Mitsui one of the richest in the world.
2. The House of Mitsui should withdraw entirely from managing Mitsui Dry Goods Shop (which in 1904 had been reorganized, from being an unlimited partnership to being a joint-stock company, and

renamed Mitsukoshi Drapery; at that time the House of Mitsui withdrew from managing the company directly by selling a stake in it).

3. The intention was to make the House of Mitsui a great financier family like the Rothschild and Morgan families through the establishment of a new financing institution to succeed Mitsui Bank and to get rid of its commercial banking business.

The leaders of the Mitsui group decided to take the opportunity to carry out the plan on condition that a thorough survey would be made before carrying it out. The plan was to be carried out by Masuda, following the directions of Kaoru Inoue, an adviser to the Mitsui family.

Masuda, representing the Control Department, and three representatives of Mitsui Bank left for Europe and the United States to survey the organizational and business aspects of European and American banks. The real purpose of the tour had been to make preparations for the withdrawal of the House of Mitsui from management of the bank, rather than to make recommendations on how to reform the bank. Inoue and Masuda changed their minds about the bank after the tour, however. In 1909 Mitsui Bank was reorganized from an unlimited partnership to a joint-stock company, capitalized at 20 million yen by the Mitsui General Family Council.[5]

When in 1909 the Mitsui General Family Council incorporated the Control Department of the Council as Mitsui Gomei, an unlimited partnership, it decided not to make Mitsui Bank the financing arm of Mitsui Gomei. As a result, Mitsui Bank, as a joint-stock company, was able to keep its commercial banking business and had to be responsible for developing the securities business and other types of investment banking business, instead of Mitsui Gomei.

Mitsui & Co.'s support for efforts to rescue Mitsui Bank seemed to be carried out in two ways. One was to help Mitsui Bank establish new areas, such as its foreign exchange business. The other was to gain control of companies like Oji Paper and shore them up so as to help Mitsui Bank wipe out its bad loans.

Mitsui Bank as the In-house Bank of Mitsui Family (1914–29)

Traders-oriented Lending Policy

When the First World War broke out, foreign trade was stopped, and the Japanese economy became chaotic until the following year, 1915, when exports started to increase sharply and the total foreign trade balance was a favourable 1.4 billion yen, which it remained between 1915 and 1918.

Domestic industries, especially trading companies, enjoyed wartime prosperity. Under these conditions Mitsui-affiliated companies like Kanebo and Oji Paper also made rapid strides into becoming top-ranking companies in their fields. Their bad loan problems, a cause of concern to Mitsui Bank for a long time, were completely resolved. Mitsui Bank moved into new areas of business to secure prosperous customers as its major borrowers; this resulted in sharply increasing deposits and the resolution of its bad loan problem during the wartime boom. The bank's main hope at the time was to secure prominent trading companies as its major borrowers, and to expand its foreign exchange transactions with trading companies. Needless to say, the bank's special relationship with Mitsui & Co. was the motivation behind the move.

Mitsui & Co. increased the scale of its transactions enormously during the First World War and became an unrivalled giant among the country's trading companies, alone accounting for about 20 per cent of the value of Japan's total imports and exports.

The scale of Mitsui Bank's transactions with Mitsui & Co. increased proportionately. The total amount of its credit to Mitsui & Co., including its trading finance, reached about 60 million yen by the end of the First World War. Mitsui & Co. had become far and away the bank's major borrower, whereas before the First World War it had not needed huge loans from the bank in spite of being the bank's highest priority borrower except during depressed economic conditions.

The total balance of credit granted by Mitsui Bank to Mitsui & Co. amounted to about 36 million yen by the end of October 1917, and about 60 million yen by the end of April 1918, or 17 and 25 per cent of the bank's balance of credit at the end of December 1917 and June 1918, respectively, after taking account of the two organizations' different accounting periods.

The Mitsui zaibatsu was forced to reform part of its policy for the management of Mitsui Bank before and after the end of the First World War. Until then the bank had followed a strict policy of collecting stable funds at low interest rates and loaning them to reliable business customers. This policy, forced on the bank by Inoue and Masuda, was very effective at improving the bank's business during depressed times, but it caused business to stagnate during the prosperous days of the First World War.

Two reforms were made. One was to allow the bank to reverse its sound loans policy and to take positive steps to increase deposits and loans. The other was to allow the bank to become more independent of Mitsui Gomei's control by allowing the bank to offer 300,000 of 800,000 new shares to the public and transferring power to a board of managing directors to be newly established. The old system whereby a holding company with diversified businesses had control over a financial institution was unworkable and had become more and more anachronistic as time went on.

Of all the zaibatsu-related banks, it was Sumitomo Bank that had shown the others the way to be a genuine modern commercial bank with efficient headquarters by offering new shares to the public. Sumitomo Bank had been established in 1895, nineteen years later than Mitsui Bank, and had been reorganized into a joint-stock company with an authorized capital of 15 million yen in 1912, three years later than Mitsui Bank. But in the matter of issuing new shares to the public, it was able to precede Mitsui Bank by two years. Within a year of offering 30,000 of 150,000 new shares to the public in 1917, Sumitomo Bank increased the number of its managing directors from one to four, chose an outside director from among the major customers subscribing to its new shares, and finally established its board of managing directors with a broad authority to make independent decisions. By spring 1918 the bank finished organizing the Head Office into a general headquarters consisting of six departments. This move suggests that in those days the creditworthiness of banks had more effect on the bank as an institution than its owners did.[6]

Following Sumitomo Bank's lead, Mitsui Bank also increased its authorized capital from 20 million yen to 100 million yen in 1919. Then 300,000 of 800,000 new 100-yen nominal shares were offered to the public. Although more than 70 per cent of these 300,000 new shares were concentrated among fifty-five people to whom 1,000 or more shares were allocated, such a public offering was a very effective step towards making the bank more independent of Mitsui Gomei control. According to a former director of the bank, under Mitsui Gomei's strong control prior to 1919, the bank had to submit for Mitsui Gomei approval plans showing even the sizes of things like drainpipes and gutters for any new branches.

Strangely enough, it was not until September 1919 that a provision giving each Mitsui Bank managing director authority to make decisions on his own was approved, even though its three managing directors had been elected and the division of duties among them had come into being already a decade before. Lack of such a provision had prevented the bank's board of managing directors from being established. In those days, the establishment of a bank headquarters that was supervised firmly and effectively by a board of managing directors was indispensable if a bank was to maintain supremacy over industrial enterprises.

The provision, however, did not cover the appointment of new personnel to Mitsui Bank directorships. According to the recollections of a former managing director in charge of personnel affairs of the bank from 1923 to 1931, even after the relationship between Mitsui Gomei (the holding company) and Mitsui Bank had been altered, Mitsui Gomei and the House of Mitsui still exerted a great influence on the appointments of new Mitsui Bank directors.[7]

Senkichiro Hayakawa, at the top of the Mitsui Bank managing directors' list, resigned from the bank to become vice-president of Mitsui Gomei in 1918 and finally in 1919 left Mitsui to become president of the Bank of Chosen, a state-owned bank. At that time Seihin Ikeda replaced Hayakawa at the top of the Mitsui Bank managing directors' list. Until then Ikeda had held real power both over the examination of loan applications from the bank's major borrowers and over the management of its fund position.

The bank increased the number of its managing directors from three to four in 1919 and then in 1921 established a stronger headquarters consisting of six departments supervised by four managing directors: Foreign and Research (Seihin Ikeda), Domestic (Naojiro Kikumoto), Secretariat and Inspection (Hirokichi Kameshima), and General Accounting and Financing (Rikisaburo Imai).[8]

By the end of 1924 Mitsui Bank seemed to have regained its leading position among those major banks that were aiming at establishing more efficient organizations than before, when it created a Foreign Exchange Department in the Head Office to take charge of the bank's foreign exchange business (the Foreign Department remained in control of foreign business in general). At the time the bank ran twenty-three places of business.

Overspecializing in the Transactions with Major Customers

Mitsui Bank partially succeeded in transforming itself from a bank for the House of Mitsui to a bank for major corporations in the 1920s after the first public sale of its shares.

The amount of idle money that commercial banks had on hand began to grow during the post-First World War recession of 1920. Needless to say, Mitsui Bank was no exception in this matter, especially since it had not completely reversed its restrictive lending policy.

By the end of April 1920 the balance of credit granted by the bank to Mitsui & Co., Mitsui Mining, and Mitsui Gomei stood at about 94 million yen, or about 26 per cent of the balance of credit the bank granted at that time. Of the 94 million yen, the balance of credit to Mitsui & Co. is estimated to have been over 70 million yen, since that to Mitsui Gomei was 20 million yen or so and that to Mitsui Mining was almost negligible. The balance of credit the bank granted to these three companies decreased by about 40 million yen just one year later.[9]

No doubt Mitsui & Co.'s sudden repayment of its debts to banks caused this rapid decrease in Mitsui Bank's balance of credit, seeing that Mitsui Gomei had decided it would pay back the 20 million yen borrowed from the bank as a subscription for Mitsui Mining in 20 semiannual instalments of one million yen each. Thus the amount of cash reserves at the bank's Head Office rose and the bank's idle money surged after August 1920. Part of the idle money was used as unbudgeted funds available to the bank's major borrowers, in addition to the budgeted funds already available to them.

All the major private banks, including Mitsui Bank, made joint efforts to give relief loans to various industries during the post-First World War recession. Mitsui Bank played a crucial role in giving relief loans to sugar refining companies. These were the first relief loans that the bank gave, and the bank was able to supply them in cooperation with Mitsui & Co., which took the initiative in asking the government, the Bank of Japan, and major commercial banks to help the sugar refining industry. Mitsui & Co. had established an interest in the industry by signing an exclusive sales agency contract with Taiwan Sugar Refining, an affiliate of Mitsui.

It was clear that Mitsui & Co. still remained eager to introduce its customers to Mitsui Bank for large loans even years after the bank's reconstruction. Mitsui Bank's share of the total amount of relief loans that major commercial banks gave the sugar refining companies and the sugar dealers was about 53 per cent.[10]

Though Mitsui Bank's history of loans to electric companies dates back to 1905, it was during and just after the recession of 1920 that the bank began to increase such loans drastically. Mitsui Bank loans to electric companies were so large that the bank's total amount of loans exceeded those of other banks, and they were directly the result of the bank's objective of putting to use its huge amount of idle money.[11]

After the establishment of the Foreign Department in the Head Office, Mitsui Bank stationed liaison representatives in New York and London in 1916 and established the Shanghai branch, its first overseas branch. This was followed by the establishment of a New York agency in 1922, London and Bombay branches in 1924, and a Surabaya office in 1925.

In addition to the expansion of its network of overseas branches in 1924, the bank reformed its Foreign Department in order to introduce a clear separation of the supervisory operations at its headquarters from its other role as the largest branch. (Strangely enough, the Foreign Department in the bank's Head Office had fulfilled both functions at the same time since its establishment in 1913.) In the reform, the bank created in 1924 a Foreign Exchange Department to oversee foreign exchange transactions, leaving the existing Foreign Department at the Head Office to control foreign business in general.

In those days, the bank's principal foreign exchange transactions were to establish credit by making overdraft contracts with major European and American banks, in order to settle import bills for cotton, and to clear its debt to the foreign banks with the money that the bank gained through the purchasing of export bills for raw silk. The bank annually purchased about 50 million yen in export bills in the early 1920s.

The bank's dash towards expansion of foreign exchange transactions started from the beginning of 1925. The amount of funds allocated to foreign exchange transactions was almost doubled, from 39.6 million yen to 78.5 million yen.[12] The profit margin on the bank's foreign exchange transactions was slightly higher than that on its domestic lending in the mid-1920s.

Mitsui Bank was keen to foster a securities business, so in 1926 the bank established a Securities Department at its Head Office to handle securities-related businesses previously handled by the Accounting Department. The bank underwrote a huge volume of corporate bonds for electric power companies and electric railway companies, to most of which it also pro-vided loans on a large scale. It is also worth noting that the bank was espe-cially eager to be involved in the flotation of foreign currency bonds, which proved to be successful for Japan's five largest electric power companies in the British and American financial markets. This eagerness seemed to translate itself into activity in two areas: foreign exchange and securities.

To get its foreign exchange business off to a good start, the bank chose Daido Electric Power Co.'s bonds (valued at US$15 million) issued in 1924. As one of the remittance banks acting for the company, the bank sent the proceeds from the sale from the United States to Japan. All of Japan's five largest electric power companies sold foreign currency bonds in and after the mid-1920s, with Daido Electric Power the first to do so. Mitsui Bank sent the proceeds of at least three of these eight bond issues: twice for Daido Electric Power Co. and once for Toho Electric Power Co.

According to the recollection of a Daido manager familiar with the flota-tion in 1924, while Dillon, Read & Co. underwrote the bonds, General Electric Co. of the United States, one of the largest exporters of electrical equipment to Japan, mediated between Daido and Dillon, Read & Co.[13] Mitsui & Co., the sole agent for the import of General Electric Co. products into Japan, was also supposed to play an important role as a mediator between the United States and Japanese companies. In the background of this situation was the US rivalry with Britain, which was pursuing a Buy British policy through its Trade Facilities Act to stimulate exports.

Mitsui Bank was the trustee for bonds valued at US$15 million that Toho Electric Power Co. sold in 1925. This was the first time the bank acted as a trustee for foreign currency bonds issued by any of Japan's five largest electric power companies. Essentially this kind of activity belonged to the securities business in a broad sense. Guaranty Co., a security affiliate of Guaranty Trust Co., underwrote the bonds.[14] Guaranty Trust made good use of this opportunity to participate in, and after a while play a leading role in, underwriting the foreign currency bonds for Japan's five largest electric power companies.[15]

As Mitsui Bank continued to step up its loans in the years following the recession of 1920, many of the country's largest companies were num-bered among its major borrowers. A 1924 list of major borrowers with a debt to the bank of five million yen or more was headed by Mitsui & Co., with 38 million yen. Most of the debt stemmed from Mitsui & Co.'s foreign exchange transactions with the bank. There were five prominent trading companies and two electric power companies among these major borrowers.

Thus the bank succeeded in establishing three main target areas for using excess funds: its lending business, its foreign exchange business, and its securities business; at the same time it acted as an intermediary for its best customers, especially trading companies and electric power companies, on the British and American financial markets.

Family Control in Trouble Again

Mitsui Bank's policy of targeting major corporations as customers began to encounter serious difficulties during and after the Financial Panic of 1927. Though the bank had pushed ahead with a policy of avoiding bad loans by careful screening of its loan clientele, ironically enough such a course of action eventually caused the bank even more serious trouble. The bank's first problem derived from its loans to Suzuki & Co., a large Japanese trading company; its second problem resulted from its loans to Tokyo Electric Light.

Some of Mitsui's leaders were of the opinion that the bank was being handicapped by the House of Mitsui (or Mitsui Gomei) because they sometimes would force the bank to pursue a conservative lending policy and sometimes would ask, directly or indirectly, the bank to provide specific customers with loans. Such unsuitable influence from the family more or less tended to prevent the bank from screening applicants for loans quickly and objectively. Thus the House of Mitsui's control over the bank started to be questioned again towards the end of the 1920s.

The Financial Panic of 1927 caused runs on many commercial banks including such powers as Mitsui Bank and Yasuda Bank, when at the height of the Panic customers entertained doubts about their reliability. Mitsui Bank had a serious run on its Kyoto branch, but immediately after that its deposits began to swell. Table 5.1 shows that its total deposits came to 560 million yen by the end of 1927, an increase of over 100 million yen in one year that reflected the trend towards concentration of deposits in the five largest banks. As a result, Mitsui Bank became more concerned about how to use its excess funds than before. The bank thereafter strove to inject these funds mainly into its foreign exchange and securities businesses. Yet before long these activities also ended up jeopardizing the bank's credibility.

First consider the bank's loans to Suzuki & Co., which went bankrupt during the Financial Panic of 1927. According to my calculations, the bank's loans to Suzuki & Co. in a broad sense rose to between 60 million yen and 70 million yen just before the bankruptcy of Suzuki & Co. in the

Table 5.1. *Increase in Japans' five largest commercial banks' deposits, 1923–30*

Year end	Mitsui (A) (¥1,000,000)	Mitsubishi (B) (¥1,000,000)	(B/A) (%)	Sumitomo (C) (¥1,000,000)	(C/A) (%)	Dai-Ichi (D) (¥1,000,000)	(D/A) (%)	Yasuda (E) (¥1,000,000)	(E/A) (%)
1923 (X)	418	307	74	344	82	344	82	569	135
1924	409	303	74	377	92	346	85	573	140
1925	440	312	71	416	95	366	83	572	130
1926	456	329	72	435	95	391	86	623	137
1927	560	471	84	553	99	521	93	713	127
1928	606	562	93	643	106	597	99	722	119
1929	660	600	91	663	100	629	95	658	100
End of June 1930 (Y)	649	593	91	671	103	634	98	637	98
(Y − X)/X (%)	55	93		95		84		13	

Source: Mitsui Bank, 'Special Edition of Research Division's Weekly Report (17 February 1931)', in The Collected Research Division's Weekly Reports, from Sakura Bank Archives (unpublished).

spring of 1927. More exactly, the loans should be divided into three categories: loans to Suzuki & Co. itself, which amounted to about 14 million yen; loans to Suzuki & Co.'s four affiliates, which totalled about 21 million yen; and call loans amounting to 39 million yen to the Bank of Taiwan, which had maintained an extremely close relationship with Suzuki & Co.

The loans were so large that Mitsui Bank could see it was in potential danger of falling victim to a chain-reaction bankruptcy with Suzuki & Co. and the Bank of Taiwan. Unfortunately, the bank's course of action made matters worse, because the bank stuck to its restrictive lending policy too doggedly so as to protect its own interests, rather than considering the public role it needed to play in the situation as Japan's largest commercial bank. The bank's action of calling in its loans to the Bank of Taiwan and Suzuki & Co. was so quick that it was criticized for triggering their bankruptcies—and the 1927 Panic itself.

Mitsui Bank, through the Securities Department it had established at its Head Office, rushed into fostering its securities business by using its increasing excess funds along with its foreign exchange profits after the Panic in 1927. At the time, the bank achieved success, especially in underwriting public and corporate bonds, conducting trust business related to electric power companies' foreign currency bonds, and buying and selling domestic and foreign short-term securities.

Although the bank's deposits increased by 170 million yen from the end of March 1927 to the end of 1929, the bank's funds for domestic lending were fixed at around 400 million yen during the period. The majority of the increase in deposits was put into its securities and foreign exchange businesses, while the rest of the increase was set aside for adding to its reserve fund held by the Accounting Department at its Head Office.

As the bank's reserves swelled, its whole outlook changed considerably. When the bank's reserves reached more than 70 million yen at the end of May 1927, the amount of reserves it deposited in noninterest-bearing current accounts at the Bank of Japan also rose to more than 60 million yen. Until the Panic of 1927, the bank had been able to provide a large number of call loans to such government financial institutions as the Bank of Taiwan, thereby turning its reserve into working funds. It is clear that the bank had too much idle money on its hands.

Keeping pace with other major commercial banks, the bank rapidly escalated its investment in public and corporate bonds sold at home and abroad after the Panic of 1927. As a result, the bank's total security holdings increased by about 110 million yen (broken down into 93 million yen, 1.2 million pounds sterling, and 4.7 million dollars) from the end of 1926 to the end of 1928.

Although the huge amount of idle money the bank had was deeply relevant to the rapid increase in investment in securities and the amount of underwritten bonds, it was not necessarily the only reason for the bank's new activities. Another factor was the bad loan problem. The bank had been compelled to collect existing bad loans and to find some way to avoid exacerbating its bad loan problem. As the bank considered the securities business, especially the underwriting of corporate bonds, to be quite effective for solving such problems, it underwrote corporate bonds for some customers and then urged them to pay off their debts to the bank by using the proceeds from these bonds. This method can be seen at work in the case of Tokyo Electric Light Co.

Though not a Mitsui affiliate, Tokyo Electric Light was one of the bank's major borrowers. After the company suffered serious damage from the Great Kanto Earthquake of 1923, it faced cutthroat competition from some of the five largest electric power companies that were after its market share. The bank's loans to Tokyo Electric Light soared rapidly after 1926. At the end of March 1928 such loans reached 85.8 million yen, or about 21 per cent of its total outstanding balance of loans (excluding call loans) at that point, due to the substantial amount of relief loans it had extended in 1927.

In return for providing the relief loans, the bank insisted on the company's reform being given priority, and it assisted by sending three business leaders to take seats on the company's board of directors. One of the main reasons the bank dared to deviate from its sound loan policy was that Takuma Dan (1858–1932; in 1914 he had assumed the presidency of Mitsui Gomei) demanded the bank take such action, for he feared that the bankruptcy of Tokyo Electric Light would have a bad influence on Mitsui & Co. and Mitsui Mining. In spite of the bank's sound loan policy, the bank accepted the request from Mitsui & Co. with little resistance, because of the long-standing relationship between the two.[16]

Fortunately, the bank managed to collect the relief loans before they deteriorated into bad loans. Of the total debt of 85.8 million yen, 19 million yen was repaid from the proceeds of a flotation of the company's domestic bonds in May 1928, and 49.3 million yen was repaid from the proceeds of two sales of the company's foreign currency bonds (one valued at 4.5 million pound sterling and the other valued at 70 million dollars) in June 1928. As a result, the bank's outstanding loans to the company were reduced to zero.[17]

How eager Mitsui Bank and other large banks were to collect their outstanding loans to electric power companies by using foreign currency bond flotation is supported indirectly by several instances concerning Toho Electric Power bonds and Tokyo Electric Light bonds underwritten by Guaranty Co. The proceeds of such bonds were to be used in part to pay those electric power companies' outstanding bank loans.

The most urgent problem that Mitsui Bank had to solve after the Panic of 1927 was how to use as much money as possible to reduce its pile of excess funds.

First of all, the bank invested about 20 million yen in British and American government bonds, valued respectively at 1.19 million pounds sterling and at 4.7 million dollars, using them as collateral for overdrawing from major British and American banks in 1927. The bank particularly aimed at becoming creditworthier in the international financial market by establishing closer relationships with such top British banks as Barclays. In those days the bank's management used to call it the 'self-sufficiency of exchange funds' principle.[18]

Naturally enough, the bank focused its efforts on expanding purchases of export bills and the settlement of import bills, especially with Mitsui & Co. and Toyo Menka, an affiliate of Mitsui & Co. Table 5.2 shows Mitsui & Co.'s exchange transactions with eight major domestic and foreign banks headed by Yokohama Specie Bank in the late 1920s. Although the ranking of each of the eight major banks had not been fixed, no doubt some kind of pecking order had been formed before the Bank of Taiwan faced its financial difficulties. In the early 1920s Mitsui Bank ranked third or fourth, with Yokohama Specie Bank and the Bank of Taiwan at the top of the list.

Mitsui Bank, however, expanded its foreign exchange transactions with Mitsui & Co. after 1926. Finally, after 1928, the bank was able to take over the leading position, ranking alongside Yokohama Specie Bank in foreign exchange transactions with Mitsui & Co. Table 5.3 shows that all the bank's various financial transactions with Mitsui & Co. and its affiliates at the end of the 1920s amounted to a good deal over 100 million yen, reflecting the expansion of the bank's foreign exchange transactions with these companies.

Table 5.2. *Mitsui & Co.'s exchange transactions with banks, 1926–9 (¥ 10,000)*

	First-half 1926		First-half 1927		First-half 1928		First-half 1929	
	Amount	(%)	Amount	(%)	Amount	(%)	Amount	(%)
Mitsui	5,731	17.1	4,981	17.0	7,335	23.2	7,231	21.3
Yokohama Specie Bank	8,647	25.8	6,727	23.0	7,787	24.6	8,202	24.1
Taiwan	3,647	10.9	1,533	5.2	258	0.8	449	1.3
Chosen	844	2.5	1,695	5.8	635	2.0	1,043	3.1
Sumitomo	171	0.5	190	0.6	1,264	4.0	797	2.3
Hong Kong and Shanghai	1,928	5.7	1,921	6.6	1,791	5.7	1,510	4.4
Chartered	1,997	5.9	1,340	4.6	1,097	3.5	1,565	4.6
International	1,493	4.4	2,128	7.3	1,734	5.5	1,784	5.2
Other banks	3,478	10.4	2,911	10.0	3,619	11.4	3,759	11.1
House bills	5,803	17.3	5,855	20.0	6,144	19.9	7,671	22.6
Total	33,568	100.0	29,311	100.0	31,664	100.0	34,011	100.0

Source: Mitusi & Co., Semiannual Reports, from MRISEH Archives (unpublished).

Table 5.3. *Mitsui Bank's credit to Mitsui & Co. and its affiliates, 1928–30 (¥1,000)*

Item	Mitsui & Co.		Toyo Menka		Southern Cotton Co.		Total	
	31/3/28	31/12/30	31/3/28	31/12/30	31/3/28	31/12/30	31/3/28	31/12/30
Bills discounted	4,022	2,380	7,998	—	—	—	12,020	2,380
Loans on bills	1,820	10,562	5,698	40	—	—	7,518	10,602
Overdraft	2,657	1,846	10,241	1,057	—	435	12,899	2,903
Foreign exchange purchased	36,054	29,709	13,569	7,560	2,501	6,636	52,123	43,905
Interest bills	10,893	349	557	1,561	7,178	—	18,628	1,911
Others	11,221	303	—	—	—	—	11,221	303
Guarantee and endorsement	306	—	—	—	—	—	306	—
Total	66,973	45,150	38,063	10,219	9,678	7,070	114,714	62,439
Acceptance	13,910	139	1,270	1,460	—	—	—	—

Source: Mitsui Bank, Documents on the Bank's Substantial Credit to Customers, from Sakura Bank Archives (unpublished).

Towards Seceding from the House of Mitsui (1930–43)

Even though most of Japan's zaibatsu-related banks had, during the 1920s, taken various steps to make themselves public companies instead of private companies, in the 1930s they still in essence remained banks managed by their respective zaibatsu families, as before. As a result, they did not as a rule feel responsible for bailing out any of Japan's major industries that were on the verge of collapse.

Before long, however, they encountered various troubles and were asked to meet various demands from major industries and the government, such as financial support for the reorganization of industries and industrial mobilization for war. The government's financial authorities interfered in private banks' affairs and strengthened control over the funds of these banks as a controlled economy developed in Japan. The most interesting thing about the relationships between the government and private banks under the controlled economy was that not only the financial authorities but also the Ministry of Commerce and Industry aggressively interfered in private banks' affairs. The Ministry of Commerce and Industry continued to be interested in switching banks' sound loan policies, which the Ministry considered to be excessively conservative and selfish, to policies that would be expansive enough to include extending loans to the heavy and chemical industries.

Until the Showa Depression, Mitsui Bank deserved attention for being the largest, oldest, and most influential zaibatsu-related bank. After the Showa Depression, the bank warranted attention for taking the initiative in assuming responsibility for the banking affairs of major industries in all sectors of the economy, not merely of Mitsui businesses.

In fact, the bank was the only large bank capable of separating itself almost completely from the control of its zaibatsu family before the zaibatsu were dissolved immediately after the Second World War. It accumulated bad loans and faced uncertainty with regard to its creditworthiness twice during the Showa Depression. It was only natural that the House of Mitsui gradually came to lose interest in managing a commercial bank.

Changing Mitsui Bank's Lending Policy

Although Mitsui Bank began to be troubled in the late 1920s with such potential bad loans as its loans connected with Suzuki & Co. and its loans to Tokyo Electric Light, the bank successfully extricated itself from the trouble without changing its conservative lending policy. The bank was able to call in its loans to the Bank of Taiwan and Suzuki & Co. very quickly and to urge Tokyo Electric Light to pay off its debt by using the proceeds from the corporate bonds the bank underwrote.

During and just after the Showa Depression that started in 1930, however, the bank was troubled by bad loans more seriously than before. In addition, the bank was also worried about the deteriorating economic environment, which badly affected its foreign exchange business. To tide itself over such a situation the bank was forced to change its lending policy drastically.

The amount of its bad loans increased in the second-half of 1932 and in 1933, though the Showa Depression had bottomed out in 1931. One reason was that the bank's loans to Tokyo Electric Light soared rapidly again from the second-half of 1929, and there is little doubt that such loans turned into bad ones after 1932. If the huge amount of bad loans to Tokyo Electric Light are added in, at the end of 1932 the total amount of bad loans would reach one-fourth of the bank's total outstanding loans. Let us see how and why the bank's loans to Tokyo Electric Light finally degenerated into really bad loans.

In April 1930, after the company had failed in a bid to raise funds by selling foreign currency bonds, the group of British and American banks underwriting the bonds began to pressure the company to reform itself more drastically.[19] Burnett Walker, the vice president of both Guaranty Trust Co. and Guaranty Co., came to Japan as a representative of the syndicate and demanded such action as the dismissal of then president Shohachi Wakao and a reduction of the dividend rate from 6 per cent to zero.

When the company did not comply with his requests, Walker asked the government to intervene. The government was vulnerable in that it would have to convert its 5 per cent sterling bonds (valued at 23.44 million British pounds and becoming due in January 1931) with the help of the group of British and American underwriters, and it would be badly hurt in the conversion of the bonds by Tokyo Electric Light's financial difficulties.[20]

The key men in the affair were Thomas Lamont, a partner of J.P. Morgan & Co. staying in London as a representative of the British and American underwriting syndicate for the Young loans made by the German Government, and Junnosuke Inoue, the Minister of Finance responsible for the conversion of the bonds. As a result of a series of negotiations, a memorandum of acceptance of some of Walker's requests was handed over to Walker and a contract for converting the Japanese Government bonds was signed by the representatives on the same day, 9 May.[21] In effect, Walker succeeded in achieving most of what he had asked for. According to the memorandum, the dividend rate would be lowered to 5 per cent and Wakao's rank would be lowered from that of president to that of vice-president.

But at the company's shareholders' meeting of June 1930 many large shareholders unexpectedly protested against the management, and eventually all the managing directors and directors representing the group headed by Wakao were forced to take responsibility upon themselves and resign.[22]

As only the three directors whom Mitsui Bank had sent to the company remained on the board of directors, the bank was in effect forced to get involved in the company's management and to place the company under the bank's supervision on behalf of the British and American underwriting syndicate. There were the circumstances behind the bank's bad loans to Tokyo Electric Light.

Debate about the bank's sound loan policy increased vigorously inside and outside the bank after the second-half of 1929, when the government decided on a return to the gold standard. For example, one member of the management proposed a reform plan under which the bank would be set free from the House of Mitsui's control to build a closer relationship between the bank and industry. Contrariwise, Mitsui & Co., which still wielded considerable influence on the bank's lending policy, insisted that all Mitsui enterprises should unite themselves under the House of Mitsui's control and wanted the bank to take closer responsibility for the family's banking affairs.[23]

Outside the bank, the government opposed the sound loan policies of all the large commercial banks. In particular, the Ministry of Commerce and Industry was eager to reverse the sound loan policies of zaibatsu-related large banks. This was because the Ministry needed these influential private banks to work closely with industry to let industry reorganize itself and rationalize its operations.

Japan's Industrial Rationalization Policy, introduced at the end of the 1920s, was based on American and German models; it was mainly aimed at promoting productivity by introducing more efficient machines into factories, improving the efficiency of business operations, cutting production costs, and the like. One of the most remarkable features of Japan's Industrial Rationalization Policy, compared with its foreign counterparts, was that it was accompanied by plans to cut excess capacity and workers on a large scale through corporate mergers. This was intended to deal with the problem of excessive competition among companies too small and weak to compete with foreign companies.

The Ministry of Commerce and Industry tried to intervene among companies in major industries facing trouble, with the aim of putting them together into one company or a small number of companies.[24] The loans of private large banks to companies, extended at the Ministry's request for making the merger projects successful, were relief loans in most cases. In the case of Mitsui Bank, though, such loans contravened its sound loan policy. The government's failure to obtain assistance from private large banks so that it could push on with merger projects became a good argument later for government control of private banks' funds and for ranking those industries that would have first priority for loans.

Mitsui Bank's leaders took excessive precautions against the foreseen possibility that the bank's cash position might tighten. That is why Mitsui Bank was unable to reverse its old-fashioned lending policy, and why the bank did not accept the government's requests. Behind such precautions were the considerable pressure on the bank from its loans to electric power companies such as Tokyo Electric Light, given that the British and American underwriting syndicate was showing signs of turning its back on Japan's electric power companies.[25]

In 1931 the bank attached greater importance to foreign exchange and securities businesses to use its growing excess funds more profitably. The performance of these two businesses reached its peak before the Second World War.

There was an increase of 35 million yen in the bank's average deposit balance and a decrease of 33 million yen in its average balance of domestic loans at the end of the first-half of 1931 over the end of 1930. As a result, about 68 million yen emerged as funds to be placed somewhere during this half year. The bank put most such funds into domestic and foreign short-term securities and foreign currency deposits in five big commercial banks and a merchant bank in the United Kingdom. Table 5.4 shows that the bank bought Indian Treasury Bills valued at 20.3 million rupees and sold or retired them valued at 12.25 million rupees during the first-half of 1931, leaving a total balance of Indian Treasury Bills valued at 11.05 million rupees at the end of June 1931. Table 5.4 also shows that the bank bought Exchequer Bills valued at 1.05 million pounds for the first time during the first-half of 1931, but did not sell or retire any of them at the end of that period. Furthermore, the bank's balance of deposits at the financial institutions at the end of June 1931 was 1,650 thousand pounds.[26]

The bank became more enthusiastic than before about purchasing British Exchequer Bills in the second-half of 1931, to expand the short-term operation of otherwise idle funds. In most of these purchases, the bank used pounds sterling obtained by exchanging dollars originally secured in the purchase of export bills destined for the United States. The bank bought British Exchequer Bills valued at 7.92 million pounds sterling during the second-half of 1931, or about seven and a half times more than what it purchased during the first-half of the year. Besides British Exchequer Bills, the bank also purchased Indian Treasury Bills and Indian Government Sterling Bonds.

Oddly enough, to increase returns from the investment the bank omitted making forward sales exchange contracts that would enable it to avoid probable exchange risks involved in the purchase of British Exchequer Bills. The bank made forward sales exchange contracts amounting to $16,330,000 instead in an amount of pounds sterling to match the bank's

Table 5.4. *Short-term securities bought by Mitsui Bank in the first-half of 1931*

	Securities bought and deposits		Profit margin (%)	Balance at term end	
	Amount	Book value (¥)		Amount	Book value (¥)
Japanese Treasury Bills	¥83,870,000	83,648,461	2.19	¥35,450,000	35,363,523
Rice certificates	¥11,842,886	11,808,526	3.48	—	—
5% Japanese Treasury Bonds	¥3,550,000	3,545,800	5.02	¥3,550,000	3,545,800
5.5% Indian Government Sterling Bonds	£500,000	4,771,433	6.14	£500,000	4,664,615
6% Indian Government Sterling Bonds	£500,000	4,894,030	6.21	£500,000	4,894,030
Indian Treasury Bills	Rs 20,300,000	14,763,636	4.21	Rs 11,050,000	7,888,201
Exchequer Bills	£1,050,000	10,280,992	2.45	£1,050,000	10,280,992
Deposits at foreign financial institutions	£2,450,000	24,113,682	2.73	£1,650,000[a]	16,226,612
Total book value		157,826,560			82,863,773

[a] £1,650,000 is broken down as follows: £500,000 in Midland, £400,000 in Barclays, £300,000 in Rothschild, £250,000 in Lloyds, and £200,000 in Natwest (formerly National Provincial).

Source: Mitsui Bank, Semiannual Reports to Mitsui Gomei, from Sakura Bank Archives (unpublished), esp. the report for the first-half of 1931.

purchase of British Exchequer Bills. Two errors were involved in those transactions. One concerned the kind of currency, and the other concerned the amount of forward sale exchange contracts sufficient to cover the bank's purchase of British Exchequer Bills.

Unfortunately, as soon as the United Kingdom abandoned the gold standard on Monday, 21 September 1931, pound sterling began to weaken quickly. Crucially, the bank had an overbought position of £8,541,000 and an oversold position of $16,334,000 on Saturday, 19 September 1931. It was not the difference, but the sum, of these that was left exposed to the provable exchange risk at the time. To cover its oversold position, it promptly purchased $16 million from the Yokohama Specie Bank to make settlement possible on 21 September 1931. On the other hand, it continued to have an overbought position, while its latent exchange losses expanded rapidly in proportion to the pound sterling's depreciation.

The bank's overbought position of £8,541,000 consisted mainly of British Exchequer Bills valued at £4,410,000, Indian Government Sterling Bonds valued at £1,320,000, British Consols valued at £2,760,000, and deposits in British commercial and merchant banks valued at £900,000 (£400,000 in Barclays, £300,000 in Midland, and £200,000 in Rothschild).

The bank's latent exchange losses generated by the pound sterling's depreciation of 30 per cent was estimated to be about 24 million yen. The bank was being driven into such a corner that it would have to disclose its huge amount of exchange losses in its financial results for the six months ending 31 December 1931. If that were to happen, doubtless the bank would have to face concern about its creditworthiness and there would be runs on the bank. The only solution to this problem was for Japan to abandon the gold standard and allow the yen to depreciate.

Then a dramatic change was made to the government's administration. On 13 December the Finance Minister of the new administration quickly reintroduced a gold embargo and put a stop to gold conversion. As a result, the yen depreciated quickly, so that by the end of 1931 the yen exchange rate against the British pound was almost restored to the level it had been before the UK's abandonment of the gold standard. This was how Mitsui Bank's problem of foreign exchange losses was solved.

Though the yen kept depreciating in 1932, giving the bank handsome foreign exchange profits thanks to its enormous overbought position in pound sterling, it simultaneously made the bank's bad loan problem more serious, for the yen's depreciation caused Japan's five large electric power companies (among them Tokyo Electric Light), which had issued dollar bonds, serious foreign exchange losses. This new problem, coupled with exhaustion owing to the domestic depression, drove the power companies into financial difficulties.

Tokyo Electric Light first failed in its attempt to convert its domestic bonds of 40 million yen that were maturing at the end of October 1932 because of a shrinking of the domestic bond market. Of course, Mitsui Bank was almost equally to blame. To do nothing would not only have caused financial difficulties for the company, it would also have triggered concern about the bank's creditworthiness.

Although the bank made an effort to ask the bond holders to subscribe to the refunding bonds, the total amount subscribed was ¥2,762,000, or less than 7 per cent of the amount of the refunding bonds to be issued (Table 5.5). The table shows that the bank was prepared, reluctantly, to subscribe to all the remainder on its own. If it did so, however, the bank's total amount of credit to Tokyo Electric Light would reach about 100 million yen (Table 5.6). In short, it was also clear that the remaining unsold bonds were too much for the bank to subscribe to by itself.

In cooperation with the Industrial Bank of Japan, Mitsui Bank was able to find a way out of its difficulties by promises of mutual help. To help Mitsui Bank, the Industrial Bank of Japan subscribed ¥14,309,500 for the

Table 5.5. *Allotment of Tokyo Electric Light's refunding bonds, 1932 (yen)*

Date	Holders of matured bonds	Mitsui Bank	IBJ
At time of issue of refunding bonds	2,762,000	37,238,000	—
On 25 October	2,762,000	27,928,500	9,309,500
In November	2,762,000	22,928,500	14,309,500

Source: The Secret Story and Documents about Mitsui Bank, from Sakura Bank Archives (unpublished).

Table 5.6. *Mitsui Bank's credit to Tokyo Electric Light in October 1932 (¥1,000)*

Unsecured loans	45,000
Loans to Toden Securities	15,000
Loans on Tokyo Electric Light's bonds	870
Loans on Tokyo Electric Light's shares	9,090
Subtotal (a)	69,960
The remaining unsold bonds (b)	28,000
Total (a + b)	97,960
The bank's total outstanding loans	approx. 400,000
Paid-in capital	60,000
Authorized capital	100,000

Source: The Secret Story and Documents about Mitsui Bank, from Sakura Bank Archives (unpublished).

refunding bonds, as shown in Table 5.5. At the same time, to help the Industrial Bank of Japan, Ikeda, the executive director of Mitsui Bank, persuaded Mitsui leaders, who were apprehensive about the idea of accepting the Industrial Bank of Japan's offer, that Oji Paper, a Mitsui affiliate, would benefit from acquiring Karafuto Kogyo, to which the Industrial Bank of Japan had extended a huge amount of bad loans. Passage of the agreement became easier when Takuma Dan, president of Mitsui Gomei and the most influential opponent of such an acquisition, was shot and killed by a young rightist in March 1932. On 18 October 1932 it was announced that the two sides had reached an agreement that Oji Paper would, the following May, consolidate three large paper manufacturing companies—Oji Paper, Fuji Paper (an affiliate of Oji Paper), and Karafuto Kogyo—into one company with ¥150 million in authorized capital under the name Oji Paper. Thus the Industrial Bank of Japan's bad loans to Karafuto Kogyo were quickly changed into good loans to Oji Paper, newly established in 1933.

Things began to improve with regard to the five large electric power companies' financial difficulties in 1933, as their foreign exchange loss problem receded a little and demand for electric power began to recover. These companies still needed a decline in their fund-raising costs, which they achieved by converting their outstanding high-interest-bearing bonds into low-interest-bearing bonds, to escape finally from their financial difficulties.

Major banks and trust companies formed many underwriting syndicates for refunding electric power bonds at a lower interest rate. For example, seven banks and two trust companies, headed by Mitsui Bank as a trustee bank, formed underwriting syndicates for refunding bonds for Tokyo Electric Light at a lower rate in 1934 and 1935. In this way even Mitsui Bank's bad loans to Tokyo Electric Light were changed into good loans to the company by 1935.[27]

While Japan's munitions and export industries were boosted both by the increase in the government's war expenditure after the Manchurian Incident and by the yen's depreciation after Japan's abandonment of the gold standard, Mitsui Bank tended to stick to its previous policy of making loans mainly to major companies, especially Mitsui & Co. and its affiliates, because the foreign exchange business still had great appeal to the bank—even though the purchase of foreign bonds and bills was prohibited by such laws and orders as the Foreign Exchange Control Law.

This was the primary reason why the bank lost its competitive ability to attract deposits and why deposits in the bank remained stable until 1935, whereas deposits in other large banks (except Mitsubishi Bank) increased markedly, as Table 5.7 shows. Table 5.7 also shows that both Mitsui Bank and Mitsubishi Bank intentionally reduced their balance of loans for about three years even after the second-half of 1932, while other large banks slowly and steadily expanded their loan balances.

Table 5.7. *Deposits and loans of Japan's six largest banks, 1931–7 (¥ 1,000,000)*

	Mitsui	Mitsubishi	Dai-Ichi	Sumitomo	Yasuda	Sanwa
Deposits						
30/6/31	710	647	659	684	610	—
30/6/32	620	616	648	679	607	—
30/6/33	696	705	769	815	730	—
30/6/34	759	696	816	827	800	1,063
30/6/35	759	752	868	886	818	1,080
30/6/36	824	805	940	970	891	1,151
30/6/37	904	903	1,054	1,093	1,023	1,263
Loans						
30/6/31	413	313	371	402	438	—
30/6/32	441	344	394	423	460	—
30/6/33	386	324	406	472	507	—
30/6/34	366	259	409	426	519	489
30/6/35	380	265	432	471	571	494
30/6/36	437	341	450	543	616	526
30/6/37	531	441	657	691	744	577

Source: The Mitsubishi Bank, *Mitsubishi Ginko shi* [History of the Mitsubishi Bank] (Tokyo: The Mitsubishi Bank, 1954), 216–17, 230, and 232.

Mitsui Bank put the newly available funds resulting from the increase in the balance of its deposits and the decrease in its loan balance into its foreign exchange and securities businesses. In rough figures, the bank put to work ¥220 million in new funds, ¥160 million of which came from an increase in deposits and ¥60 million from a ¥60 million decrease in loans during the approximate period from the end of March 1932 to the end of June 1935, by buying long-term government bonds valued at ¥180 million and expanding its foreign exchange operations by ¥40 million. However offensive such use of the funds looked, it contained essentially an old-fashioned and extremely conservative attitude towards taking responsibility for banking transactions with industry.

It started changing its policy of lending mainly to major companies after 1935, when the bank's bad loan problem eased and at the same time it was patently clear that the bank was losing out to other large banks in attracting deposits and giving loans.[28] It established a Committee to Promote Transactions with Firms in 1935, and followed this up with a reform of its foreign exchange operations and the abolition of its Securities Department at the Head Office in 1936. These steps were taken to discontinue the policy of using excess funds on its foreign exchange and securities businesses.

To promote transactions with firms, first of all the bank tried to target all Mitsui enterprises. Table 5.8 shows that the bank's outstanding loans to Kanegafuchi Spinning Co. were about ¥72 million at the end of June 1937,

Table 5.8. Mitsui Bank's transactions with Mitsui enterprises, 1937–43 (¥1,000)

Name	30/6/37 Loans	30/6/37 Deposits	30/6/39 Loans	30/6/39 Deposits	31/12/40 Loans	31/12/40 Deposits	31/3/43 Loans	31/3/43 Deposits
Mitsui Gomei	— (—)	— (—)	15,000 (15,270)	5,689 (5,689)	0	1,929	—	—
Mitsui & Co.	(38,356)	(22,115)	6,578 (53,788)	29,065 (33,131)	84,862 (128,295)	65,667 (68,706)	(137,177)	(84,962)
Mitsui Mining	—	—	12,509 (14,732)	2,805 (2,806)	29,768 (32,095)	7,982 (7,985)	(43,425)	(4,452)
Toshiba	—	—	2,500	1,955	10,800	2,455	(36,637)	(20,785)
Oji Paper	(13,693)	(4,828)	6,897 (13,742)	2,608 (2,608)	24,357 (50,239)	1,548 (1,552)	(22,831)	(7,074)
Toyo Menka	(35,358)	(1,671)	1,862 (33,372)	973 (1,761)	703 (21,929)	3,410 (8,454)	(17,293)	(1,743)
Kanegafuchi Spinning	(71,764)	(11,882)	45,172 (67,496)	7,226 (7,255)	41,713 (57,859)	8,474 (9,055)	(67,455)	(12,438)
Nippon Steel	—	—	1,325	4,239	6,250	13,918	(10,309)	(39,043)
Nihon Seifun	—	—	2,565 (24,229)	571 (408)	17,441 (17,565)	2,345 (2,347)	—	—
Toyo Koatsu	—	—	13	0	1,340	3	(10,540)	(83)
Others	—	—	9,829	41,831	20,385	50,051	—	—
Total (A)	—	—	104,250	96,962	237,619	157,782	—	—
Total (B)	—	—	236,296	101,683	346,757	166,455	—	—

Note: Figures in parenthesis taken from Mitsui Bank's Documents on Mitsui Bank's Substantial Credit to Customers. Total (B) is the total of the figures in parenthesis (i.e. from Mitsui Bank's 'Documents') plus the figures for Mitsui Gomei (only for 31/12/40), Toshiba, Nippon Steel, Toyo Koatsu, and others (which are only available from the 'Monthly Reports'). Because figures given in 'Documents' are based on Mitsui Bank's 'Auditor's Reports', they are thought to be more reliable than those given in 'Monthly Reports'.

Sources: Mitsui Bank, 'Monthly Reports of the Bank's Transactions with Mitsui-Related Companies in Loans and Deposits', in Japan Business History Institute (ed.), *Historical Materials on Mitsui Bank*, v (Tokyo: JBHI, 1978), 564–87; Mitsui Bank, Documents on Mitsui Bank's Substantial Credit to Customers, from Sakura Bank Archives (unpublished).

as a result of a remarkable expansion in loans to firms beginning around 1935. After 1937, a stream of Mitsui enterprises followed Kanegafuchi Spinning Co.'s lead and turned into the bank's major commercial borrowers.

Merger with Dai-Ichi Bank

After the outbreak in 1937 of war with China, Mitsui Bank began to face a serious fund shortage problem; at the same time it became concerned that its loans to munitions companies would turn into bad loans during the probable postwar recession. To overcome these problems the bank accelerated a move to change its lending policy drastically, and it finally decided to set itself free from the restraints of House of Mitsui control, which was seen as the major obstacle to such a change.

As the bank responsible for the banking affairs of all Mitsui enterprises, the bank not only had to meet the funding requirements of Mitsui affiliates, but also had to provide loans to external munitions companies and to buy government bonds to fulfil an important public role imposed on the leading banks. As a consequence, the bank became unable to meet by itself the demands for funds made of it. To solve this problem the bank first formed syndicates with other banks, then it adopted a policy of having as many branches and offices as possible, and finally it decided to prepare for a bank merger.

To control private banks' use of funds, a few items of legislature such as the Law for the Extraordinary Adjustment of Funds of 1937 and the Order Concerning the Operation of Funds by Banks of 1940 were introduced to back up the Foreign Exchange Control Law of 1933.

Under such circumstances, Mitsui Bank's transactions with Mitsui affiliates changed a great deal. First of all, the bank's outstanding loans to Mitsui-controlled companies trading under the Mitsui name expanded rapidly. Second, Mitsui Mining, Tokyo Shibaura Electric, Japan Steel Works, Ltd., Toyo Koatsu Industries, Inc., and Mitsui Chemical Industry Co., Ltd., all of which were beginning to accept orders from the military, finally joined Oji Paper as the bank's major commercial borrowers. Third, the balance of the bank's outstanding loans to Mitsui affiliates (twenty-two companies) reached almost 30 per cent of its total outstanding balance of loans, 10 per cent higher than the approximately 20 per cent of the mid-1930s.[29]

Junshiro Mandai (1883–1959; chairman of Mitsui Bank from 1937 to 1943) worked out a merger strategy at the beginning of 1938. It not only aimed at making the bank Japan's largest through such a merger, but it also was intended to solve the long-standing problem of separating the bank from the Mitsui zaibatsu. He was concerned that the bank, which had huge loans to munitions companies, would be faced with financial difficulties

during the probable postwar recession and that the bank's crisis might lead
to the ruin of the House of Mitsui. Learning of the merger plan from
Mandai, the House of Mitsui finally accepted it on condition that the
family (through Mitsui Gomei) would remain a major shareholder and that
the Mitsui family name would live on in the new bank to be established
through the merger.[30] Mandai's merger plan, however, was finally rejected
by the bank that Mitsui Bank wanted to merge with, Dai-Ichi Bank.

Mitsui Bank's loans to Mitsui & Co., which had acquired a shareholding
division through the merger with Mitsui Gomei (a holding company),
expanded remarkably and reached about ¥140 million at the end of March
1943. This put heavy pressure on the bank. The bank's managers became
preoccupied with this problem and decided, just before the end of 1942, to
resume merger talks with Dai-Ichi Bank.

At this point the House of Mitsui was forced to make considerable con-
cessions and withdrew its earlier demands. The family's only condition was
that the new bank to emerge from the merger would provide loans to Mitsui
businesses. In return for that, the family promised Dai-Ichi Bank to
renounce retention of the name Mitsui and to accept not having the right to
be a major shareholder in the new bank. To safeguard these two House of
Mitsui pledges against nonperformance, Dai-Ichi Bank not only obtained a
written promise from Mitsui Bank before the governor of the Bank of Japan
as a witness, it also asked the Ministry of Finance to make them conditions
for the Ministry's informal approval of the merger. Mitsui Bank and
Dai-Ichi Bank finally did merge, establishing Teikoku Bank in March 1943.

Teikoku Bank was the first bank with the opportunity to be responsible
for the banking affairs of major industries on a nationwide scale. In order
to fulfil these objectives, it planned to adopt a new policy of extending
more long-term loans over a one-year period, to be supplied for war production in line with national goals. The bank, however, soon began to face
a serious fund shortage problem. The problem emerged around the end of
June 1943, only three months after the start of its operations, and forced the
bank to abandon its expansion of long-term lending. After January 1944 it
pushed on with its strategy of asking the Industrial Bank of Japan to provide long-term loans to the designated munitions companies that Teikoku
had made its prime borrowers, while intensifying loan prioritization.

Conclusion

In the interwar years, Mitsui Bank, aiming to become a genuine commercial bank, tried to be faithful to the principle that it should prefer the

discounting of commercial bills to loaning on bills, and short-term lending to long-term lending. In putting such a lending principle into practice, the bank seemed to attach extremely great importance both to the foreign exchange business (with such major trading companies as Mitsui & Co.) and to the securities business (with companies in debt to the bank).

As far as the period prior to the war between Japan and China beginning in 1937 was concerned, the bank was to all practical effects successful in keeping the average loan period to less than two months, even as it met the demand for long-term capital funds from Mitsui-affiliated companies, electric power companies, and electric railway companies.[31] The bank duly regulated the average loan period, which grew longer as a result of the expansion of the bank's loans to electric power companies in the years 1926–7 and in the years 1930–3. It was able to do so mainly through underwriting bonds issued by the electric power companies to pay off bank loans.

After the mid-1930s the way of combining a securities business with a lending business came to play a more important role in restricting the average loan period and was eventually extended by the bank to financing munitions companies. In this manner, the bank succeeded in keeping the loan period down to under two months even after 1937. Still, it was becoming more and more difficult for the bank to meet fully the demand from munitions companies for long-term capital funds, because of the shrinking of its foreign exchange and securities businesses. Before long, its modus operandi was brought to an end when the government expected commercial banks to provide more long-term loans. At the beginning of the 1940s, Teikoku Bank, established through a merger of Dai-Ichi Bank and Mitsui Bank, faced the problem of a serious shortage of funds, almost causing it to abandon the expansion of its long-term loan business.

NOTES

1. This chapter is a revised and abridged version of chapters 1 and 2 in Shinji Ogura, *Banking, the State and Industrial Promotion in Developing Japan, 1900–73* (Basingstoke and New York, NY: Palgrave, 2002) reproduced with permission of Palgrave Macmillan.
2. Mitsui Bank, *The Mitsui Bank: A History of the First 100 Years* [English edition] (Tokyo: Mitsui Bank, 1976), 68.
3. Mitsui Bunko [Mitsui Research Institute for Social and Economic History, abbreviated to MRISEH hereafter], *Mitsui jigyo shi* [The history of Mitsui business enterprises], vol. 3, pt. 1 (Tokyo: MRISEH, 1980), 3–22.
4. Mitsui Bank, 'The Minutes of the Branch Managers' Meeting Held in October 1904', in Nihon Keieishi Kenkyusho [Japan Business History Institute,

abbreviated to JBHI hereafter] (ed.), *Mitsui Ginko shiryo* [Historical materials on Mitsui Bank], ii (Tokyo: JBHI, 1977), 84; The Mitsui General Family Council, 'The Minutes of the Council's Control Department', pt. 1, *Mitsui Bunko ronso* [Mitsui Research Institute Review], 7 (1973), 335.

5. 'Memoirs of Tomozo Toyama', in Memoirs of Former Executives of Mitsui Bank, from Sakura Bank Archives (unpublished).

6. Sumitomo Bank, *Sumitomo Ginko 80-nen shi* [The 80-year history of Sumitomo Bank] (Osaka: Sumitomo Bank, 1979), 195–201.

7. 'Memoirs of Hirokichi Kameshima', in Memoirs of Former Executives of Mitsui Bank, from Sakura Bank Archives.

8. Mitsui Bank, Directives from the Head Office, from Sakura Bank Archives (unpublished).

9. Mitsui Bank, 'Telegrams about the Bank's Fund Position', in JBHI (ed.), *Historical Materials on Mitsui Bank*, v (Tokyo: JBHI, 1978); Mitsui Bank, The Minutes of the Board of Directors, no. 859 (14 May 1920), no. 860 (28 May 1920), and no. 864 (23 July 1920) (unpublished); Mitsui & Co., The Minutes of the 8th Branch Managers' Meeting, from MRISEH Archives (unpublished); Mitsui Mining, *Semiannual Reports*.

10. Mitsui Bank, *The Mitsui Bank*, 95; The Secret Story and Documents about Mitsui Bank, in four volumes, from Sakura Bank Archives (unpublished); Mitsui Bank, The Minutes of the Board of Directors, no. 858 (23 April 1920); Mitsui Bank, The Supplement to the 'Hochi' [the Bank's internal newspaper], no. 2421 (27 April 1920) (unpublished).

11. Mitsui Bank, The Minutes of General Managers' Meetings, from Sakura Bank Archives, especially the minutes of the meeting of 25 February 1930 (unpublished).

12. Mitsui Bank, 'Telegrams about the Bank's Fund Position', in JBHI (ed.), *Historical Materials on Mitsui Bank*, v; Mitsui Bank, Semiannual Reports to Mitsui Gomei, from Sakura Bank Archives (unpublished), especially the Semiannual Reports for 1923–6.

13. Seiji Moroo, *Jigyo kin'yu jimbutsu: Daido Denryoku 20-nen kin'yu shi ko* [Business, finance, and leading figures: A study of 20 years of Daido Electric Power Co.'s raising of capital] (Nishinomiya, Hyogo Prefecture: private publication, 1940), 89–241, and especially 271–3.

14. Mitsui Bank's New York Branch, Report on an Investigation into Investment Bankers (1925), from Sakura Bank Archives (unpublished). According to this report, the bank negotiated with Bankers Trust Co. first to ask it to underwrite bonds. The negotiations, however, ended in failure.

15. US Congress, Senate Committee on Finance, *Sale of Foreign Bonds or Securities in the United States* (Washington, DC: Government Printing Office, 1931–2), 959.

16. 'Memoirs of Naojiro Kikumoto', in Memoirs of Former Executives of Mitsui Bank, from Sakura Bank Archives.

17. Mitsui Bank, Documents on the Bank's Substantial Credit to Customers, from Sakura Bank Archives (unpublished); The Secret Story and Documents about Mitsui Bank.

18. Mitsui Bank, Semiannual Reports to Mitsui Gomei, especially the report for the second-half of 1927; Mitsui Bank, The Minutes of the Board of Directors, no. 1036 (8 July 1927).

19. Seihin Ikeda, *Zaikai kaiko* [Memoirs of the Japanese business circle] (Tokyo: Sekai no Nihonsha, 1949), 230–1.

20. *Tokyo Asahi Shimbun* [The Tokyo Asahi], news reports from April and May 1930.
21. Inoue Junnosuke Ronso Hensankai (ed.), *Inoue Junnosuke Den* [The life of Junnosuke Inoue] (Tokyo: Inoue Junnosuke Ronso Hensankai, 1935), 607–10.
22. *Asahi Keizai Nenshi* [The Asahi Economic Chronicle] (Osaka: Asahi Shimbunsha, 1932), 112–25.
23. Mitsui & Co., The Minutes of the 10th Branch Managers' Meeting, from MRISEH Archives, 1931, 158–9 (unpublished).
24. The Ministry of International Trade and Industry (MITI) (ed.), *Shoko seisaku shi* [The history of the Ministry's industrial and commercial policies], ix (Tokyo: MITI, 1961), 12–31.
25. Mitsui Bank, The Minutes of General Managers' Meetings, from Sakura Bank Archives.
26. Mitsui Bank, Semiannual Reports to Mitsui Gomei, especially the report for the first-half of 1931.
27. Mitsui Bank, 'An Investigation into the Bank's Loans to Mitsui-Related Companies and Their Executives', in JBHI (ed.), *Historical Materials on Mitsui Bank*, v, 543–4.
28. Mitsui Bank, 'A Summary of the Chairman's Address to the Branch Managers' Meeting Held on 2 October 1935', in Mitsui Bank, The Collected Chairman's Addresses to Branch Managers' Meetings, from Sakura Bank Archives (unpublished).
29. Mitsui Bank, 'Monthly Reports of the Bank's Transactions with Mitsui-Related Companies in Loans and Deposits', in JBHI (ed.), *Historical Materials on Mitsui Bank*, v, 564–87; Mitsui Bank, Documents on the Bank's Substantial Credit to Customers, from Sakura Bank Archives (unpublished); Mitsui Bank, The Bank's Audit Report for the First Quarter of 1943, from Sakura Bank Archives (unpublished).
30. 'Memoirs of Junshiro Mandai', in Memoirs of Former Executives of Mitsui Bank, from Sakura Bank Archives.
31. Mitsui Bank, 'Semiannual Reports of Mitsui Bank', in JBHI (ed.), *Historical Materials on Mitsui Bank*, i (Tokyo: JBHI, 1978); Mitsui Bank, Semiannual Reports to Mitsui Gomei, especially the reports for 1926–43. The average loan period is equal to 12 times [the quantity] the sum of both average balances of loans on bills and bills discounted divided by [the quantity] the sum of loans on bills and bills discounted.

PART II

UNIVERSAL BANKING

6

The French 'Banques d'affaires' in the Interwar Period: The Case of Banque de Paris et des Pays-Bas (Paribas)

ERIC BUSSIÈRE

Introduction

This contribution tries to analyse the consequences of the First World War and the effects of the economic context of the interwar period on the structure of activities of the French 'banques d'affaires', and especially the most important of them, the Banque de Paris et des Pays-Bas (Paribas). Created in 1872, Paribas had as its first objective participation in the flotation of an international loan intended to pay the reparations due from France to Germany after the Franco-Prussian War of 1870. Market activities, and especially bond issues for governments, remained the key activity of Paribas from its birth up until the First World War. These financial activities were conducted on an international scale through syndicates in which Paribas played a leading role when the French market was involved. Relations with enterprises constituted the second kind of activities engaged in by Paribas, especially utilities such as railways, gas, and electricity, whose development generally generated important stock and bond issues. Banking activities were the counterpart of market activities, but they began to develop significantly only at the beginning of the century and played only a secondary role at Paribas before the First World War.

The specific role of banques d'affaires is best understood if one considers the division of labour that existed in the French banking structure toward the end of the nineteenth century. Deposit banks, especially the three major ones of Crédit Lyonnais, Société Générale, and CNEP, spread out wide networks and developed their banking activities essentially by using their deposits in short-term operations such as discounting. Thanks to their networks they played an important role in issuing operations as the leaders of placement syndicates, whereas Paribas and other banques d'affaires often played the leading role in underwriting syndicates.

The First World War brought about major changes to the conditions under which banks operated. Economic conditions were deeply changed by inflation and the depreciation of the French franc between 1919 and 1926–8, as well as by the specific needs of industrial reconstruction. As a consequence of these new conditions, financial resources were primarily used for national needs; very few were available for international investments up to 1928. This new context naturally had profound implications for Paribas, which had to change the structure of its activities. This study tries to analyse what kind of effects this economic and political context had on Paribas's strategy and the structure of its activities, especially during the twenties. Because it had initiated before the war an emphasis on its banking activities, especially those connected with enterprises, Paribas was pushed by the climate of the war and the reconstruction after it to accentuate this trend. In some respects, the model of the French banque d'affaires became similar to the model of the universal bank, as A. Pose has pointed out.[1] We shall see, however, that the economic conditions of the 1920s, in particular inflation, forced the bank progressively to alter its projects.

Towards a New Model of the French 'Banque d'affaires' after the First World War?

As in other countries in Europe, inflation strongly affected the French economy after the First World War as a consequence of the huge costs of the war itself and of the reconstruction between 1919 and 1926. The progress of inflation was especially strong in 1919–20 and then again between 1923 and 1926, when the French franc was subjected to strong speculative attacks that induced imported inflation, especially in 1925–6. Although the level of industrial output was around 30 per cent above the prewar level in July 1926, the assets of the six major deposit banks were still one-third below their prewar levels at this time.[2]

Paribas, like other French banks, was strongly affected by this turn of events, which reduced its means of intervention in the economy. As a banque d'affaires, its capacity to make direct investment in the economy through investment and portfolio activities was of utmost importance. These investments determined special relationships with enterprises that were clients for its banking and financial activities. As portfolio investments depended on the bank's equity capital, the ability to preserve the latter

Table 6.1. *Equity capital and deposits (million francs)*

	Equity capital			Deposits		
	Six major deposit banks	Paribas	% of Paribas	Six major deposit banks	Paribas	% of Paribas
1913	1,180	232	19.7	5,955	346	5.8
1920	1,570	264	16.8	17,650	892	5.0
1925	1,717	344	20.0	26,113	2,783	10.7
1926	1,740	345	19.8	28,620	2,487	8.7
1929	3,541	582	16.4	42,608	3,285	7.7

Sources: Data from Paribas archives; A. Plessis, 'Les banques, le crédit, l'économie', 348.

from inflation was one of the things that determined the impact of its activities in the economy. As Table 6.1 suggests, because of bad conditions on the financial market during periods of inflation, none of the French banks was able to preserve the level of its equity capital during the interwar period. Paribas's capital was raised from 100 to 150 million francs in 1919, to 200 million in 1922, and to 300 million in 1929. Nevertheless, its equity capital went down in real value between 1922 and 1929, and it was still far below its prewar level in 1930 and below the level of the major deposit banks. Still, Paribas decided to maintain a higher level of portfolio investment than the prewar ratio permitted: its portfolio represented 69 per cent of its equity capital in 1913 and 93 per cent in 1929.

In the area of deposits, Paribas fared better than the credit banks. Like other banques d'affaires, Paribas had no network in France in that time and began gradually to canvass deposits from its clients around 1900. But efforts in that direction became a priority after the end of the war. As Table 6.1 shows, the search for deposits was successful, partially as a result of the systematic efforts of the banking department and, as we shall see later, to a closer relationship with enterprises. Because the level of deposits was low at the beginning of the period, there is nothing surprising about the rapid increase in deposits collected by Paribas between 1920 and 1925. But without a network, Paribas's campaign reached its limits and was effectively offset after 1926 by the very strong development of networks by the major deposit banks; for instance, Crédit Lyonnais had 408 agencies in France in 1919, 858 in 1926, and 1,354 in 1930. Still, the real value of deposits collected by Paribas in 1929 was above its prewar level and seemed capable of supporting more vigorous banking activity.

What were the effects of inflation on the assets of the bank? Were its resources able to meet the needs of its activities, especially during the 1920s, a period of fast economic growth in France?

As deposits grew faster than in deposit banks, especially in the first half of the 1920s, one would expect that Paribas's banking activities during this period would develop faster. This was particularly true for short-term credits through discounting, which represented 35.5 per cent of Paribas's assets in 1926 and 31.5 per cent in 1930, against 15.5 per cent in 1913. The trend is more specific for current account credits, which were the usual way for banques d'affaires to provide funds to enterprises. Their relative weight revealed a stabilization rather than an increase, with 35.8 per cent of the assets in 1913, 35.5 per cent in 1926, and 31.5 per cent in 1930. But this stabilization in fact reveals a behaviour very different from that of credit banks, whose market share of current account credits fell sharply during the mid-1920s, as shown in Table 6.2. Therefore, while for the deposit banks the search for security and for liquidity seemed to be a priority during the first-half of the 1920s, the search for diversification and for the ability to satisfy the financial needs of enterprises seemed to be the priority of Paribas. This analysis is supported by the changes in the kind of short-term credits delivered by banks. During the greater part of the 1920s, and especially during the years of inflation, the major portion of short-term assets of banks consisted of treasury bills.[3] Paribas shows the same tendency at the beginning of the period, but it saw a very sharp reduction of these treasury bills in the middle of the 1920s: at the end of 1923 treasury bills represented 56 per cent of Paribas's short-term assets, 38 per cent at the end of 1924, and an average of about 5 per cent during the year 1926.

This trend is on line with the specific role played by current account credits at Paribas during the middle of the 1920s. The important role of current

Table 6.2. *Current account credits: Paribas and the two major credit banks (FF 1,000,000)*

	Crédit Lyonnais	Société Générale	Paribas	% of Paribas to CL	% of Paribas to SG
1919	1,289	1,466	210	16.3	14.3
1920	1,435	1,890	296	20.6	15.7
1921	944	1,783	295	31.3	16.5
1922	1,017	1,316	398	39.1	30.2
1923	1,316	1,804	570	43.3	32.6
1924	1,614	2,183	847	52.5	38.8
1925	1,677	2,356	1,157	69.0	49.1
1926	1,957	2,514	1,133	57.9	45.1
1927	2,448	2,641	1,680	68.6	63.6
1928	3,810	3,674	1,781	46.7	48.5
1929	4,660	4,325	1,870	40.1	43.2
1930	5,227	4,576	1,333	25.5	29.0

Source: H. Bonin, 'Les banques françaises en économie libérale (1919–35)'.

Table 6.3. *Gross profits of Paribas*

	Financial activities		Banking activities	
	Current FF 1,000,000	(%)	Current FF 1,000,000	(%)
1913	18.2	70.9	7.5	29.1
1922	27.1	46.6	31.1	53.4
1923	22.9	39.3	35.3	60.7
1924	32.5	41.7	45.5	58.3
1925	23.1	31.0	51.5	69.0
1926	35.2	32.5	73.3	67.5
1928	61.6	51.4	58.3	48.6
1929	85.0	57.0	64.1	43.0
1930	83.9	57.7	61.3	42.3
1932	35.5	38.1	57.8	61.9
1933	39.0	38.4	62.2	61.6
1934	24.5	32.2	51.6	67.8
1935	25.4	35.5	46.1	64.5
1936	23.0	36.2	40.5	63.8
1937	38.2	44.0	48.8	56.0

Source: Paribas archives.

account credits and the quasi-disappearance of treasury bills from the assets of the bank reveals a strong involvement in industry financing and even, as empiric analysis will show, a relative lack of means during the period of strong inflation and depreciation of the franc. As Table 6.2 shows, the stabilization of the franc by Poincaré in 1928 induced a shift in these tendencies, with a return to better conditions on the financial market.

Table 6.3 helps us to fine-tune our analysis of the global strategy of the bank in reaction to the economic environment of the period. The development of banking activities appears clearly to have been, over the long-term, more than a kind of contracyclical way to stabilize profits during the period of inflation as well as during the Great Depression. Before the First World War, financial activities represented the structural basis of the profits of the bank; thus, between 1909 and 1913 they never represented less than 70 per cent of the gross profit of Paribas in France: 70.9 per cent in 1913, 80.8 per cent in 1909. During the interwar period, according to data at our disposal, they never reached that level again, and only three times did they exceed the 50 per cent level: in 1928, 1929, and 1930, when financial activities on the market of Paris reached a peak (in 1930 the volume of issuing at Paris—9.6 per cent of the GDP—exceeded the prewar high of 9.2 per cent of the GDP in 1913). As a consequence, banking activities became the new structural basis for Paribas, maintaining a level of about 60–65 per cent of gross profits during both the period of inflation and the period of the Depression.

One must, however, avoid separating these two kinds of activities; in most cases the development of banking activities at Paribas was linked to its position as shareholder of enterprises and led to a better integration of the services offered by the bank to its clients in the banking and in the financial fields. An internal report on the investment portfolio of the bank written at the beginning of 1939 indicated that the importance attributed to this portfolio was justified both by the return it offered and by the leverage it gave to the bank to promote its commercial and financial services. The strategy that the bank intended to follow during the ensuing years was to sell those shares that gave no leverage and to seize opportunities to acquire new ones that would create new relations with firms.

A more detailed analysis of the results of the financial activities of Paribas allows us to specify their nature and their role in the global activity of the bank. In the internal accounts of the bank, financial profits were divided into three major sources: capital gains realized through trading activities on stock markets; revenues from the portfolio; commissions obtained from issuing and underwriting activities. As one might expect, the capital gains were more volatile than portfolio revenue or commissions and very dependent on stock exchange quotations (Tables 6.4 and 6.5). These gains represented 50.3 per cent of the results of financial activities in 1928, and they remained high in 1929 (with a maximum of 46.8 million francs) and 1930 (33.7 million). Gains fell sharply after 1930, dropping to 22.9 million in 1931 and 13.9 in 1932.

Table 6.4. *Results of financial activities: 1*

	Capital gains		Portfolio revenue		Commissions		Others	
	Current FF 1,000,000	(%)	Current FF 1,000,000	(%)	Current FF 1,000,000	(%)	Current FF 1,000,000	(%)
1922	10.6	39.1	10.1	37.3	6.1	22.6	0.3	1.0
1923	9.6	42.1	7.3	32.0	5.4	23.7	0.6	2.2
1924	11.3	35.4	12.5	39.1	6.8	21.3	1.3	4.2
1925	5.4	22.9	13.6	58.0	4.1	17.5	0.4	1.6
1926	8.9	25.4	18.5	52.8	6.2	17.7	1.5	4.1
1927	21.6	42.9	21.1	41.7	7.5	14.8	0.4	0.6
1928	31.0	50.3	20.0	31.8	9.3	15.1	1.8	2.8
1934	5.0	20.4	10.7	43.8	4.4	17.9	4.4	17.9
1935	6.8	26.9	10.5	41.2	5.0	19.8	3.1	12.1
1936	8.9	38.9	10.9	47.6	1.5	6.3	1.6	7.2
1937	14.3	37.3	14.5	38.0	8.4	22.0	1.0	2.7

Source: Paribas archives; internal reports from the general secretariat.

Table 6.5. *Results of financial activities: 2 (current FF 1,000,000)*

	Capital gains	Portfolio revenue
1929	46.8	18.9
1930	33.7	23.5
1931	22.9	19.6
1932	13.9	13.9

Note: Some partial data are available for the years 1929–32.

Source: Paribas archives.

Commissions were more connected than one might have expected with other activities of the bank. Paribas faced, in that area, strong competition from deposit banks supported by their large networks. Floating activities, especially the floating of treasury and railway bonds, which represented large amounts of capital, were controlled by major credit banks; Paribas's share in these syndicates was rarely more than a few points.[4] So banques d'affaires were mainly concerned with underwriting activities, especially in the case of issues of stocks. In these transactions Paribas used its connections to lead the syndicates and play the role of major underwriter; this was especially true in regard to oil and electricity companies, which were the source of many issues during the period.

As the portfolio of the bank included mainly shares, its revenue remained comparatively stable, especially during the Depression, with a high point of 23.5 million francs in 1930 and no low below 10 million during the 1930s. One can easily understand, then, why Paribas management considered this portfolio an essential element in the bank's activity, not only for its returns but also for the connections with enterprise that it generated.

Besides inflation, legal restrictions on long-term exports of capital were another major change in the economic environment that obliged Paribas to alter its prewar strategy. Controls on capital exports were especially effective for long-term issues, but they also had an effect on direct industrial investments. As a result, between 1919 and 1928 only a few operations were permitted by the financial authorities when political or major national economic interests were involved. Any return to international activities between 1928 and the beginning of the 1930s was for a short period and in limited areas, thanks to the monetary restrictions of the 1930s. After 1934, when France had to deal with several periods of capital outflows, French banks were no longer able to play any significant international role.

Table 6.6 shows the consequences of these restrictions of activity on Paribas's share portfolio. The reduction of investments in Europe was due

Table 6.6. *Paribas's share portfolio: a breakdown by geographical distribution (%)*

	France	Europe	America	Asia and Middle East	Africa	Miscellaneous
1913	23.3	27.8	35.3	7.5	2.0	4.1
1919	32.5	13.3	38.2	8.1	4.2	3.7
1928	41.0	18.5	17.2	14.6	4.8	3.9
1943	53.0	15.6	5.6	7.4	18.4	—

Source: Paribas archives.

Table 6.7. *Paribas's share portfolio: a breakdown by areas of activity (%)*

	Banks, financial companies	Utilities	Industry	Miscellaneous
1913	38.4	43.8	11.3	6.5
1919	40.5	37.8	10.9	10.8
1928	45.6	14.1	33.3	7.0
1945	45.0	14.0	34.0	7.0

Source: Paribas archives.

to losses in Russia and Central and Eastern Europe in spite of a partial resurgence in this last area for political reasons during the 1920s; thus the majority of investments in Europe were concentrated in Western Europe, especially in Belgium. As for the major interests of Paribas in Latin America, the bank progressively withdrew these interests during the 1920s and 1930s. The most striking development was the concentration of investment in areas of national interest, not only in France itself but also in the Empire: Africa, and especially Morocco.

This concentration on national interests is confirmed in Table 6.7. The column for banks and financial companies shows a permanent commitment; the reduction of utilities is explained by a retreat from overseas holdings, despite the strong interests of the bank in electricity in France and in the Empire during the 1920s and the 1930s. The growth of interests in industry, however, represents the major change in this period. As we shall see later, it began at the end of war itself, and this new shape of the Paribas portfolio, with a priority given to industry, especially national industry, was going to be a permanent feature of Paribas investment strategy up to the 1960s.

It is now possible to propose a general description of the major changes in the structure of Paribas activities during the interwar period. One must, for a good understanding of the changes, take into account the economic and political environment. As we shall see in the next section of this study, the political context of the war led to a concentration of economic efforts on the national interest with the aim of reinforcing national industry. This political trend was backed up by monetary constraints that reinforced this orientation. In the case of Paribas, this environment explains its new involvement in financing national enterprises, especially industrial firms. Still, inflation and unfavourable conditions in the financial market implied the financing of enterprises by credit, especially in the mid-1920s. The need to diversify sources of profit as well as the new relationship with enterprises explains the growth of Paribas's banking activities during the 1920s. The model of the French banque d'affaires was more like the model of the universal bank than it had ever been. Because of a lack of deposits and of equity capital, however, this change had to be carried out in rather unfavourable conditions.

Financing Industry

This section tries to bolster our general analysis with a more empiric description of Paribas's handling of an overall industrial strategy during the 1920s.

While it had some experience of financing enterprises before the First World War, the interwar period represents a real shift in the approach of Paribas towards industry. The change that took place during the 1920s was in the development of an industrial project, a kind of globalization of the relationship with enterprises and the birth of a specific organization inside the bank for the management of its industrial interests.

Paribas already had some experience of industrial financing before the war. Around 1895–1905 it was involved in a series of initiatives in Europe connected with the new technologies of the second industrialization and stimulated by boom conditions. In Russia Paribas invested in huge projects to create new capacities for steel production in the Ural area that had been initiated by French industrialists like Chatillon-Commentry and Schneider. In Norway the bank was associated with the creation of Norsk-Hydro, in the chemical industry, which was developing a new process of nitrogen synthesis. Paribas was also involved in the development of electrification through several interests in firms such as Compagnie Parisienne de Distribution d'Électricité (created in 1907) or in the Société Générale Belge d'Entreprises Électriques. While ventures in the electricity sector were successful, Paribas suffered serious setbacks in its steel and chemical ventures. In Russia, serious mistakes by management caused the failure of

Volga Vichera and Ural Volga, which were liquidated in dire financial conditions. In Norway, Paribas and its partners were confronted with technological risk: the development of the Birkeland-Eyde process was longer and more difficult than expected and Paribas had to allocate much more money than planned, but this enterprise was saved and largely benefited by the war. In each of these last three cases, Paribas was drawn into the venture by external initiatives, had no real control over management decisions, and had to take charge of the restructuring of the firms—both the technical and the financial aspects in the Russian companies, and only the financial aspect in the case of the Norwegian company.

The consequences of these difficulties in the industrial field was a profound distrust by top management at Paribas toward industrial investments. In 1905 Director Dupasseur, in charge of the liquidation of the Volga Vichera venture, said, 'We do not have the requisite personnel to carry on a business in metallurgy in Russia by ourselves...I will never try to persuade my board to start up a new one'.[5] In 1909 H. Finaly, who would become managing director of Paribas in 1919, wrote: 'You know, doubtless, that the activity of our establishment for the last few years is not much oriented towards industrial ventures.' And in fact, in 1913 industry represented only 11.3 per cent of Paribas's share portfolio.

The First World War was indubitably a turning point towards a new strategy in the industrial sector. Instead of being involved in industrial projects as a result of external initiatives, Paribas took active steps to launch, inside a short period, ventures in several areas. Most of these initiatives were taken between 1916 and 1920 in the context of industrial mobilization resulting from the war and the subsequent reconstruction. The overall aim was not only military victory but also a transformation of France's industrial structure so as to be better able to compete with Germany after the conflict. This global project was initiated not only by the bank but also by a group of people composed of industrialists, politicians, high civil servants (especially engineers), and diplomats. In each area the major decisions were taken after joint analysis by the bank in collaboration with high civil servants from several ministries: War, Industry, Marine, and Foreign Affairs. Four or five areas were especially of interest.

In the metallurgy industry, Paribas assisted the group Delaunay-Belleville, a manufacturer specializing in motor cars and in steam engines, to turn its activity toward such military needs as trucks, light armoured cars, airplane engines, and shells. Paribas's contribution consisted in the floating of several bond issues and in current account credits. In 1916 R. Delaunay-Belleville was elected a director on the board of Paribas.[6] At the end of the war Paribas was involved in the creation of a new shipbuilding yard as part of the reconstruction of the French merchant fleet, which had been nearly destroyed during the war. The project was born in the Marine Ministry's administration but taken in charge by industrialists: a steel maker, an automobile maker, and several building contractors. Chantiers Navals Français (CNF) was established in 1917. Paribas became a shareholder of this company in 1918 when its equity was raised to 30 million francs and the bank managed the floating of 30 million francs' worth of bonds in 1919.[7] The third major initiative of Paribas in the metallurgy area was the reorganization of the iron and steel industry in 1918–20. Paribas had ancient links with one of the major iron and steel makers in the North of France: Forges et Aciéries du Nord et de l'Est, which became one of the leaders of the reorganization of the steel industry after the war by taking over some of its important competitors in northern France and by creating a new important subsidiary in the eastern part that went on to acquire an import-ant plant previously owned by Germans.

Electricity was another of the areas in which Paribas developed a global strategy at the end of the war. This strategy was based on the aim of building, in France and in Belgium, an integrated group on the German model, from the building of equipment to the production and distribution of electricity. Using its Belgian connections and abilities,[8] the bank reached an agreement with English Electric Company (EEC), which wanted to expand its activities on the Continent. The industrial programme, elaborated in 1918, involved the creation of two companies—Constructions Électriques de Belgique and Constructions Électriques de France—which were to benefit from the processes and patents of their British partner. The CEF was established in 1920, with Paribas one of its major shareholders. In 1922, the CEF had started up at Tarbes, in southwestern France, a new plant designed to build electric locomotives for railway companies and equipment for power stations.[9] The group enlarged its activities in 1923 through participation in the hydroelectrification of France by the creation of Énergie Électrique du Rouergue. With the creation of this new company, the Paribas group wanted to participate in the creation, in southwestern France, of a large regional network for the distribution and production of electricity. The Rouergue began to build a new dam on the Tarn River in 1924.[10]

Paribas also played a major role in developing new fields of activity in which French industry was up against strong foreign competition, especially from the British and the Americans. This was the case in telecommunications and in the oil industry.

In telecommunications, Paribas had prewar experience with the telegraph through its participation in the CFCT, which managed a network of wires between France and overseas areas. The development of wireless telegraphy before and during the war, with the strong domination by British interests through Marconi's wireless, was considered a field of activity in which the French industry had to be present for political reasons.[11] Supported by the Ministry of Foreign Affairs, Paribas united French interests in this field of activity and created Compagnie Générale de TSF (CSF) in 1918. During the following years, this company developed an international network for radiocommunications, as well as the first French broadcasting company in 1923.

The oil industry is one of the areas in which Paribas evolved the most active policy after the war. Here again the aim was to create a national capacity for production, refining, and distribution. Paribas developed three major initiatives in this field. The first was to acquire interests in Romania by the acquisition of German interests in the Steava Romana; the second consisted in an alliance with the American Standard Oil of New Jersey through the creation of Standard Franco-Américaine in 1920, which went on to develop its distribution capacity during the 1920s; the third was the creation of a national company in 1924—the Compagnie Française des Pétroles, or CFP— whose initial role was to take charge of French interests in the Near East.

As Paribas was developing this global strategy in the industrial field, it had progressively to adapt its organization and expertise in industrial management. In the months following the end of the war, Paribas's managerial blood was revivified with the arrival of a large number of engineers. At the top of the bank, Horace Finaly was appointed general manager in 1919; although a lawyer, he had successfully taken over the monitoring of some of the most important industrial interests of Paribas before the war, such as Norsk-Hydro. During the war, he actively supported the industrial mobilization and the programme of industrial development described above. Under the general manager were directors of departments. An organization chart of 1927 tells us that, besides stock exchange and bank operations, there were business operations. At that time these were not yet strictly specialized, but two of them were clearly oriented towards industrial affairs.

Louis Wibratte was the most important of the subordinate directors. He was a graduate of the Ecole Polytechnique, the most famous state engineering school in France; he began his career in railway companies in Africa and South America, especially as president of the Brazil Railway Company in 1918–20. He was appointed a Paribas director in 1920 and took over special charge of the industrial interests of the bank. In 1927 he was helped in the management of his department by E. Caudrelier, who was deputy manager; a graduate of Polytechnique, he had been recruited in 1919 as an engineering consultant. At the head of their secretarial staff one finds one lawyer and another graduate from Polytechnique. Wibratte and Caudrelier had under their control the technical services, with two engineers in charge of technical studies for the bank. In addition to Wibratte, there was a second director in charge of industrial affairs: A. Roudy. Recruited, like Caudrelier, as an engineering consultant, he too was a graduate of Polytechnique. One must also mention the prominent role of H. Urban at the top of the Bruxelles branch of Paribas; he strongly influenced the industrial strategy of the bank, especially in the field of electricity. He also was an engineer.

While the strong involvement of Paribas in new industrial ventures at the end of the war can be attributed to H. Finaly and to the strong personal connections he had with ministries, the bank was also influenced from 1922 by L. Wibratte, who became Finaly's 'theoretician' of industrial rationalization. As we shall see later, several ventures in which Paribas was engaged suffered problems that were brought to light by the depression of 1920. Wibratte, who played an important role in the reorganization of these enterprises, extended this reorganization into a plan for rationalizing industrial structures at the national level in such a way that the banks, and especially the banques d'affaires, would fulfil the roles of initiative and arbitration. In these roles, banks would be helped by the shortage of disposable credit, which would enable them to influence industrial decisions.[12] As we shall see, this forecast would be wrong and the bank would be unable to put this plan into effect.

Technical risk and management mistakes were the first reasons for the difficulties that affected some of the industrial ventures in which Paribas was involved, but the depression of 1920 and inflation (especially in 1925–6) actually revealed and increased them. One of the major problems Paribas had to solve was the increasing financial needs of numerous enterprises in a period (1921–7) of narrow activity on the French financial market, especially in the area of stock issues. We shall examine some of these problems that were particularly difficult to solve.

First there was the Delaunay-Belleville group, whose profits were insufficient to amortize the heavy investments made during the war. Above all, the Delaunay group did not carry out any adequate industrial redeployment in civil manufacturing; in 1920, its motor cars and steam engines were out of date.[13] Then there was CNF; the world crisis in shipbuilding was the main cause of its difficulties, but these were increased by additional costs due to postwar inflation at a time when the shipyard had not yet been firmly established. In these two cases, Paribas was aware of the difficulties in the middle of 1920 because of the sudden increase in requests for short-term credits from these firms. As a director of Paribas wrote: 'The Chantiers Navals affair causes me much uneasiness. The more we look at it, the more we find large and badly explored needs. Our credits grow, however, very quickly.'[14] In these two cases, Paribas had to manage the restructuring of these firms. As the bank had an early realization of the seriousness of the difficulties, it appealed to external expertise to establish the technical reorganization programme. In the case of the Delaunay-Belleville group, technical assistance was obtained from Fiat in Italy, and especially from Marine-Homécourt, a major firm in the French metallurgy industry. In the case of CNF, assistance was asked of E. Mercier, one of the most emin-ent state engineers in France. In both cases it was decided to avoid a winding-up, even if the situation for the Delaunay group was considered to be highly dangerous.

The consequence of these difficulties was a very heavy financial involvement of Paribas in the financing of these affairs. Even though a financial restructuring of the Delaunay group was carried out between 1920 and 1924, including capital reductions and consolidation of short-term debts, Paribas's financial risks grew very quickly:

31/12/1920: 6.07 MF
31/12/1921: 16.2 MF
31/12/1922: 22.4 MF
31/12/1923: 34.6 MF
31/12/1924: 49.0 MF (including 39.4 MF credits)
31/12/1925: 41.2 MF.[15]

In the case of CNF, 28 million francs of credits were granted both by Paribas (13.5 million) and by Crédit Lyonnais in 1920; these were converted to 28 million in bonds in 1922. Then, as it was decided to keep CNF alive, new credits were granted whose total amount stood at around 60 million francs at the beginning of 1929 (Paribas: around 29 million).[16] Other ventures in metallurgy suffered difficulties during the period of reconstruction. This was true for the group Nord et Est, whose reconstruction programme was more costly than expected. Here again Paribas had to support the firm by credits, but its involvement was greatly eased in 1923 when Compagnie des Mines de Lens, the biggest and most prosperous coal mine in France, became the major shareholder of the firm.

Paribas suffered similar problems in the electricity sector. The Constructions Électriques de France (CEF), supported by important orders from the Compagnie du Midi, built in southwest France, at Tarbes, a new plant for locomotives. But the locomotives broke down as a result of initial manufacturing defects, resulting in financial penalties and delays in payment; at the end of 1924 a technical reorganization of CEF was successfully undertaken with the assistance of EEC, but the consequences of the problems were heavy to bear, both for CEF and for the bank. In 1927 Paribas, which had made advances to the firm of over 28 million francs, decided on a complete financial reorganization: the capital was reduced from 50 to 20 million francs, and then raised to 67.5 by the conversion of debts into shares. In addition, the Rouergue experienced financial problems between spring 1925 and the end of 1927 because of additional costs on the building of the Pinet Dam in a context of fast inflation and currency depreciation. These difficulties were solved through a 3.5 million florin loan raised in Holland and help from new shareholders like Vieille Montagne, a Belgian firm dealing in nonferrous metallurgy, which took part of a new 40-million-franc capital issue. In spring 1928 new advances amounting to 54 million francs were obtained, mainly from a new partner, the Union Financière d'Électricité, one of the major French enterprises in the field of electricity.[17]

In all the cases we have examined, mistakes of management and technical difficulties were largely magnified by the context of inflation, which increased the uncertainty of any financial forecasting by the firms and the needs for more credits from the banks. Paribas reacted to these difficulties by providing credits and by increasing its own means of intervention by increasing its deposits, as we saw earlier in this chapter. But the efforts to gain deposits reached their limits in 1926–7 when some of the enterprises supported by Paribas were in transition and needed huge amounts of credit to achieve their reorganization. Paribas also reacted internally by developing its own technical expertise and methods of industrial management. As soon as he was appointed at Paribas, L. Wibratte took charge of difficult cases like the Delaunay group as well as other difficult cases in the electricity sector. As we mentioned, Wibratte thought that the stabilization of the French franc would offer to the banks, and especially to Paribas, the opportunity to influence the conditions whereby a general rationalization of French industry would become possible, and to solve the problem of the lack of liquidity. In fact, however, the experience would prove that this idea was an illusion.

Electricity offers a nice example of what happened because of the special involvement of Paribas and because of the personal role of Wibratte in that field. In the electrical industry, the initiative for rationalizing the sector came from industrialists themselves; the foundation of Alsthom was decided by the top management of the two leaders of the branch in France: Thomson–Houston and Alsacienne de Constructions Mécaniques. Their two heads, A. Petsche and A. Detoeuf, approached Paribas in 1927 when the idea of merging CEF and the embryonic Alsthom was first raised. This project was realized two years later when CEF had by then recovered, both technically and financially. As CEF was still a middle-sized enterprise in a vulnerable position owing to its narrow specialization, Paribas seized the opportunity and decided to accept a merger. A scheme to integrate CEF and Alsthom was devised in October 1929 and came into effect in April 1930. The merger was formally achieved in 1932.[18] These decisions are to be compared with the help received from the Union Financière d'Électricité, the Petsche group, in the financing of the Rouergue in 1928; in these two cases, the bank decided to leave the leadership to industrialists and to forsake its industrial ambitions.

Other sectors where Paribas had specific projects just after the war show the same development. In the case of CNF, a strong reorganization was achieved in June 1928 through the winding-up of the firm followed by an arrangement with creditors and the taking in charge of the shipyard by a group of new industrial partners. Paribas could finally sell its shares in 1943. In the case of the Delaunay-Belleville group, a new financial reorganization was set up in 1927 and the company began to sell its equipment in 1928. The same kind of development occurred in other sectors, such as the oil industry, as happened in the case of Standard Franco-Américaine. During the 1920s Paribas contributed to the financing of its numerous sub-sidiaries (such as Standard Franco-Américaine de Raffinage, created in 1929). But Standard Franco-Américaine never became the active basis for a real industrial cooperation between Paribas and the American group. The conclusion of this venture was the regrouping of all the interests of the American group in France in Franco-Américaine de Raffinage and the winding-up of Standard Franco-Américaine during the 1930s. The example of telecommunications also shows how hard it was for the bank to influence the reorganization of industry; between 1927 and 1932 the bank tried to promote a merger between the CFCT and Radio France—cable and radio communications—on the British and American models. But this project was only partially achieved in 1932 and the merger itself did not take place.[19]

So, while the movement for rationalization of industrial structures at the end of the 1920s was helped by good conditions on financial markets, the major enterprises in each branch benefited by it more than the banks. This can be shown by the two different ways in which Paribas and the Petsche group made use of the new opportunities offered by the market. While the bank managed to obtain new resources by raising its capital in 1929, it also tried to lighten its financial effort by creating new financial subsidiaries like the Compagnie Financière d'Électricité. This company was created in March 1928 with an initial capitalization of 25 million francs, raised to 50 million in 1929. The initial contribution of the bank was made up of a part of the stocks in its portfolio that concerned electricity. Paribas kept for itself the controlling shares of this new holding and benefited from the help of external partners like the American bank Kuhn Loeb, and also from the Union Financière pour l'Industrie Électrique, the holding company of the Petsche group.[20] Given the nature of the shareholding of the Financière d'Électricité, one cannot consider this creation a means to improve its abil-ity to influence the strategic decisions of the major actors of this branch of the economy. In the case of the Petsche group, the Union Financière pour l'Industrie Électrique, created in 1924, was used to gain more financial independence from the banks, especially at the end of the 1920s, when Petsche obtained the right to participate in the issuing operations formerly reserved to the banks. Petsche also managed to increase competition between banks in these operations; Paribas, for instance, had to concede in 1930 the leadership for the bond issues of the Union d'Électricité—which was in charge of the distribution of electricity in the Paris area—to Crédit Lyonnais, following some tough discussions with A. Petsche.[21] So the main objective of Paribas at the end of the 1920s clearly appears not that of try-ing to gain influence on strategic decisions in that area but that of benefit-ing by the revival of the financial market and by the huge amount of issues in the sector of electricity, where volume quadrupled between 1922–6 and

1927–30.[22] This was also true in other areas of development such as the oil industry, for instance.

Conclusion

The choices made by Paribas at the end of the war can be explained by the political context of that time, the influence of several of its top managers (such as the Belgian H. Urban), and the necessity to concentrate investments on national interests for economic reasons. These tendencies led the bank toward the model of universal banking as it was practised in Belgium, where Paribas had its most important foreign subsidiary. During the 1920s Paribas acquired the services of experts/specialists, especially when it was confronted with difficulties and obliged to rationalize its industrial participation. However, even some of its most efficient top managers had illusions about the bank's ability to lead a global strategy toward industry, and inflation and a lack of resources forced the bank to retreat from its ambitions. The trend towards the universal bank model was stopped. These decisions were taken in the context of a return to the prewar division of labour between commercial banks and banques d'affaires after the French franc recovered in 1928. For the banques d'affaires, this period of high level of activity on financial markets offered them an opportunity to reduce their current account credits and to return to more liquid assets when it was difficult for them to compete with credit banks, which were making strong and successful efforts to gain deposits. On the other hand, this period offered an opportunity for high profits through underwriting commissions and capital gains. So the shift in the global strategy of the bank, largely due to its managing director H. Finaly, was essentially a pragmatic adjustment to the new context existing at the end of the 1920s.

The 1930s were for Paribas, as for all the French banks, a period of a very low level of activity. Deposits declined more at Paribas than at Crédit Lyonnais for several reasons (Table 6.8). Paribas decided from the autumn of 1929 on a strong reduction of its short-term foreign investment activities and on repaying large amounts of the time deposits that were used to finance them. This attitude was stressed at the beginning of 1931. Between 1931 and 1933, Crédit Lyonnais and the other big deposit banks benefited by huge amounts of new foreign and domestic deposits because of the security offered by the French franc, the Paris market, and the big banks. This was not true for Paribas because of the specific risks that were connected with the banques d'affaires. After 1933, all French banks were affected by withdrawals because of hoarding by domestic depositors and

Table 6.8. *Crédit Lyonnais and Paribas: equity capital and deposits (FF 1,000,000)*

	Equity capital			Deposits		
	Crédit Lyonnais	Paribas	% of Paribas to CL	Crédit Lyonnais	Paribas	% of Paribas to CL
1930	1,214	616	50.7	13,460	3,117	23.2
1935	1,221	598	49.0	10,706	1,643	15.3

Source: A. Pose, *La monnaie et ses institutions*, 683, 692–3.

outflows of capital from France.[23] As regards assets, the reduction of economic activities and the search for security led to a sharp reduction of current account credits—1,333 million in 1930 to 581 million in 1935 at Paribas, 5,228 million in 1930 to 3,368 million in 1935 at the Lyonnais—and to a change in the short-term portfolio structure with an increasing amount of treasury bills.

As for business results, the deposit banks were less affected by the crisis than the banques d'affaires: the Lyonnais was able to maintain stable profits throughout the 1930s while the net profit of Paribas was reduced to zero in 1934, 1935, and 1936. In fact, Paribas was severely affected by the crisis and had to suffer a sharp depreciation of its share portfolio, from a potential gain in value of more than 450 million francs in 1929 to a potential loss of 75 million in 1935. As for its discount portfolio and its current account credits, the stock of bad debts grew to around 200 million in 1934.

However, Paribas did not suffer any of the runs experienced by numerous French banks, including its most important competitor as a banque d'affaires, the Banque de l'Union Parisienne (BUP), which was affected by a run in 1931 and obliged to reorganize in 1932 and in 1934. The depreciation in the share portfolio of Paribas was reduced to zero in mid-1937, and a provision of 56 per cent was made for doubtful debts in 1936.

Why did Paribas get through the crisis in better shape than other banks? One of the more likely explanations is Paribas's policy of reorganization and of retreat from important industrial responsibilities between 1928 and 1930 and the transfer of a significant part of the bank's industrial risks to the hands of major industrial groups. This attitude was combined with a strong policy of writing off bad debts and making provisions for doubtful debts so that in 1930, when they amounted to about 75 million francs, provision was made for them at a level of 77 per cent. However, during the 1930s, the bank remained indisputably an enterprise bank. Its most important credits were given to industrial firms or utilities. In 1929 oil, electricity, trade, food, and iron and steel constituted the majority of the current account credits; in 1935 the breakdown was about the same except for an increase to the automobile sector,[24] and this allotment of credits is in accordance with the breakdown of the bank's share portfolio. But the renouncing of strategic responsibilities at the end of the 1920s led to a better distribution of risks, and the consolidation of stable relations with enterprises brought stable sources of profits for banking activities and from the share portfolio revenues.

NOTES

1. A. Pose, *La monnaie et ses institutions* (Paris: Presses Universitaires de France, 1942), 577 and 694.
2. A. Plessis, 'Les banques, le crédit, l'économie', in M. Lévy-Leboyer and J-C Casanaova, *Entre l'Etat et le marché: L'économie française des années 1880 à nos jours* (Paris: Gallimard, 1991), 347.
3. Ibid., 351–2.
4. Some examples are given in H. Bonin, 'Les banques françaises en économie libérale (1919–35)', Ph.D. thesis (University of Paris X-Nanterre, 1995, 1022/V–VI), 487 and 491–6.
5. O. Lebel, 'Politique industrielle et investissements directs de la Banque de Paris et des Pays-Bas dans l'industrie russe: 1896–1914', Master's thesis (University of Paris IV-Sorbonne, 1993), 90.
6. Paribas archives 561/1, 561/8, 562/100, and 590/4.
7. Paribas archives 550/1 to 4; 551/8 to 10; and 537.
8. For more on these connections, see E. Bussière, 'Paribas and the Rationalization of the French Electricity Industry in the 1920s', in Y. Cassis, F. Crouzet, and T. Gourvish, *Management and Business in Britain and France* (Oxford: Clarendon Press, 1995), 207–8.
9. Paribas archives 578/6 (Constructions Électriques de France); 101/18 (Constructions Électriques de Belgique).
10. Paribas archives 574/18, memorandums 24-1-1924 and 1-2-1924.
11. P. Griset, 'Les télécommunications transatlantiques de la France, 1869–1954', Ph.D. thesis (University of Paris IV-Sorbonne, 1993), 445–6 and 526–7.
12. One can find a partial publication of one of the studies by Wibratte in E. Bussière, 'Les réflexions d'un banquier sur la situation économique du monde à l'époque de la conférence de Gênes', *Etudes et Documents*, X (1998), 259–76.
13. Paribas archives 561/01, memorandum of Wibratte 10/1922.
14. Paribas archives 561/, Atthalin to Mercier, spring 1920.
15. Paribas archives 561/8, engagements de la banque chez les EDB, mars 1928.
16. Paribas archives 551/9, crédits en cours.
17. Paribas archives 574/18, memorandums 3-3-1927; 11-3-1927; 28-3-1927; memorandum 16-5-1928.
18. Bussière, 'Paribas and the Rationalization', 211–12.

19. Paribas archives 534/31, memorandum 20-10-1927; Griset, 'Les télécommunications transatlantiques de la France', 835–43.
20. Paribas archives 582/18-21, memorandums 9-12-1927; 20-2-1928; 19-6-1929; 20-12-1929.
21. Paribas archives, Secretariat Martin: Union d'éllectricité 8, memorandum 30-6-1930.
22. A. Strauss, 'Le financement de l'industrie électrique par le marché financier en France des aanées 1880 aux aanées 1980', in Association pour l'histoire de l'électricité en France (ed.), *Le financement de l'industrie électrique, 1880–1980* (Paris: Association pour l'histoire de l'électricité en France, 1994), 238–41.
23. Plessis, 'Les banques, le crédit, l'économie', 356–60.
24. Bonin, 'Les banques françaises en économie libérale', 976–80. Bonin gives a partial breakdown of credits by sectors based on a total amount of 387 million francs of current account credits in 1929: iron and steel, 17.9%; trade, 13.5%; electricity, 11%; food, 11%; oil, 9.3%, and so on.

7

German Banks and their Business Strategies in the Weimar Republic: New Findings and Preliminary Results

HARALD WIXFORTH

Introduction

At the end of the First World War it became obvious to the greater part of German society that the world had changed considerably. The German banks and their directors, as well as the private bankers, were faced with this situation, too. During the Kaiserreich the large German universal banks like the Deutsche Bank, the Discontogesellschaft, the Dresdner Bank, and the Darmstädter Bank für Handel und Industrie played a dominant role in financing all the important branches of German industry, as well as the greater part of enterprises that were engaged in foreign trade. The universal banks that had their headquarters in Berlin, in particular, expanded in every region of the Kaiserreich by establishing a large number of branch offices, thus strengthening their influence in almost every section of German industry. Moreover, they founded several specialized financial institutions in other European countries, as well as in Asia and even South America.[1] The development of the German economy, which prospered after the crisis of 1873–8, along with relatively stable political conditions, favoured the bankers' business and their influence in the society of the Kaiserreich. At the turn of the century the large German universal banks had obviously reached the peak of their influence and power in German society.[2]

The First World War itself made no impact on the success story of German banking, which had lasted for nearly fifty years. The closure of the stock exchanges in August 1914 caused a decline in profits formerly gained by stock issues, but they then could be replaced by expanding the business of granting credits to the German government and the most important enterprises for war-production. So the majority of German bankers did not see any need to change their business or to alter their business strategies. With the end of the First World War and the collapse of the Kaiserreich, however, some of them felt that the 'first golden age of banking' had come to an end. But how were they to react to the new political conditions and economic framework? What kind of business strategy had to be adopted?[3]

The German banks were faced with a second great challenge soon after the end of inflation and the so-called stabilization of the Reichsmark, which had been introduced as the new currency in the summer of 1924.[4] Again the economic conditions and the legal framework for the business of banking changed significantly within a short time—a situation that forced the banks and their directors to adjust their business strategy to the new circumstances. Despite a short period of economic recovery from spring 1925 to autumn 1929, the outbreak of the economic depression in October 1929, and especially the severe financial crisis in Germany in June and July of 1931, signified a fundamental threat for the banking system as a whole.[5] Within a period of just thirteen years, German banks and their directors were faced with a need to make fundamental changes to their business strategies three times. The questions still remain unanswered: What decisions were made in those situations? How did the German banks react to the new challenges, and did they react successfully, or not? Was the dramatic financial and banking crisis in the summer of 1931 an inevitable result of poor business strategies taken by the financial institutions?

This chapter is an attempt to give answers to these questions. Unfortunately, we still lack analytical and detailed studies on the business strategies of German banks during the Weimar Republic. Research on German banking has not been able to deal with this subject because, on the one hand, scholars have not gained access to the archives of the banks and, on the other hand, much of the material has been lost as a result of bombing damage incurred during the Second World War. This chapter intends to present the first, and perforce only preliminary, results of research on this subject. Detailed studies that analyse and compare the business strategies of each of the large universal banks must follow in order to fill out the picture.

German Banks during a Period of Inflation

During the First World War a great number of German enterprises were able to loosen their earlier close ties with their banks. Companies engaged in war production in particular gained enormous profits. The demand for bank credits was reduced, and consequently the control of banks over their clientele. On the other hand, bank deposits rose considerably over the course of the whole war. Lacking other forms of lucrative business, the banks uniformly decided to invest these deposits in treasury bills to cover the rapidly rising demand for credit from the German government. Even after the end of the war the banks continued with this investment strategy. A close connection between the banks and public finance became a specific feature during the first years of the Weimar Republic. A study of the composition of assets of the nineteen most important German universal banks shows that the percentage of bills and treasury bills rose from 20.9 per cent in 1913 to 48.5 per cent in 1920. In the balance sheets of the eight 'Berliner Großbanken' this percentage even amounted to 60 per cent in 1920.[6]

The banks were well aware of the fact that they had no better ways to invest the deposits, which were rising steadily as a result of accelerating inflation. For example, the Dresdner Bank wrote in its annual report of 1918: 'The greater part of the money we received we had to invest in government treasury bills, in treasury bills issued by the German federal states, or in municipal loans, because, like the other banks, we were not able to find enough other useful possibilities of investment.'[7]

In this respect it seemed reasonable for the banks to pursue this kind of investment strategy. Moreover, the German Reichsbank did not hesitate to discount even large amounts of treasury bills. The banks believed that they could rely on these guaranteed profits. It is hardly surprising that the percentage of treasury bills in the composition of assets of the Berlin universal banks reached an all-time high of about 65 per cent in the spring of 1921. Then, at the same time as the sharp decline in the value of the German mark, the percentage of bills in bank assets fell considerably. The question still remains: did the directors of the Berlin banks notice that the depreciation of the mark would accelerate in the month ahead, and if they did, when? On the one hand, from spring 1921 experts in German banking had started to criticize the close connections between public finance and the Berlin banks. They believed it dangerous that the greater part of bank assets consisted of public liabilities denominated in marks and that the banks were thus put at risk by a forthcoming depreciation.[8] On the other hand, we have only a few hints that the real causes and the further development of inflation had been discussed by the boards of directors of Berlin banks during the first years after the war. Like the greater part of the German population, including economists and experts, the directors of the banks did not see the faults in the discount and credit policy of the German Reichsbank as being the main reason for inflation. Many of the bankers were convinced that in the case of a settlement of reparations, the value of the mark would stabilize, and that the German currency would even regain its former strength.[9] For example, a member of the board of directors of the Dresdner

Bank, Walter Frisch, in his report on the development of his bank, describes the stages of inflation in detail. But he does not mention any discussions among the members of the board regarding the origins, causes, and results of inflation. According to Frisch's report, the Dresdner Bank ignored the real causes of inflation. So it is not surprising that the bank did not change its business strategy during these years and pursued a policy of investing its deposits in treasury bills or public loans.[10]

The rapid depreciation of the mark in spring and summer 1921, however, must have been noticed by the banks and their directors. They became cautious about buying and discounting treasury bills and other public liabilities and started to invest their assets as deposits in other banks, especially in other countries. In 1922 and 1923 this became the most favoured type of investment, with the result that its share in the composition of bank assets increased from 7.3 per cent in 1920 to 30.9 per cent in 1923, thus representing the most important kind of asset in these years. Meanwhile, the share of treasury bills declined from 48.3 per cent in 1920 to a mere 2.2 per cent in 1923.[11]

Another change in business strategy indicates that the banks must have been aware of the dangers of inflation. In 1921 each one of the Berlin banks tried to strengthen its ties with financial institutions in other countries, in order to find 'safe harbours' for their deposits. Apart from private British bankers, financial institutions in the Netherlands, especially in Amsterdam, played a prominent role in this respect. The Dresdner Bank, for example, established the private bank Proehl & Gutmann there and ran it as a branch in the Netherlands. The Discontogesellschaft, another important Berlin universal bank, followed suit when it moved its branch in Antwerp, Albert de Bary & Co., to Amsterdam in 1921. The Deutsche Bank, the Commerz- and Privatbank, and some of the most important German private bankers acted similarly, when they opened branches in Amsterdam in this year. Thus, establishing their own affiliates in Amsterdam and transferring the greater part of their deposits to them could be regarded as a special strategy of all the important German banks to protect their assets against the effects of inflation at home.[12]

The rapidly increasing importance of stocks in the balance sheets of the banks shows that they believed in an intensified engagement in stock issuing as another measure to protect their money against the inflationary depreciation of the mark. Participating in stock issues or even intensive stockjobbing was quite a common feature of all banks, especially after 1921. Because of the increasing volume of money, it was easy to found new stock companies. A great part of the German population was interested in and willing to purchase the shares of new companies or newly issued stocks of already existing firms. Many of these enterprises intended to increase their capital in order to adjust it to the demands of an inflationary period. An increasing number of stock issues occurred every day on

German stock exchanges: this guaranteed the banks high profits, because they organized this kind of business.[13] In addition, the banks tried to invest their deposits directly in shares of almost all the important companies, and for two reasons. First, they wanted to gain profits by stockjobbing; second, they intended to gain control over an increasing number of industrial companies. The banks were successful only in the first respect, however, and they failed to widen their influence or control over industry. On the contrary, most of the companies were able gradually to dissolve their former ties with the banks. As a result of high liquidity and the expanding volume of money, they could finance their businesses by new stock issues, for example, so as a result they did not have to rely on bank credits. Nevertheless, the banks' decreasing business in granting credits could be compensated for by rising profits in stock issuing or stockjobbing.[14]

All in all, the year 1921 marked a turning point in the business strategies of Berlin's universal banks and perhaps of the majority of German banks. Quite clearly, the bankers had noticed the dangers of the depreciation of the mark. Moreover, they had understood the peculiarities of business in a period of inflation. They had learnt that long-lasting and traditional patterns of business had lost their usefulness and would have to be replaced by new ones. The banks that were ready and willing to change their investment strategies and to look for opportunities to protect their deposits against inflationary effects, could participate in the 'benefits' of the depreciation of the mark. At the moment there still is insufficient detailed information on whether or not this change in business strategies was the result of a specific process of decision making by boards of directors. What kind of discussions were held, what information was obtained and used, what specific entrepreneurial strategy was fixed—all these questions can hardly be answered in detail. Only the result of the discussions and decisions made in the board of directors meetings—a change in business strategies in 1921—can be observed.

Needless to say, these questions deserve a more detailed and profound answer. Some German banking historians have criticized the role of the banks in the inflation period. They argue that the financial institutions did not pursue an adequate business strategy during this period, with the result that they ended up as losers to inflation, whereas other parts of German industry, like heavy industry, the chemical industry, and engineering, were able to increase their influence in the economy and were among the winners in the inflationary period. The criticism is based on a comparison between the balance sheets of the years 1913 and 1924, when the banks were forced to publish balances in the newly introduced currency, the Reichsmark, for the first time. This comparison shows that the banks had in fact lost nearly 66 per cent of their capital and around 69 per cent of their reserves. The Berlin banks had lost around 43 per cent of their capital and 50 per cent of their reserves.[15] These figures indicate, many banking historians argue, that the position of the banks in the German economy after 1923 was weaker than it was at the beginning of the First World War. Unfortunately, these historians did not take into account how and when this depreciation of capital actually happened. If we look at the balance sheets of Berlin universal banks for 1913 and 1918, we can observe that their capital in 1918 had already depreciated to 35.7 per cent of its 1913 value. This development continued in 1919. By the end of this year the Berlin banks had already lost 90 per cent of their capital and 87 per cent of their reserves, as compared with 1913.[16]

If we look at the 'destruction of the capital basis of the German universal banks'—the theme of so many articles on this subject—one has to admit that this 'destruction' had already occurred by the end of 1919. The balance figures of 1924, however, shows a loss of only around 43 per cent of the capital and half of the reserves. This indicates that the banks had succeeded in regaining at least a part of their capital basis during the years 1920–3. How did this happen?[17]

The argument that this outcome is closely linked with the change of business strategies after spring 1921 seems to be reasonable. As soon as the banks stopped buying treasury bills or other kinds of public loans, as soon as they refused to discount bills to the extent they had done during previous years, they were successful in restoring their capital basis. Two measures were important in this respect. Most banks received their deposits in 'Papiermark', the German currency that was steadily depreciating. A substantial part of these deposits was changed into foreign currencies and then transferred as deposits in banks in other countries. If necessary, however, the German banks paid their clientele in 'Papiermark', which meanwhile had depreciated even further. Another portion of these deposits remained as deposits in financial institutions abroad and formed thereby the basis for capital restoration of the German banks.[18]

The same purpose was served by other measures. A large portion of customer deposits was used to buy industrial shares, real estate, or gold-based foreign currencies. The effect was the same: while the clientele of the German banks received depreciated 'Papiermark', the banks themselves benefited by this kind of investment, because the value of these assets increased in step with the rate of inflation. The banks profited from the effects of inflation by their credit policy. They acquired money and loaned it to their clientele. The rate of interest for these loans was lower than the rate of inflation, but higher than the rate the banks paid for the deposits. The difference between the two rates created substantial profits for banks, especially in 1921 and 1922.[19]

In conclusion, banks were able to benefit from inflation once they decided to change their business strategies in spring 1921. The criticism that the banks had chosen a business policy that was not suitable in the specific circumstances of the inflation period does not seem to be justified.

The banks and their directors had been aware not only of the risks but also of the benefits of currency depreciation, and they were able to react and to choose a business policy that brought back a substantial part of the capital and reserves lost in previous years. In this respect, the banks were among the winners and not the losers in the specific situation existing in the period from 1921 to 1923. The criticism of some banking historians that the banks reacted too late is in this case misleading. During the First World War and even the first year after it ended, no politician, no banking expert, and only a few economists, analysed the real causes of the inflation. So why should the German bankers be expected to have known them? Unfortunately, the banks had lost a substantial part of their capital and their reserves during the war and especially in 1919, whereas other parts of the economy had enlarged their operational basis. Comparing the situation of the German banks at the beginning and the end of the decade between 1913 and 1923, one has to admit, however, that they were in fact among the losers at this point in time—a heavy burden to bear during the following years.

German Banks after Inflation and the Stabilization of the Reichsmark

After the end of inflation and the stabilization of the new German currency, the Reichsmark, in the summer of 1924, the large Berlin universal banks were faced with the fact that their position in the German economy had changed considerably. They had lost influence compared with the industrial combines in heavy industry, the chemical industry, and engineering. Their position in the German credit system also had weakened during the inflation period. Other financial institutions such as special industrial branch banks or saving banks and 'Kreditgenossenschaften' in rural regions had gained a greater percentage of the banking business.[20] The directors of the Berlin universal banks knew that one of the important targets for the coming years was to restore the position of their institutes in the credit system and their overall influence in the economy. For example, one of the members of the board of directors of the Discontogesellschaft, Georg Solmssen, pointed out in 1925 that 'in contrast to industry the banks were not able to "escape" into real values during the inflation period, with the result that they became one of the prominent victims of the depreciation of the currency'.[21] His colleague Oscar Wassermann, member of the board of directors of the Deutsche Bank, agreed, when he said that the banks were not able to feed the capital demand of industry because they had lost a substantial part of their own capital.[22]

These observations show that the German banking system suffered from a shortage of capital after the period of inflation. This was especially true for the smaller provincial banks, but some of the Berlin universal banks also were forced to admit that they had lost their former operational basis. Moreover, all financial institutions suffered from increased administrative expenses, which had risen from 45 per cent (1913) to 77 per cent (1925) of gross profits. The banks therefore had to reorganize their business and strengthen their ties with their clientele, if they wanted to stand up to competition from other financial institutions, especially from abroad. As a consequence, most banks reduced their staffing levels, which had risen rapidly during the inflation period. Moreover, some of the nonprofitable branches were closed.[23] Further reductions in transaction and administrative costs were achieved by concentrating on large-scale, well-established industrial customers, because a small number of large credits could be supervised much more cheaply and easily than a large number of smaller credits.[24] In almost all German banks discussions regarding new business strategies were held. The crucial point was to find out which strategy would be suitable to the changed conditions of banking. As a result of these discussions, the directors of the Berlin banks decided that the managers of the provincial branches should have limited responsibility and flexibility in granting credits. The Deutsche Bank, for example, prohibited its branches from granting credits in excess of 100,000 marks without the consent of the head office—a consent that was only rarely granted. But since branch managers were not compensated in line with the profitability of their branch, they had little incentive to utilize even the scope they had.[25]

This new business strategy had certain consequences for the relations between the banks and their customers. After the period of inflation had ended, most of the smaller industrial companies suffered from a considerable shortage of capital and an inadequate credit supply. Many of them were now faced with the fact that the managers of the Berlin bank branches in the provinces refused to grant credits or to give them access to long-term overdraft facilities. The inadequate capital supply of many of the smaller and medium-sized companies in the provinces can be seen as a consequence of the credit policy of the large Berlin universal banks. These banks preferred to feed the demand for capital of their larger industrial customers, probably at the expense of small-sized industry. For the Berlin banks, it was considered more profitable to carry out business transactions with large combines, which needed large credits and financial support to restore their position on international markets. On the other hand, the control of a great number of smaller credits granted to smaller enterprises meant increasing costs for most of the Berlin banks.[26]

In addition, the large enterprises could always rely on various credit facilities offered by a multitude of banks at home and abroad. They could compensate for the paucity of money in the German capital market by issuing stocks or by seeking funds in Great Britain or the United States.[27] Therefore, the assumption that the credit policy of the banks strengthened the position of the great combines in German industry and made their further expansion possible, seems to be justified. On the other hand, smaller businesses seem to have been neglected as customers, especially by the large Berlin universal banks. In addition, these smaller companies were not able to arrange issues of stock on the German capital market or in other countries. As a result of this development, the capital shortage of small and medium-sized German industry intensified in the second-half of the 1920s. Some experts in German banking, like Alfred Lansburgh, editor of the well-known financial journal *Die Bank*, recognized a considerable gap in the German banking system.[28]

Although concentration within German industry and the expansion of combines were accelerated by the credit policy of the large universal banks, the banks themselves criticized this development, because it was believed to be a substantial obstacle to their regaining their previous position in the German economy, as well as a further step by the larger economy to emancipate itself from the former influence of the banks. And the results of several empirical studies do, in fact, reveal little evidence of a dominance of the banks over industry. On the contrary, one gets the impression that the larger combines could in some respects dominate the banks, particularly in regard to their credit policy. After the period of inflation, the large combines could increase the number of their business relations with banks from both home and abroad. The iron and steel concern Phoenix raised the number of its banking relations to forty-eight, the Gutehoffnungshütte to forty-three, and the Deutsch-Luxemburgische Bergwerks- und Hütten AG to as high as fifty-five. The largest and most important company in Germany's heavy industry during the Weimar Republic, the Vereinigte Stahlwerke—a trust established in 1926 by the merger of six combines—maintained business relations with fifty-six banks.[29] Although we lack comparable data, the same happened with the large companies in the electrical and chemical industries. The two large combines of the electrical industry in particular, the Siemens combine and the AEG, and the 'giant' of the chemical industry, the IG Farbenindustrie, maintained business relations with a multitude of banks in several different countries.[30]

In addition, during inflation some of the combines set up their own investment companies, or 'house banks'. For example, in 1923 Krupp established the 'AG für Unternehmungen der Eisen- und Stahlindustrie'. By purchasing shares in the various enterprises of the Krupp combine, its 'house bank' provided the combine with investment capital. The Oberhausener Kohle- und Eisenhandelsgesellschaft functioned similarly for the Gutehoffnungshütte, the Montana AG—a Swiss investment company—for the Eisen- und Stahlwerk Hoesch, Thyssen & Co. and the

Bank vor Handel en Scheepvaart in Rotterdam for the Thyssen combine, and the Phoenix-Trust-Maatschappij—a Dutch holding company established by German shareholders of the Phoenix, Dutch banks, and the Dutch iron and steel works Hoogovens—for the Phoenix. The Sichel combine—a 'mixed' combine that arose rapidly in the inflation period—acquired the Westbank AG and reorganized it as its 'house bank'. BASF bought the majority of stock of the Deutsche Länderbank and reestablished it as a 'house bank', and it even became the 'house bank' of the IG Farben when BASF joined the IG.[31]

The increasing number of banking relations as well as the setting up of house banks and investment companies further undermined the formerly close credit relations between the Berlin universal banks and their large industrial customers. As well, many American and British banks had money enough to lend to foreign industrial companies on easy terms. These banks wanted to strengthen their ties with German industrial companies in order to get new customers. In this situation, the German banks were unable to keep their foreign rivals off the market. The increasing number of business relations and the keen competition among the banks, resulting from the internationalization of the capital market, prevented a restoration of the German banks' former influence among the larger industrial companies as well as in industry as a whole. In addition, the intensified presence of banks from abroad caused an increasing dependence on foreign capital, which was to become one of the greatest threats to the German economy in the time of the Great Depression.[32]

Despite the fact that bankers were still often present on the supervisory boards of large companies and combines, these personal networks lost their importance compared to what they were in Kaiserreich times. Their industrial clientele succeeded in intensifying competition among banks by giving all of them the same degree of inside information, in order to reduce risks resulting from an asymmetry of information among the competitors. This meant that the same instrument that had functioned as a 'bridgehead' to control the business policy of their industrial customers during the Kaiserreich, turned out to be an important tool in (re)establishing entrepreneurial independence—possibly even despite a strong demand for external financing. A question still remains as to the extent to which this was a common feature in the relations between banks and industry in Weimar Germany, or whether this was only valid for the connections between the great combines and their financial institutions.[33]

The large universal banks in particular tried to pursue business strategies by which operational costs could be reduced and relations to large-scale industry in Germany could also be strengthened. At first sight this seemed a reasonable attempt to restore their former position, but in fact these strategies caused severe flaws in the German banking system. Some of the combines, financed by large bank credits, expanded rapidly and had no solid operational basis in times of crisis. The universal banks, on the other hand, neglected a wide range of their earlier customers, thus becoming dependent on the development and standing of their large-scale clientele. Several combines, for example, benefited from relatively low interest rates for the credits they had received. This was obviously a consequence of the competition among banks at home and elsewhere.[34] On the other hand, the profit margins in the credit business of the banks remained comparatively low as a result of the keen competition. So the profits the banks gained after 1925 were insufficient to guarantee a satisfactory liquidity and to form solid financial reserves. This became obvious when the financial crisis of 1931 led to the collapse of the German banking system.[35]

We still lack sufficient empirical evidence to know whether or not the directors of the large universal banks noticed that their business strategies could lead to problems. If we look at the credit policy of the Darmstädter- und Nationalbank and its director Jacob Goldschmidt, for example, as well as the business strategies of the Dresdner Bank, the assumption that many of the bankers were not aware of the risks in their business seems to be justified. Granting credits on easy terms to maintain close relations with customers and to prevent a further decline of influence in industry seemed to be the most important aim of the business strategies pursued by these two financial institutions.[36] Attempts to restore their former position in the German economy eventually led to the opposite effect—this was the dilemma of the large German banks in the 'golden twenties'.

German Banks during the Great Depression

In the years 1931 and 1932 economists, experts in German banking, and several bankers discussed whether the financial crisis of 1931 could have been foreseen and who could have foreseen it.[37] The essence of this discussion was that nobody had recognized the real origins of the crisis. The business policy of the banks had not been recognized as one of the most decisive mainsprings of the crisis and of the collapse of the German banking system. The unwise credit policy of the German Reichsbank as well as the sudden crash of the Austrian Creditanstalt für Handel und Gewerbe did play a more important role in this respect. So the majority of participants in this discussion argued in their analysis. But was this assessment correct?

Analysis of the real origins and causes of the financial crisis of 1931, as well as of the 'great slump' in Germany, is a complex and difficult task, as recent debates on this subject have shown.[38] This might be why we still do not have a detailed study of the German banking crisis that includes all the different aspects of the banks' failures and is based on sufficient empirical material from bank archives. Some economic historians and experts in German banking have therefore dealt with this subject by presenting different points of view in their analysis. Whereas authors of some older studies have stated that competition in German banking as well as the credit policy of the banks in the late 1920s led to the crash,[39] other scholars in more recent works have modified this picture. Hardach, for example, has argued that the complexity in foreign policy played just as important a part in the story as the 'business events' did. James pointed out, citing some material from archives, that German speculation against the Reichsmark, based on 'insider information', initiated the withdrawals of deposits in the spring and summer of 1931, and that foreign withdrawals came only in the aftermath of this event.[40] Several articles have been written with the intention of proving how reliable different memoranda and memoirs of German bankers could be, as well as those of German politicians on this subject. Most of these studies have been written after the end of the Second World War. They can only be regarded as a kind of *ex post facto* justification. For example, there has been a long discussion on the question of whether or not the Deutsche Bank had helped the Darmstädter- und Nationalbank by discounting their bills, or to what extent the Reichsbank refused to discount the bills of the Danatbank in those dramatic days in July 1931. For the present, it seems difficult to decide what measures taken by the Reichsbank, the German government, or the Berlin universal banks were useful in preventing the collapse of the banking system. A detailed answer on these questions will only be possible if sufficient archival material on the role of the Danatbank, the Dresdner Bank, and the Deutsche Bank becomes available.[41]

Nevertheless, some remarks can be made on the situation of the banks that were primarily involved in the banking crisis. Even after the collapse of the New York stock exchange in October 1929 the German bankers continued to pursue their business policy as before. Some alarming signals besides the major financial scandals, however, such as the bankruptcy of the FAVAG, one of the largest German insurance companies in those days, or the financial troubles of the Karstadt store and the Schultheiss-Patzenhofer brewery, must have caused the German bankers to take notice. Despite this, the Danatbank and its leader Jacob Goldschmidt presented in the annual reports for 1929 and 1930 an optimistic view on the further development of industry and banking. Another director of the Danatbank, Doerner, who had joined the bank one year before the crisis, revealed that this kind of optimism was totally misleading. At the beginning of 1930 he discovered that the bank had so many bad accounts and losing subsidiaries that he was convinced it would sooner or later run into serious troubles, because its capital and reserves were insufficient for the size of its engagement. So Doerner was sceptical when Goldschmidt turned down a plan for a merger between Deutsche Bank–Discontogesellschaft and the Danatbank that was being discussed at the time. Goldschmidt did not even accept the suggestion of a merger with one of the other remaining major Berlin banks, or at least a substantial capital increase to widen the financial basis of the Danatbank. He only signed a friendship and mutual cooperation agreement with the Dresdner Bank and with the Berliner Handelsgesellschaft.[42] Doerner then informed Goldschmidt about the critical situation of the Danatbank. And it was Doerner, too, who after a good deal of detective work revealed in May 1931 that the Nordwolle combine, one of the Danatbank's largest clients in the German textile industry, was nearly bankrupt. Goldschmidt understood immediately that this could signify more than serious trouble for his bank. The rest of the story is well known. It seems worth pointing out, however, that Goldschmidt, the brilliant leader of the Danatbank, with all his optimistic statements about a prosperous future for his institute, had evidently been badly informed about the situation of the companies he had praised so highly. Moreover, he did not trust his colleagues on the board of directors of the Danatbank and withheld information from them as long as possible. This attitude must be corroborated by some other archival material, but all in all it reveals that the directorate of the Danatbank did not have a distinct strategy to overcome the crisis.[43]

The Dresdner Bank was faced with a similar situation. According to Frisch's report, the directors of the bank, such as Henry Nathan, knew that some of the credit arrangements were full of risks. For example, the bank lost money in its credit operations with the NSU automobile enterprise and other companies of this sort. Also, the takeover of the Ostbank für Handel und Gewerbe in Posen soon became a costly venture for the Dresdner Bank, with no benefits. As Frisch pointed out in his report, he was against this transaction, but the other directors decided on undertaking the business when he was on a holiday so that he could not oppose it.[44]

Dubious and perhaps even hazardous credit operations, as well as bad and hasty decisions by directors, were some of the main causes of the serious difficulties that some of the German banks had in 1931. Needless to say, these were not the only reasons. The political destabilization of the Weimar Republic, with increasing numbers of votes for the extreme right- and left-wing parties, caused a withdrawal of foreign capital as well as the sudden and unexpected collapse of the Austrian Creditanstalt. The unsuccessful journey of the president of the German Reichsbank, Luther, destroyed public confidence in the stability of the currency and the German banking system further. From this point of view and in retrospective, the collapse seemed to be inevitable. On the other hand, it is worth noting that the two large banks that got into difficulties had had the most dubious and risky accounts, whereas other financial institutions could better withstand the withdrawal of deposits and the coming crisis. The assumption that banks (like the Deutsche Bank or the Berliner Handelsgesellschaft) that pursued a less risky business strategy could survive the crisis, seems to be justified.[45]

Otherwise, under 'normal' conditions the Dresdner Bank and the Danatbank could have withstood losses in some credit operations and difficulties in some of the relations with their customers. In the business of banking such events had occurred several times. But until 1931, the Dresdner Bank as well as the predecessor of the Danatbank, the Darmstädter Bank für Handel und Industrie, had never been faced with such heavy losses that could lead directly to an immediate collapse.[46] Members of the board of directors, especially Goldschmidt, probably believed at first that they could solve the problems when the first dubious transactions with its clientele occurred. Most of the bankers had had this experience several times before, so why should they act differently this time? Moreover, they were convinced that the German Reichsbank would support the banks in times of trouble, as it had done several times before.[47] Confidence in the functioning of the 'lender of the last resort' and the experience of how to overcome problems in banking were probably another reason for hasty and unwise conclusions and reactions to the actual situation. Also, despite all the optimism in the annual reports of the Danatbank and in statements made by Goldschmidt, times were obviously not 'normal'. The political environment for banking was in a process of destabilization. Moreover, there had been signs of weakness in the international monetary system, not only in the German banking system.[48] Probably some of the directors of the large universal banks had ignored these 'environmental' problems in their business. This attitude, which emerged after the period of inflation as a result of the desire to do business as before the First World War, might be another reason for the impending crisis. So far, we only have evidence that the leaders of the Deutsche Bank and the Discontogesellschaft had recognized the risks and difficulties in banking comparatively early, that is in 1926, when they had started the first negotiations for a merger of the two banks. When this merger occurred in October 1929, the new Deutsche Bank–Discontogesellschaft (later known as the 'De-Di-Bank' or Deutsche Bank) was in such a strong position that it could easily settle all difficulties in this time of crisis.[49] In this respect, it was probably a great mistake that the Danatbank and the Dresdner Bank did not go through with the merger they had discussed, as their great rivals had done. So a somewhat destructive competition between these banks as a consequence of the daily struggle for lucrative transactions with large industrial clients, as well as dubious accounts and a narrow profit margin, remained characteristic of the business policy of these two banks, which all in all led to the collapse of the whole German banking system in those dramatic days of July 1931.

Concluding Remarks

Compared with the 'golden age' of German capitalism and banking during the Kaiserreich, the Weimar Republic was a period full of problems for most segments of the German financial system. The universal banks were especially affected by war and inflation. During the First World War and the years directly after its end they had already lost most of their capital and assets. Some of these banks, like the large Berlin universal banks, succeeded in regaining a part of their capital basis when they changed their business strategy in 1921. This restoration, however, was insufficient to compensate fully for what they had lost. The banks, therefore, became one of the losers of the inflation that occurred in Germany, despite benefiting from its effects in several aspects of their business. Moreover, their relations with their customers had been reduced and their position in the German economy had been weakened.

After inflation came to an end the banks, especially the large Berlin universal banks, tried to restore their former position and to reestablish former close connections with their clientele. These clients, however, had gained a considerable freedom of manoeuvre, because a great number of banks at home and in other countries wanted new customers. The large industrial combines, for example, could choose from a great number of banks to satisfy their capital demand. In contrast to the banks from other countries, the German institutes were at a disadvantage because they did not have enough funds to feed the credit demand of the large industrial enterprises. Strong and often destructive competition and rivalry among the banks was the consequence of this new situation in the German banking system. Risky credit transactions and dubious accounts on their balance sheets were other results of competition that led to narrow profit margins and to a hazardous business policy in several cases. Whereas the directors of some of the large Berlin banks like the Deutsche Bank or the Discontogesellschaft recognized the risks in this situation, others did not and refused to take adequate measures against the risks. These banks preferred to continue the business policy they had pursued during the Kaiserreich.

But shortly after the beginning of the Great Depression it became obvious that the German banking system was suffering from a structural weakness, one that was additionally intensified by 'environmental' problems like political destabilization. The banks that had lent under the most unfavourable terms and that had pursued the most risky business policies fell into serious troubles in the financial crisis of 1931, whereas others could withstand these turbulent times. The attempt by the government, the directors of the Reichsbank, and even the Deutsche Bank to isolate these banks from the others failed completely. As a result, the whole German banking system collapsed, thus aggravating an already severe economic crisis. The process of economic and political destabilization was thereby intensified and the way paved for the collapse of the Weimar Republic.

NOTES

1. For the financing of export and establishing of branches abroad see the recently published works of B. Barth, *Die deutsche Hochfinanz und die Imperialismen: Banken und Außenpolitik vor 1914* (Stuttgart: Steiner, 1995), and of M. Reitmayer, *Bankiers im Kaiserreich: Sozialprofil und Habitus der deutsche Hochfinanz* (Göttingen: Vandenhoeck & Ruprecht, 1999).
2. A good survey of the development of German banking during the Kaiserreich is given by R. Tilly, 'German Banking, 1850–1914: Development Assistance for the Strong', *Journal of European Economic History* 15/1 (1986), 113–52; idem, 'Universal Banking in Historical Perspective', *Journal of Institutional and Theoretical Economics (JITE)* 154/1 (March 1998), 7–32; D. Ziegler, 'The Influence of Banking on the Rise and Expansion of Industrial Capitalism in Germany', in A. Teichova, G. Kurgan-van Hentenryk, and D. Ziegler (eds), *Banking, Trade and Industry: Europe, America and Asia from the Thirteenth to the Twentieth Century* (Cambridge: Cambridge University Press, 1997), 131–56; M. Pohl, 'Festigung und Ausdehnung des deutschen Bankwesens zwischen 1870 und 1914', in Institut für Bankhistorische Forschung (ed.), *Deutsche Bankengeschichte* 2 (Frankfurt: Knapp, 1982), 223–352.
3. See, for example, the reaction of Simon Alfred Oppenheim, the director of the Cologne private bank Sal. Oppenheim jr. & Cie., in November 1918, at the end of the German Kaiserreich, in M. Stürmer *et al., Wägen und Wagen: Sal. Oppenheim jr. & Cie. Geschichte einer Bank und einer Familie* (Munich: Piper, 1989), 331–2.
4. For the introduction of the Reichsmark, see H.-O. Schötz, *Der Kampf um die Mark 1923–24: Die deutsche Währungsstabilisierung unter dem Einfluß der nationalen Interessen Frankreichs, Großbritanniens und der USA* (Berlin: de Gruyter, 1987). For the situation of the German banks after 1924 see T. Balderston, 'German Banking between the Wars: The Crisis of the Credit Banks', *Business History Review* 65/3 (autumn 1991), 554–605.
5. The most informative study on the German banking crisis in the summer of 1931 still is K. E. Born, *Die deutsche Bankenkrise 1931: Finanzen und Politik* (Munich: R. Piper, 1967). See also R. E. Lüke, *13. Juli 1931: Das Geheimnis der deutschen Bankenkrise* (Frankfurt: Knapp, 1981) and T. Balderston, 'The Banks and the Gold Standard in the German Financial Crisis of 1931', *Financial History Review* 1/1 (April 1994), 43–68.
6. R. W. Goldschmidt, *Das deutsche Großbankkapital in seiner neueren Entwicklung* (Berlin: E. Ebering, 1928), 59; A. Lansburgh, 'Die Berliner Großbanken 1920', *Die*

Bank (1921), 321; F. Grüger, 'Die Wirkungen des Krieges und der Kriegsfolgen auf das deutsche Bankwesen mit einem Rückblick auf die Vorkriegszeit', in Bankenenquetekommission (ed.), *Untersuchungen des Bankwesens 1933, I. Teil, Vorbereitendes Material*, vol. 1 (Berlin: Carl Heymanns Verlag, 1933), 48.

7. See the annual report of the Dresdner Bank of 1918, in Bundesarchiv Koblenz, Akten der Reichskanzlei, R 43/1, 643, Privatbanken.

8. See A. Lansburgh, 'Die Berliner Großbanken im Jahre 1921', *Die Bank* (1922), 546; C. Schmitt, 'Die Probleme der Bankgewinne', *Die Bank* (1922), 22 and 101; G. Speer, 'Die Politik der Reichsbank gegenüber dem Bankwesen: Die Inflationszeit', in Bankenenquetekommission (ed.), *Untersuchungen des Bankwesens 1933, I. Teil, Vorbereitendes Material*, vol. 2 (Berlin: Carl Heymanns Verlag, 1933), 159–86.

9. G. D. Feldman, 'Die Deutsche Bank vom Ersten Weltkrieg bis zur Weltwirtschaftskrise', in L. Gall *et al.*, *Die Deutsche Bank 1870–1995* (Munich: C. H. Beck, 1995), 185; idem, 'Banks and Banking in Germany after the First World War: Strategies of Defence', in Y. Cassis (ed.), *Finance and Financiers in European History 1880–1960* (Cambridge: Cambridge University Press, 1992), 246.

10. Historical Archive of the Dresdner Bank AG, Frankfurt (HADrB): Walter Frisch, Die Dresdner Bank von Versailles bis Hitler, unpublished report, 7–13.

11. Goldschmidt, *Das deutsche Großbankkapital*, 59.

12. See especially J. Houwink ten Cate, 'Amsterdam als Finanzplatz Deutschlands (1919–23)', in G. D. Feldman *et al.* (eds), *Konsequenzen der Inflation* (Berlin: Colloquium, 1989), 152–65.

13. Schmitt, 'Die Probleme des Bankgewinne', 24; Lansburgh, 'Die Berliner Großbanken im Jahre 1921', 552; Grüger, 'Die Wirkungen des Krieges', 46; V. Wellhöner and H. Wixforth, 'Unternehmensfinanzierung durch Banken—ein Hebel zur Etablierung der Bankenherrschaft', in D. Petzina (ed.), *Zur Geschichte der Unternehmensfinanzierung* (Berlin: Duncker & Humblot, 1990), 24.

14. H. Wixforth, *Banken und Schwerindustrie in der Weimarer Republik* (Cologne: Böhlau, 1995), 506–12.

15. Centralverband des deutschen Bank- und Bankiersgewerbes (ed.), *Materialien zur Vorbereitung der Bankenenquete* (Berlin, 1933), 120; M. Pohl, 'Die Situation der Banken in der Inflationszeit', in O. Büsch and G. D. Feldman (eds), *Historische Prozesse der Inflation* (Berlin: Colloquium Verlag, 1978), 89.

16. Goldschmidt, *Das deutsche Großbankkapital*, 53–55; Centralverband, *Materialien*, 121.

17. L. von Mering, 'Die deutschen Banken unter dem Einfluß der Inflation', *Bankwissenschaft* (1924/25), 622; L. Merzbach, 'Zur Lage im Bankgewerbe', *Bankarchiv* (1924/25), 55.

18. A. Lansburgh, 'Die Berliner Großbanken 1922', *Die Bank* (1923), 471.

19. Feldman, 'Strategies of Defence', 244; W. Prion, *Kreditpolitik: Aufsätze und Reden* (Berlin: Verlag Julius Springer, 1926), 109.

20. C.-L. Holtfrerich, 'Die Auswirkungen der Inflation auf die Struktur des deutschen Kreditgewerbes', in G. D. Feldman (ed.), *Die Nachwirkungen der Inflation auf die deutsche Geschichte 1924–1933* (Munich: Oldenbourg, 1985), 200–1.

21. G. Solmssen, 'Entwicklungstendenzen und weltwirtschaftliche Aufgaben der deutschen Großbanken', in G. Solmssen (ed.), *Beiträge zur deutschen Politik und Wirtschaft 1900–1933*, ii (Berlin: Verlag Duncker & Humblot, 1934), 526.

22. Speech of Oscar Wassermann at the sixth general meeting of German bankers (VI. Allgemeiner Deutscher Bankierstag) in Cologne, 1925.
23. See the overview of the development of the branches of the German 'Großbanken' in *Untersuchungen des Bankwesens 1933*, part 2, statistics (Berlin: Carl Heymanns Verlag, 1933), 179.
24. H. James, *The German Slump: Politics and Economics 1924–1936* (Oxford: Clarendon, 1986), 139–46; Wixforth, *Banken und Schwerindustrie*, 510–11.
25. G. D. Feldman, 'Banks and the Problem of Capital Shortage in Germany, 1918–23', in H. James *et al.* (eds), *The Role of Banks in the Interwar Economy* (Cambridge: Cambridge University Press & Éditions de la Maison des Science de l'Homme, 1991), 60; H. James, 'Banks and Bankers in the German Interwar Depression', in Cassis, *Finance and Financiers in European History*, 272–3.
26. R. Schirmer, 'Das Kreditproblem der Mittel- und Kleinindustrie', *Deutsche Wirtschaftszeitung* 24/42 (20 October 1927); P. Schulz-Kiesow, 'Das langfristige Kreditproblem der mittleren Industrie', *Bankarchiv* (1927/28), 341.
27. Several examples are given in Wixforth, *Banken und Schwerindustrie* and in K. Lehmann, *Wandlungen der Industriefinanzierungen mit Anleihen in Deutschland (1923/24–1938/39)* (Stuttgart: Franz Steiner Verlag, 1996). See also Balderston, 'German Banking between the Wars', 568–9.
28. A. Lansburgh, 'Die Finanzierung des Kapitalbedarfs der Mittel- und Kleinindustrie', in B. Harms (ed.), *Kapital und Kapitalismus* (Berlin: Verlag Reimar Hobbing, 1931), 131; W. von Radzibor, *Das Problem des langfristigen Kredits für die kleinere und mittlere Industrie* (Rostock: C. Hinstorffs, 1929); Ausschuß zur untersuchung der Erzeugung und Absatzbedingungen der deutschen Wirtschaft. Unterausschuß für Geld-, Kredit- und Finanzwesen (ed.), *Der Bankkredit* (Berlin: E.S. Mittler & Sohn, 1930), 162–8.
29. See Archive of the Mannesmann AG (MA), P 1 25.26.2, P 1 25.29; Haniel-Archive (HA), 300/71/52–3; Archive of the Thyssen AG (TA), FWH 126/53, 126/54; 527/03; TA, A 768/3, A 815/1, A 771/1; TA VSt 955, VSt 4141.
30. See W. Feldenkirchen, 'Unternehmensfinanzierung in der deutschen Elektroindustrie der Zwischenkriegszeit', in D. Petzina (ed.), *Zur Geschichte der Unternehmensfinanzierung* (Berlin, 1990), 42–7; G. Plumpe, *Die I.G. Farbenindustrie* (Berlin: Duncker & Humblot, 1990), 123.
31. See Historical Archive of the Fried. Krupp GmbH, 41/2-198; HA, 300/193/000; Hoesch-Archive, A 3 b 24; TA, A 522/2; MA, P 1 25.38. See also P. Ufermann, *Könige der Inflation* (Berlin: Verlag für Sozialwissenschaften, 1925), 44 and 62; W. Hagemann, *Das Verhältnis der deutschen Großbanken zur Industrie* (Berlin: Verlag für Sozialwissenschaften, 1931), 21; M. Wittkowski, *Großbanken und Industrie in Deutschland 1924–31* (Tampere: Hameen Kirjapaino Oy, 1937), 17, and the chapters on these enterprises in Wixforth, *Banken und Schwerindustrie*.
32. M. Gehr, 'Das Verhältnis der Banken zur Industrie in Deutschland 1850–1931', Ph.D. thesis (University of Tübingen, 1960), 86–7; G. Hardach, 'Banking and Industry in Germany in the Interwar Period 1919–1939', *Journal of European Economic History* 13/2 (1984), 217; Balderston, 'German Banking between the Wars', 576–7.
33. D. Ziegler, 'Die Aufsichtsräte der deutschen Aktiengesellschaften in den zwanziger Jahren: Eine empirische Untersuchung zum Problem der Bankenmacht', *Zeitschrift für Unternehmensgeschichte* 43/2 (1998), 194–214.

Several examples of the role of bank directors on the supervisory boards in heavy industry are given in Wixforth, *Banken und Schwerindustrie*.

34. Several examples are given in Wixforth, *Banken und Schwerindustrie, passim*.

35. J. Blatz, *Die Bankenliquidität im Run: Statistische Liquiditätsanalyse* (Cologne: Selbtsverlag, 1971); F.-W. Henning, 'Die Liquidität der Banken in der Weimarer Republik', in H. Winkel (ed.), *Finanz- und wirtschaftpolitische Fragen der Zwischenkriegszeit* (Berlin: Duncker & Humblot, 1973), 156. The contemporary criticism was formulated by, for example, Alfred Lansburgh, 'Die Liquidität der Banken', *Die Bank* (1930), 1945–7 and Balderston, 'German Banking between the Wars', 581.

36. See, for example, Frisch, Die Dresdner Bank von Versailles bis Hitler, 40–50; G. D. Feldman, 'Jacob Goldschmidt: The History of the Banking Crisis of 1931 and the Problem of Freedom of Maneuver in the Weimar Economy', in C. Buchheim *et al.* (eds), *Zerissene Zwischenkriegszeit* (Baden–Baden: Nomos, 1994), 305–24.

37. H. Fuchs, 'War die deutsche Geldkrise vorauszusehen und wer hat sie vorausgesehen?', *Zeitschrift für handelswissenschaftliche Forschungen* 25 (1931), 67; G. Katona, 'Die Banken in der Krise', in *Der Deutsche Volkswirt* (17 April 1931); H. Priester, *Das Geheimnis des 13. Juli* (Berlin: Georg Stilke, 1931); H. Scheffler, 'Die Geschäftspolitik der großen Kreditbanken im Lichte der Bankenkrise', *Zeitschrift für Betriebswirtschaft* (1933), 523.

38. See the various contributions that were published in the 'Borchardt controversy' that started in German economic historiography in 1981 and still continues even today. Some of the most important contributions from the German point of view should be mentioned here: K. Borchardt, 'Zwangslagen und Handlungsspielräume in der großen Weltwirtschaftskrise der frühen dreißiger Jahre: Zur Revision des überlieferten Geschichtsbildes', in K. Borchardt (ed.), *Wachstum, Krisen, Handlungsspielräume der Wirtschaftspolitik: Studien zur deutschen Wirtschaftsgeschichte des 19. und 20. Jahrhunderts* (Göttingen: Vandenhoeck & Ruprecht, 1982), 165–82; C.-L. Holtfrerich, 'Alternativen zu Brünings Wirtschaftspolitik in der Weltwirtschaftskrise?', *Historische Zeitschrift* 235 (1982), 605–31; C.-D. Krohn, 'Ökonomische Zwangslagen und das Scheitern der Weimarer Republik', *Geschichte und Gesellschaft* 8 (1982), 415–26; and G. Plumpe, 'Wirtschaftspolitik in der Weltwirtschaftskrise: Realität und Alternativen', *Geschichte und Gesellschaft* 11 (1985), 326–57.

39. See Karl-Erich Born, *Die deutsche Bankenkrise 1931* and the majority of articles published in *Untersuchungen des Bankwesens*, part 1, vols. 1 and 2.

40. G. Hardach, 'Banking and Industry in Germany in the Interwar Period', *Journal of European Economic History, Supplement: Banks and Industry in the Interwar Period* 13/2 (1984), 221; idem, *Weltmarktorientierung und relative Stagnation: Währungspolitik in Deutschland 1924–31* (Berlin: Duncker und Humblot, 1976); H. James, 'The Causes of the German Banking Crisis in 1931', *Economic History Review*, 2nd ser. 37/1 (1984), 68–87.

41. For more on this subject, see Feldman, 'Jacob Goldschmidt', 307–27.

42. Feldman, 'Jacob Goldschmidt', 323; Bundesarchiv, R 43/1, Akten der Reichskanzlei, 648, Privatbanken, annual reports of the Danatbank for 1929 and 1930.

43. Feldman, 'Jacob Goldschmidt', 325; Priester, *Das Geheimnis des 13. Juli*, 24.

44. Frisch, Die Dresdner Bank von Versailles bis Hitler, 44–50.

45. Balderston, 'German Banking between the Wars', 585; Feldman, 'Jacob Goldschmidt', 326.

46. For the crisis of the Dresdner Bank in 1900–1 see H. Wixforth, 'Bank für Sachsen oder Bank für das Reich? Zur Geschichte der Dresdner Bank von 1872–1914', in S. Lässig and K. H. Pohl (eds), *Sachsen im Kaiserreich: Politik, Wirtschaft und Gesellschaft im Umbruch* (Weimer: Böhlau, 1997), 309–42.

47. L. Gall, 'Die deutsche Bank von ihrer Gründung bis zum Ersten Weltkrieg 1870–1914', and G. D. Feldman, 'Die Deutsche Bank vom Ersten Weltkrieg bis zur Weltwirtschaftskrise', both in L. Gall *et al., Die Deutsche Bank 1870–1995.*

48. T. Balderston, 'The Banks and the Gold Standard in the German Financial Crisis of 1931', 46–63.

49. See Feldman, 'Die Deutsche Bank vom Ersten Weltkrieg bis zur Weltwirtschaftskrise', 285.

PART III

INSURANCE AND SECURITIES

8

A Historical Account of Japan's Life Insurance Companies in the 1920s and 1930s

MARIKO TATSUKI

Introduction

The Japanese life insurance industry had two dimensions in its early days. At first, basic life insurance was provided by traditional friendly societies, which had developed in the proto-industrial days of the Tokugawa era. This was referred to as 'pseudo-life-insurance' after the introduction of modern insurance in the late nineteenth century. Modern scientific life insurance, on the other hand, was introduced from the West after the Meiji Restoration, and it competed with pseudo insurance.

The pseudo-insurance companies had taken root so deeply in the life of the populace that they continued to prosper for quite some time after modernization following upon the Meiji Restoration. These companies had no scientific standards such as mortality tables or policy reserves. When the government conducted an investigation of the life insurance industry in 1894, it found among the several dozen companies it checked that only ten or so kept mortality tables. Governmental regulations on life insurance started with the enactment of a systematic law on the management of life insurance to regulate the insurance companies because pseudo-life insurance often dealt heavy blows to people's livelihood, especially in urban areas. When the government introduced supervisory directives, together with the enactment in 1898 of the former Commercial Code, many life insurance companies were unable to remain in business because they had no actuaries. This clearly reveals the generally weak foundations of life insurance companies at that time.

By contrast, the big life insurance companies established in and after the 1880s introduced the Western insurance system and had clear business plans. Their management was based on scientific statistics and their premiums were high. As a result, their clients were limited to people of the upper middle class or higher. With the promulgation of the Insurance Business Law in March 1900, Japan's insurance industry came under the supervision of an exclusive law and a licensing system based on free competition and public announcements. However, the government met with criticism to the effect that stipulations concerning policy reserves were too strict, and it was compelled to permit use of the Zillmers method, whereby reserves are built up in stages.[1] Apparently only three companies had adequate policy reserves at that time: Meiji Life Assurance, Teikoku Life Assurance, and Nippon Life Assurance.

In 1898, when the government first introduced supervisory directives, seven life insurance companies (including Meiji, Teikoku, and Nippon) organized a Life Insurance Society, a forum in which they jointly undertook diverse activities, such as discussing revisions to the Commercial Code, preparing model policy provisions, and conducting campaigns to promote understanding of life insurance. When the Russo-Japanese War broke out in 1904, the life insurance companies subscribed to 7 per cent of the entire issue of war bonds, as a result of which their power was recognized in the financial community. In 1905 the life insurance companies expanded the size and scope of activities of the Life Insurance Society and renamed it the Japan Life Insurance Companies Association (JLICA), with seventeen corporate members. Following the Russo-Japanese War, the JLICA became very active, opposing and finally defeating a proposal in the Diet to nationalize the insurance industry. Competition became extremely fierce with the addition of thirteen companies that were established between 1906 and 1911. Here again, the JLICA played an important role in guiding the industry towards healthy development—by, for example, forcing unprincipled persons out of business and clamping down on unscrupulous sales activities.

In the economic turbulence of the 1920s and 1930s, when competition was again severe, the Japanese life insurance companies intensively promoted large-scale mergers and acquisitions. The biggest five life insurance companies concentrated their efforts on acquiring new contracts. As a result, the total amount of assets held by life insurance companies grew rapidly, reaching one-sixth that of banks in 1937.

Wartime economic controls were strengthened after the war between Japan and China broke out in July 1937. The government issued bonds to meet the war expenses. These bonds increased rapidly, amounting to 12 billion yen in 1937 and double that figure in 1939, and by 1941 showing a more than threefold increase. The government requested financial institutions other than banks to accept these bonds.

Life insurance companies were expected to accept bonds and were put under the fund control and supervision of the Ministry of Finance (MOF) in 1938. The share of insurance companies among holders of government bonds was less than 2 per cent until 1936. It grew to more than 3 per cent in 1937 and by 1941 was over 4 per cent. The banks' share during this period remained around the 30 per cent mark.

This chapter will review the competition, reorganization, and prosperity of life insurance companies under economic control, focusing on company strategies, especially those of Chiyoda Mutual Insurance, Meiji Life Assurance, and Nippon Life Assurance. Wartime control over life insurance is believed to have been less strict than that over banks because insurance companies resisted such control. This was mainly because the government took more interest in controlling the funds of banks than those of life insurance companies, whose total assets were still small. The companies were also aided by the industry's autonomy, which had its roots in history, in the sense that it had grown without governmental protection. This chapter will also reexamine the significance of wartime control over the industry because it brought benefits to the management and development of large companies—benefits that were of greater importance to them than the preservation of their autonomy.

The Growth of Life Insurance

In the long depression after the First World War, big companies grew steadily and the middle class grew along with them. Before the First World War there were two classes: a small number of affluent people and the remaining majority, who were poor. Banks and insurance companies were separated according to whether or not their customers belonged to the upper class. In the life insurance business, customers of the big companies were mainly upper-class people, because the insurance premiums were too expensive for everyone else. As a result of the economic boom during the First World War, office workers of big companies had increased in number and they had new insurance needs to be served.

Another change in the insurance business was the introduction of postal life insurance in 1916. Initially, postal insurance was subject to an upper limit of 250 yen in the amount insured. Contracts of less than 300 yen declined in insurance companies after the Russo-Japanese War of 1904–5, at least in the case of big companies. Postal insurance obviously inherited the basic conditions of the industry that were just pointed out above. It catered, however, for the small insurance needs of the general populace.

Big companies, on the other hand, issued more and more large contracts in the economic boom of the First World War. There is little doubt, however, that postal insurance had a decisive effect on the marketing policy of the large insurance companies, because thereafter they began to develop a variety of new policies to attract consumer interest. The upper limit of postal insurance was first raised in 1922, then finally revised to 450 yen in 1926. The insurance companies opposed each increase, but in the 1920s they were entering into large contracts exceeding 20,000 yen in steadily increasing numbers.

In 1910 Chiyoda Mutual started selling a new type of endowment insurance with an annual policy dividend. It also increased the upper limit of the insurance amount per person to 30,000 yen, two years earlier than Meiji Life did. This new product sold well, rapidly enhancing the company's new business. The company ranked fourth by insurance-in-force in 1912, its eighth year of existence. Ikunoshin Kadono, the founder and first president of Chiyoda Mutual, had previously been the vice-principal of Keio Private School, whose founder, Yukichi Fukuzawa, first introduced insurance to Japan. Kadono adopted an aggressive and successful management policy.[2]

Stimulated by the success of Chiyoda Mutual, other life insurance companies introduced various new products. Largely as a result of the economic boom during the First World War, the national income had been growing and these new products sold well. The insurance companies consequently made remarkable progress and maintained a high rate of growth even in the economic depression after the First World War (see Table 8.1).

After the First World War, two significant changes in the business took place: the zaibatsu took over life insurance companies (see Table 8.2) and the mutual companies started performing well (see Fig. 8.1). Since Japan's heavy industry began to grow during and after the First World War, the zaibatsu needed large amounts of capital to finance it, and they felt that their own resources were insufficient. They expanded their financial business (including insurance, not only life but also nonlife and trust) so as to concentrate capital held by private individuals.

The Mitsubishi zaibatsu, for instance, was the largest shareholder of Meiji Life since 1890 and occasionally sent one of its officers to become Meiji's president. The Yasuda zaibatsu established a friendly society in 1880 and reorganized it into a joint-stock company in 1900. Sumitomo, Mitsui, and other zaibatsu were late in establishing affiliated life insurance companies; Sumitomo took over Hinode Life in 1925 and Mitsui took over Takasago Life in 1926. A feature of Japanese life insurance was the fact that most contracts were of the endowment type. The insurance-in-force of these companies grew rapidly, as did their assets. In fact, the zaibatsu-affiliated insurance companies had been mostly medium-sized before they were taken over, and then they grew rapidly with the backup of the zaibatsu. Sumitomo Life, for example, ranked thirty-third among Japanese

Table 8.1. *The growth of life insurance in Japan*

Year	Number of companies	Insurance-in-force (¥1,000,000)	New business (¥1,000,000)	Total assets (A) (¥1,000,000)	Distribution of securities and loans							
					Public bonds (B) (¥1,000,000)	(B/A) (%)	Corporate bonds (C) (¥1,000,000)	(C/A) (%)	Stocks (D) (¥1,000,000)	(D/A) (%)	Loans (E) (¥1,000,000)	(E/A) (%)
1910	29	558	150	73	14	20	4	5	9	13	19	26
1920	42	2,639	694	401	44	11	63	16	61	15	79	20
1930	40	7,694	1,365	1,560	169	11	375	24	228	15	417	27
1935	33	12,536	2,677	2,510	269	11	578	23	554	22	626	25
1936	33	14,455	3,063	2,831	290	10	641	23	728	26	666	24
1937	33	16,707	3,470	3,202	340	11	656	20	919	29	763	24
1938	33	19,661	4,320	3,614	441	12	685	19	1,081	30	790	22
1939	32	24,198	5,873	4,171	621	15	779	19	1,262	30	855	20
1940	32	30,363	8,021	4,917	886	18	910	19	1,437	29	956	19
1941	29	36,494	8,576	5,852	1,278	22	921	16	1,523	26	1,147	20
1942	23	42,781	9,205	6,963	1,870	27	1,005	14	1,761	25	1,202	17
1943	22	51,710	12,251	8,243	2,595	31	983	12	2,115	26	1,245	15
1944	21	68,618	18,220	10,948	3,770	34	1,073	10	2,374	22	1,630	15

Sources: Hoken nenkan [Insurance annual], annual editions (Tokyo: Shokosho Hokenkyoku).

Table 8.2. *Total assets of insurance companies and of banks (¥1,000,000)*

Year	Total assets			Underwriting reserve		Deposit
	Life	Nonlife	Banks	Life	Nonlife	Banks
1910	73	34	1,684	62	0	1,186
1920	401	268	7,647	349	0	5,827
1930	1,560	405	11,332	1,389	180	8,737
1935	2,510	491	13,120	2,231	211	9,950
1940	4,917	807	32,589	4,486	383	24,670
1945	12,380	2,553	119,829	11,032	1,049	102,348

Sources: Hoken nenkan, annual editions; *Nihon Teikoku tokei nenkan* [Japanese Empire statistics annual], annual editions (Tokyo: Naikaku Tokeikyoku).

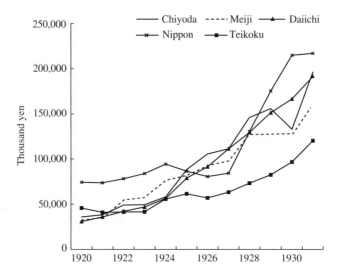

Fig. 8.1. *New business of Big Five*
Note: Chiyoda and Daiichi were mutual concerns.
Sources: Hoken nenkan, annual editions.

insurance companies in 1926 when Hinode Life was renamed Sumitomo Life, then rose to be sixteenth in 1930, tenth in 1933, and sixth in 1938.

The growth of mutual insurance companies, however, came about as a result of severe competition. They challenged the big joint-stock companies by saying that they could offer more beneficial products to customers, because, as mutual organizations, they had no need to pay dividends to shareholders. They also cultivated a new market by developing 'high-premium high-dividend' products and stimulated the speculative spirit of the upper middle class. These points will be discussed in the next section.

Competition in the 1920s and Early 1930s

During the prolonged economic slump of the 1920s and early 1930s, big banks and big life insurance companies succeeded in gaining public trust and grew bigger. In the life insurance business, new customers tended to be attracted to the big five companies, including the two large mutual concerns, Chiyoda and Daiichi. Typical of the competition between the three joint-stock companies and two mutual concerns was the rivalry that existed between Chiyoda Mutual and Nippon Life (and to some extent with Meiji Life as well). The top position in terms of new business acquisition was occupied in turn by these two: until 1924 and from 1929 onwards, it was Nippon Life; from 1925 to 1928, Chiyoda Mutual took over (see Fig. 8.1). In terms of insurance-in-force, however, Nippon Life was always at the top, and Meiji Life was usually in second place. From 1928, Chiyoda Mutual rose to second and Meiji Life fell to third.

There was a great change in Japanese social structure during these years of economic slump. The middle class, which emerged in cities,[3] gained higher incomes and had a strong tendency to prefer interest to security. The 'high-premium high-dividend' policy, introduced by mutual companies, was favourably accepted by these people. Moreover, advertising and the services offered by an expanded, more conveniently located sales network were very effective for selling insurance to the middle class. The development of high-yield endowment insurance and construction of an expanded, more conveniently accessible sales network became keys to the growth of insurance companies.

Chiyoda Mutual grew rapidly, targeting the new market that was being cultivated among the emerging middle class. The company increased the maximum insured amount per contract to 100,000 yen in 1920. At the same time, it aggressively cultivated customers among salaried workers who were able to maintain a stable livelihood as the result of a fall in prices during the economic depression, as well as among landed farmers in rural areas. It introduced various incentives to encourage large agencies, including higher agent commissions, recognition of excellence in agents, etc. It also closed down small or inferior agencies. The quality of contracts was improved, and this might explain why the surrender ratio was fairly low in the case of Chiyoda Mutual, compared with Nippon Life and Meiji Life, even though the rate of increase of new business was similar.[4]

In 1923 the Tokyo metropolitan area was hit by the Great Kanto Earthquake. The Japan Life Insurance Companies Association decided to pay insurance money immediately and in full, and to allow deferment of premium payment. They raised funds to cover these measures from the Bank of Japan. In this way, the life insurance companies won much public confidence.[5] This was the first case in which the JLICA showed strong leadership to its members.

Chiyoda Mutual, like the other life insurance companies, grew rapidly in the 1920s. It gained 58 million yen worth of new business in 1924 and 88 million yen worth in 1925. Insurance-in-force reached 304 million yen in 1924, 372 million yen in 1925, and 422 million yen in 1926. Chiyoda Mutual ranked third in 1925 by insurance-in-force and first by new business from 1925 to 1928 (see Fig. 8.1).

Following completion of post-earthquake reconstruction, Chiyoda Mutual decided to extend its business to China in 1924. President Kadono announced in 1925 a change in the company's strategy from prudential to aggressive. The company raised dividends and increased the size of the business department and the number of agents. It also introduced endowment insurance with annual dividends. The 'high-premium high-dividend' policy was favourably accepted by people with higher incomes who had a strong preference for interest. The new product was also far simpler than the old type, which paid dividends every five years. Moreover, the company made effective propaganda by saying that its business costs, insurance payments, and cancel returns were low, enabling it to offer high dividends. This policy favourably impressed the general populace. The company consequently grew faster than its three long-established rivals.[6]

Of course, Meiji Life and Nippon Life carried on similarly innovative management initiatives and did well against the mutual life insurance companies that were prominent in the late 1920s. Meiji Life and Nippon Life, however, did not promise high dividend rates to policyholders, in an attempt to keep premiums low.

Nippon Life had its headquarters in Osaka and was relatively unaffected by the Great Kanto Earthquake. But Nippon Life had its strongest footing in rural areas and therefore could not quickly respond to changes in the market during and after the First World War. As a result, it failed to acquire much new business and from 1924 on its share of new business declined (see Fig. 8.1). The company began to revise its business system, especially in cities, and to increase the number of its agents. Though the number of agents increased by 1.7 times in the decade from 1919 to 1928, the amount of insurance sold per agent declined.[7]

We can conclude that the company failed in its agent policy. In cities the company could not compete realistically with Chiyoda Mutual and Daiichi Mutual, while in rural areas its market was invaded by the two competitors. Moreover, the business environment changed unfavourably for Nippon. It seems that the entry of zaibatsu into life insurance was a blow to the company, because zaibatsu affiliates gained the trust of these upper-class people who until then had been their good customers. Among the zaibatsu, Sumitomo Life in particular was expected to become a tough rival because in Osaka no large insurance company other than Nippon Life had been holding a significant share of that market. Sumitomo, one of the biggest zaibatsu and headquartered, entered the life insurance business by taking over Hinode Life of Tokyo. Although Nippon Life maintained the highest share in the amount of insurance-in-force throughout the 1920s and 1930s, its share in new business declined until 1928. The insurance-in-force of Chiyoda Mutual consequently grew to 86 per cent of Nippon Life's by 1930, even though it had been half that of Nippon Life in 1920.

Meiji Life held a constant share even in new business. The company started marketing a new low-premium product in 1921. Confident in its 'low-premium, low-dividend' policy, it introduced an actuarial table compiled by three Japanese companies, replacing the one developed by the seventeen British companies. The new actuarial table certainly made more sense for Japanese insurers, because the life expectancy rate of forty-two and over was higher than the English one. The company devised a new idea, that of introducing the Zillmer method for calculating policy reserve and reducing costs rationally. It changed its way of business at the same time, introducing a new insurance salesperson system with efficiency wages, sales quotas, and assistant salespeople. The new product gained public favour and sold well.[8]

Meiji Life and Nippon Life had been the leading Japanese life insurance companies for more than forty years. To cope with intensified competition, however, they made all-out efforts to reduce overhead expenses, reinforce sales personnel, and develop various new products. As a result, Nippon Life just managed to retain its lead, and in 1939 Meiji Life regained the third position that it had lost in 1931 (see Fig. 8.2).

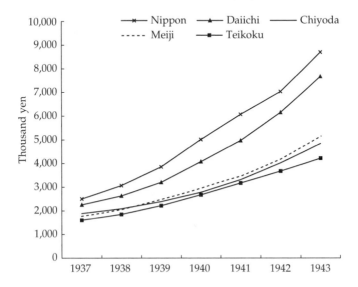

Fig. 8.2. *Insurance-in-force of Big Five*

Sources: *Hoken nenkan*, annual editions; *Seimei hoken jigyo gaikyo* [The outlook of life insurance] (Tokyo: Seimei Hoken Toseikai), annual editions.

The share in new business and insurance-in-force held by the big five increased remarkably from 1927 and exceeded 50 per cent in 1930. The main reason was that people trusted only big companies during the prolonged unfavourable economic situation. This concentration of business spread to all financial institutions, not only life insurance but also nonlife insurance and banking. Another reason was the severe competition among the big companies. Small companies were unable to offer attractive products or expand their business networks.

In the depressions of 1927 and 1930, deposits in banks declined considerably; as a result, bank assets remained sluggish until 1933. On the other hand, the assets of life insurance companies increased from 884 million yen in 1926 to 1,482 million yen in 1931, raising the total assets of the financial institutions by 9.4 per cent (see Table 8.2). As a result, the status of life insurance improved significantly in the early 1930s. In the same years the stock market suffered a severe decline. The insurance companies began to invest in loans rather than bonds and stocks because the yields of the latter were depressed. The stock market recovered after 1934 and the ratio of stocks to total assets once again increased. The percentage of bonds, on the other hand, remained around 10 per cent until 1937 (see Table 8.1).

Though the importance of stocks in assets management kept declining in the early 1930s, they still hovered around the 15 per cent mark. Life insurance companies had to cope with the stock market collapse. The government also was concerned about the problem and asked life insurance companies to buy more stocks.[9] In 1930, Kunizo Hara, president of Aikoku Life, and Tsuneta Yano, president of Daiichi Mutual, appealed to other life insurance companies to establish a Stock Holding Company of Life Insurance, in order to support the stock market and thus to secure their assets. Nippon Life and Mitsui Life at first refused to participate but finally agreed to do so. Thirty-two companies joined the Stock Holding Co.[10] This helped to prevent a fall in stock prices. It was dissolved in 1933 after successfully accomplishing its mission. The life insurance companies displayed strong autonomy in this case.

On the other hand, there were also cases in which the JLICA failed to exert the desired influence. In the long recession of the 1920s, competition among life insurance companies became severe and some companies began to undermine other companies' contracts by offering to pay higher dividends. Moreover, so-called cancelling brokers resold cancelled contracts to other companies, taking advantage of the distress caused by the unfavourable economic circumstances and people's ignorance about insurance. The JLICA established an agreement to control such unethical business practices in 1929 and new regulation of the business was begun in 1930. In spite of this measure, the problem was not solved until the Ministry of Commerce and Industry (MCI) promulgated an act aimed at controlling the insurance business and introduced a salesperson registration system in 1931.

Meanwhile, the Insurance Business Law was revised in 1927. The main points of the revision were that the policy reserve obligation was intensified, while restrictions on mergers and acquisitions were relaxed. A New Bank Act was also promulgated in 1927, and mergers were promoted. Behind these revisions was the severe competition taking place among financial companies within the prolonged unfavourable economic environment. The government gave guidance to financial institutions by means of these acts so that they would become more robust and able to meet the demand for funds for rationalization, the development of the heavy and chemical industries, and so on. When revising the Insurance Business Law, the government at first insisted on suspending the imprimatur of the Zillmer method in order to strengthen insurance companies' ability to finance. The JLICA, however, said that, if the Zillmer method were suspended, many of the small companies would not be able to attain the policy reserve level required by the net premium method and would go bankrupt. The Zillmer method was finally approved in 1926, but with a shorter redemption period. Governmental supervision of life insurance companies, as a result, was more generous than that applied to banks. Another reason that can be thought of for the lenient supervision is that the supervisory office for insurance was the MCI, while other financial institutions such as banks and trusts, were supervised by the MOF.

For the life insurance industry, the act as revised in 1927 had achieved good results in controlling unfair soliciting. Many companies were unable to achieve the required policy reserve level under the revised law because of heavy spending on sales promotion, large irrecoverable loans, or speculative, high dividends. By the early 1930s they had either merged or transferred their insurance contracts *en bloc* to other companies. As a result, there was less unfair competition and companies having sound managerial policies could conduct their business in favourable circumstances. The JLICA completed rules that all agreed on for sales and established policy, in addition to founding the Stock Holding Company of Life Insurance.

Prosperity of Life Insurance in the 1930s and Wartime Control

In 1931 the war between Japan and China broke out, and by 1933 (much earlier than in Western countries) Japan's economy smoothly recovered from the depression. The life insurance business enjoyed prosperity in the 1930s, being untouched by wartime controls. As can be seen in Table 8.1, new business in 1930 was twice what it was in 1920, and in 1936 more than

twice what it was in 1930, reaching 3 billion yen; this seems to be the result
of intensified competition among life insurance companies. The assets of life
insurance companies also increased remarkably and were mainly invested
in stocks, as the stock market had once again turned bullish. Although the
performance of the life insurance companies was more remarkable than that
of banks, they still remained outside the control of the MOF.

Some changes did take place, however, in the structure of the industry
(see Table 8.3). The big three, Nippon Life, Daiichi Life, and Meiji Life,
grew and acquired a larger share under the controlled economy. The
zaibatsu affiliates also showed rapid growth. Other companies, including
Chiyoda Mutual and Teikoku Life, which had ranked among the big five,
gradually declined (see Fig. 8.2). Chiyoda Mutual performed well in the
prewar period and celebrated its thirtieth anniversary in 1934. It acquired
the largest amount of new business in 1935 but thereafter went into
decline. This was partly a reaction to sales in its thirtieth anniversary year.
A more significant reason, however, was that the company's high dividend
policy was hampered by the low interest rate environment of wartime control. The company was compelled to reduce dividends, a development that
proved unpopular, while it was unable to offset this advantage by designing new popular products. There were also some problems in the administration of agencies as a result of the company's excessively rapid growth.
One more reason that can be mentioned is that President Kadono, who had

Table 8.3. *The concentration of insurance in wartime*

Company	1933				1940			
	Insurance-in-force		New business		Insurance-in-force		New business	
	(¥1,000,000)	(%)	(¥1,000,000)	(%)	(¥1,000,000)	(%)	(¥1,000,000)	(%)
Nippon	1,278	13.3	264	13.3	5,012	16.5	1,322	16.5
Chiyoda	1,144	11.9	215	10.9	2,782	9.2	476	5.9
Daiichi	1,142	11.9	211	10.7	4,075	13.4	1,041	13.0
Meiji	1,062	11.0	188	9.5	2,944	9.7	575	7.2
Teikoku	776	8.1	175	8.8	2,678	8.8	556	6.9
Total of the five	5,403	56.2	1,052	53.1	17,491	57.6	3,971	49.5
Yasuda	363	3.8	60	3.0	1,212	4.0	387	4.8
Mitsui	259	2.7	64	3.2	1,339	4.4	349	4.4
Nomura	216	2.3	45	2.3	1,072	3.5	214	2.7
Sumitomo	215	2.2	59	3.0	1,530	5.0	444	5.5
Total of the four	1,054	11.0	228	11.5	5,153	17.0	1,394	17.4
Others	3,156	32.8	700	35.4	7,719	25.4	2,656	33.1
Gross total	9,613	100.0	1,980	100.0	30,363	100.0	8,021	100.0

Sources: Gendai Nihon sangyo hattatsu shi [History of industrial development in modern Japan], *27 kan: hoken*
[Vol. 27: Insurance] (Tokyo: Kojunsha Shuppankyoku, 1966), 136; company histories of the above companies.

been in charge of the company since its establishment, retired in 1937 at the age of eighty-two.

In 1937 the government promulgated the Law for the Extraordinary Adjustment of Funds, which restricted life insurance companies as well as banks and trust companies in their management of funds. All financial organizations were forced to hold government bonds and to invest in war-related industries. On the other hand, the total insurance-in-force increased greatly, despite the fact that people's standard of living was depressed under wartime control. This was the result partly of aggressive sales campaigns and partly of a governmental savings campaign against the background of general wartime unrest.

The Insurance Business Law was revised once again in 1939, and life insurance companies were put under the control of the MOF in 1941. As the assets of life insurance companies grew tremendously in the 1930s, so did their share of the fund market (see Table 8.2). Expectations placed on their financing capacity grew ever larger. The government intended to tighten restrictions on them in order to make their business basis more solid through liquidation or reorganization of small, unhealthy companies. After the promulgation of the revised law, small or weak companies were absorbed by large companies or by zaibatsu affiliates. In some cases the government promoted M&A of small joint-stock companies by mutual companies. There were forty-four companies in 1925, but these had decreased to thirty-three by 1934 and to twenty-one by 1945.

Competition was moderated by the influence of wartime control. Insurance companies were compelled to buy large quantities of government bonds, which affected their return on investment and, consequently, the high reserve level, which had hitherto enabled them to offer high dividends and to win out against competitors. The twelve largest companies committed themselves to the MCI in October 1937, buying government bonds with up to 7 per cent of their total assets and up to 25 per cent of the increase in policy reserve.[11] In the following year, the sixteen largest companies promised to increase the upper limit to 10 per cent of total assets and one-third of the increase in policy reserve. The proportion of public bonds to total assets had been increasing since 1938, until it reached over 20 per cent after the Pacific War began in 1941 (refer to Table 8.1). The yield on total assets decreased as the ratio of public bonds increased. It was 5.4 per cent in 1935 but fell to 5.1 per cent in 1940 and 4.8 per cent in 1941 (see Table 8.4).

Being a private association, the JLICA could not enforce strict control over unethical business practices without the support of the government. The relationship between JLICA and the government gradually changed in the 1930s. The case of the establishment of a reinsurance company specializing in clients with disabilities shows the limitations of the private business association. At the suggestion of a medical representative of

Table 8.4. *Yield on total assets (%)*

	Nippon	Daiichi	Meiji	Chiyoda	All companies
1920	7.31	7.30	6.90	7.12	6.96
1925	7.49	7.61	7.08	8.03	6.93
1930	6.11	6.76	5.96	6.45	5.98
1931	6.08	6.35	5.89	6.34	5.82
1932	6.43	6.35	5.88	6.65	6.09
1933	6.38	6.32	5.70	6.28	7.99
1934	5.58	5.96	5.47	5.24	5.52
1935	5.33	5.63	5.41	5.02	5.40
1936	5.32	5.54	5.20	5.00	5.25
1937	5.49	5.48	5.11	5.05	5.26
1938	5.23	5.32	5.10	4.94	5.25
1939	4.91	5.23	5.17	4.92	5.12
1940	4.71	5.18	5.07	4.88	5.10

Sources: *Hoken nenkan*, annual editions.

München Rückversicherungs Gesellshaft, which had been planning to start a Japan–German joint enterprise, the JLICA established a board to investigate the insuring of people with disabilities. The board reported that it would be necessary to inquire into the circumstances of people with disabilities. Such an inquiry was impossible without the cooperation of the Ministry of Home Affairs (MHA), and the JLICA asked it (through the MCI) to support the inquiry. The report on the inquiry was published in 1933. Kyoei Life Reinsurance was planned and established on the basis of the inquiry. Much hope was placed on the reinsurance system as the company expected to handle 70 per cent of the rejected cases of clients with disabilities. When the company began business in 1936, however, most of the large insurance companies ceded scarcely any contracts of people with disabilities to the new company, as large insurance companies were performing well despite such contracts. On the other hand, small companies readily accepted as healthy clients the cases that had been rejected by large companies, without charging any extra premium. Thus, the management of Kyoei Reinsurance had a difficult time at first, but after hostilities between Japan and China broke out, reinsurance of normal life insurances increased and the company grew steadily.[12] The JLICA owed much to government support in getting Kyoei Reinsurance established, but thereafter it extended little help to the company in a highly competitive environment.

The government required the business world to give its support and cooperation immediately after the war started in China in July 1937. The JLICA accepted the request and agreed not to charge extra premiums in the cases of insured who were going to fight in the war, because the government promised that the war would be little more than a limited engagement. Contrary to expectations, however, the war spread all over China and to Southeast Asia. Militarists became increasingly despotic as the war escalated, and life insurance companies were unable to charge any extra premiums. They also had to pay insurance for the dead or injured without assessment. The only way the JLICA could protect business was to set an upper limit of insurance on people who were going to war. Payments for war deaths and injuries in 1938 were twice the amount of the year before, and in 1942 they accounted for about one-fourth of total outlays.

The MCI advised the top management of large companies to reduce dividends so as to increase capital available for public bonds. In October 1937, three months after the war broke out, the JLICA accepted the advice of the MCI and decided to reduce dividend payments by 10 per cent annually. In each of the following two years, all companies reduced their dividends by about 10 per cent in line with this agreement. The war emergency deprived the JLICA of its autonomy. As for extra premiums, the military acted much more despotically in this war than in earlier wars in which Japan had been involved.

Under the controlled economy, Nippon Life, Daiichi Mutual, and Meiji Life were life insurance companies that showed especially remarkable performance. Let us look at the situations at Nippon Life and Meiji Life. The agencies of the two companies were vigorous because attractive and innovative products were being put on the market and both presidents wielded strong leadership over the agencies. Tatsu Naruse, president of Nippon Life, and Shozo Abe, president of Meiji Life, were outstanding figures in the industry.

Naruse, the then chief executive manager, reformed Nippon Life's agency system in 1934. The new system had been in partial use for a decade when Nippon Life, suffering from a decline in new business, completed the reform in 1934. The old agents who had been the main channel of agencies located in rural areas were restricted in their role in collecting premiums, and new special agents were put in place. The new channel consisted of the special agents and salespeople sent to them by the branches. In urban areas the agency system had already been employing agents and salespeople for a year. The number of special agents increased rapidly; by 1935 there were more new agents than old ones, and by 1940 they outnumbered the old agents three to one. There was also a fourfold increase in salespeople during the same period. President Hirose died in 1936 and Naruse assumed the presidency the next year. He was a man with a modern outlook and held many important positions outside Nippon Life. He was active in building close ties between Nippon Life and big business and the government.[13]

The company cultivated the market vigorously in areas other than the Kinki region (where it was located) and performed well. The Kinki region, which had accounted for 35 per cent of the insurance-in-force in 1935, saw this figure fall to 29 per cent in 1940. On the other hand, the company's share in western areas such as Kyushu and Chugoku increased. The establishment of a large sales network was clearly a major factor in increasing new business in the period of a controlled economy. Another factor seems to have been the ability to develop new products, in which Nippon Life was also successful. In 1935 the company sold a new product offering high dividends to compete with other companies' high-dividend products. Nippon Life's share in new business, which was 12.6 per cent in 1934, grew to more than 15 per cent from 1936 onwards thanks to the new product.[14] From 1937, however, it had to reduce dividends in compliance with the decision of the JLICA.

In 1940 Nippon Life designed a new product based on a contribution plan, which at the time was an entirely new idea. The product was suited to the low-interest period and sold well. The share in new business picked up, increasing by 1.5 times over the amount of the previous year. Although it fell again in 1942, the idea was such an obviously good one that it was copied a few years later by some zaibatsu affiliates. These were newcomers to the industry and inexperienced in designing insurance products. Besides Nippon Life, many other companies also sold new low-premium products in 1940 and the years following. It was critical for all companies to lower the assumed rate of interest in order to keep operations steady and healthy. This meant that some mutual companies holding high-dividend policies were obliged to change to low-dividend policies. This seems to be one of the reasons, by the way, why Chiyoda Mutual performed rather poorly during this period.

Meiji Life conducted vigorous sales campaigns in the mid-1930s and launched a new product in 1936. The new insurance offered high dividends and was designed to be successful in a competitive environment. The new product had various merits, including the fact that it was planned to keep high dividends for the long-term, that it introduced a simple and fair dividend system, and that premiums were higher than those for existing products so that more than 90 per cent of profit could be paid back to policyholders. The assumed rate of interest was reduced for managerial stability. This new product was sold in parallel with the old low-premium insurance; this enabled the company to offer a variety of products to fit diversified needs. This is very different from the sales policy of Nippon Life, which stopped selling its old product after introducing a new one in 1940.[15]

The sales network of Meiji Life was also reformed significantly in the 1930s. The company sent several members of their staff to the United States to learn new sales methods. It had been reforming its agent system ever since introducing a low-premium product in 1922. The company invited agents with good performance records to the head office or to branches in an attempt to build up closer relationships with the owners of agencies.

This encouraged the agents to work hard, and they made important contributions to the increase in new business. In 1936 the company reformed its agency system so as to help large agencies control several subagents and a large number of salespeople. At the same time, small and nonperforming agents were closed. Shozo Abe, the managing director in charge of sales, introduced a new policy in 1938 by saying that the company should fight for supremacy by using the largest possible sales force. He drew up a plan to increase salespeople at all branches, in the hope that the company would climb to third place in the industry. The agents were inspired by his words and the salespeople's morale was raised. In 1938 Meiji Life moved into third position in new business rankings after being fifth in 1936 and 1937.

In the first phase of wartime control from the start of the war in China in 1937 to the outbreak of the Pacific War in 1941, governmental control was concentrated mainly on banks in order to raise funds for the war. This was a period in which Japan's heavy and chemical industries were developing, and economic conditions were favourable. The severe competition among life insurance companies was eased by the wartime control. Their products sold well, thanks to the government's savings campaign, and they performed well, together with other industries. They did not put up much resistance to control, and indeed there was no need to do so. However, the conciliatory attitude of the JLICA nurtured in those years turned out to be fatal for the industry when wartime controls were strengthened following the start of the Pacific War, as it culminated in the problems of special premiums for people who went to war and of payment of war risk insurance.

Establishment of the Life Insurance Control Association and Strengthened Controls

The Life Insurance Control Association (LICA) was established in 1942. The government decided to strengthen its control over all financial organizations. It had to raise funds rapidly to finance increasing war expenditures and to step up the production of war materials. Control associations were established in all the important industries in 1941, and the basic plan of a Life Insurance Control Association was announced the same year. After examining the government's plan, the JLICA announced it would not establish such an association but would reform itself to keep its autonomy, while adding three companies that had not been members of the JLICA. This plan was rejected and in 1942 the JLICA was ordered to establish the LICA. The government transferred the administration of insurance to the MOF in 1942, when the MOF exercised tighter control over life insurance companies, and government control over life insurance was tightened from then on. The JLICA, a policy initiator since its establishment, was reorganized as the Life Insurance Society and became, in effect, the industry's social club. The insurance business had finally lost its autonomy.[16]

The transfer of the administration to the MOF meant stricter control over the assets management of life insurance companies. As a result, holdings of national bonds by life insurance companies accelerated under the MOF's administration. As we can see in Table 8.1, the percentage of public bonds among total assets of life insurance companies rose as high as 22.9 per cent in 1942 and 34.4 per cent in 1944. The yield on total assets decreased as the ratio of public bonds increased: from 4.81 per cent in 1941 it fell to 4.15 per cent in 1944.

The LICA unified insurance agreements. All the insurance companies acted in unison to introduce new products such as 'Koa Insurance' in 1943. A plan for a product that did not require medical examinations was initiated in 1941 because of the wartime shortage of medical examiners. This product was in great demand, thus prompting all the insurance companies to promote its sales energetically. The industry had been paying war risks since 1937 and paid less attention to war risks than to nonlife insurance. As the war progressed, however, these contracts resulted in more and more payments on claims and seriously affected the operation of insurance companies.

The government introduced Wartime Death and Injury Insurance in 1943. This was state-run, and all insurance companies—twenty-one life insurance and thirty-four nonlife—were appointed as ceding insurers. The government made this insurance semicompulsory, especially for workers at military factories. The insurance companies found themselves playing the role of agencies receiving commissions from the government.

In 1945 the government established the Life Insurance Central Control Association (LICCA), an organization responsible for reinsurance of war risks, underwriting of Wartime Death and Injury Insurance, and other wartime measures related to life insurance. The LICCA absorbed Kyoei Life Reinsurance Co., the reinsurance company established in 1935.[17]

Mergers among life insurance companies were also strongly promoted by the government from 1939. The number of companies had fallen from thirty-three in 1938 to twenty-nine by 1941 and to twenty-one by 1944. The distinguishing feature of mergers in those years was that their aim was to strengthen the industry. Meiji Life merged with two companies: Fukuju Life Assurance (in 1942) and Yurin Life Assurance (in 1943). Prior to that, in 1936, the MCI suggested to Meiji Life that it merge with Tokiwa Life, but the company refused, for reasons that are unknown. In May 1942 the government enforced a financial enterprise reorganization act aimed at promoting mergers. Meiji Life expected that it would be compelled to reduce high dividends on shares and that capital increase would not be permitted except through mergers. Although Meiji Life did not at first know the name of the companies with which it would be asked to merge, it decided to obey the governmental order. The negotiations were in each case conducted between the parties concerned. Fukuju Life and Yurin Life were both stable medium-sized companies and had a firm business basis.[18] The

Table 8.5. *Stocks and bonds of Nippon Life and Meiji Life, held in 1941 (¥1,000)*

Name	Industry	Nippon	Meiji
Stocks			
Mitsubishi Jukogyo	Steel and Machinery	9,275	12,563
Oji Seishi	Paper	8,077	7,730
Nihon Chisso Hiryo	Nitrogen Chemicals	4,342	2,075
Mitsubishi Honsha	Holding Company	4,042	11,232
Hitachi Seisakusho	Machinery	3,919	—
Nihon Seitetsu	Iron and Steel	3,904	—
Mitsubishi Kogyo	Mining	3,828	11,696
Dainihon Seito	Sugar Refining	3,267	4,288
Tobu Tetsudo	Railway	—	7,738
Asahi Garasu	Glass	—	6,225
Tokyo Gas	Gas	—	5,565
Mitsubishi Ginko	Bank	—	5,217
Tokyo Dento	Electric	—	4,950
Total[a]		126,403	174,822
Bonds			
Nihon Hassoden	Electric	11,340	9,098
Minami Manshu Tetsudo	Railway	11,012	—
Nihon Chisso Hiryo	Nitrogen Chemicals	9,716	6,670
Chosen Shokusan	Korean Bank	8,852	6,467
Toyo Takushoku	China Investment	7,349	—
Kansai Kyuko	Railway	7,084	1,634
Tobu Tetsudo	Railway	4,648	1,295
Nihon Seitetsu	Iron and Steel	4,544	9,348
Asahi Benberg	Synthetic fibre	4,064	—
Tokyo Dento	Electric	1,184	6,507
Toho Denryoku	Electric	3,214	5,698
Nihon Kogyo Ginko	Bank	1,893	5,140
Total[a]		167,032	124,983

[a] Includes the amount of stocks and bonds that are not listed in this table.

Note: Only those companies are listed here whose stock and bond holdings by Nippon Life or Meiji Life amounted to 4 million yen (or reasonably close) or more.

Sources: Nippon Life Insurance (ed.), *Nippon Seimei hyakunen shi*; Nihon Keieishi Kenkyusho [JBHI] (ed.), *Meiji Seimei hyakunen shi shiryo* [Materials on a hundred-year history of Meiji Mutual Life] (Tokyo: Meiji Life Insurance, 1981).

mergers were profitable for Meiji Life, for it was able to gain new business in the territory that it acquired from the two companies.

Nippon Life received all the contracts (transferred *en bloc*) from two companies: Fuji Life Assurance (in 1942) and Aikoku Life Assurance (in 1945). Fuji Life was a small company, and the MCI ordered the transfer of its contracts to Nippon Life in 1941. Aikoku Life, on the other hand, was a large, well-established company that in 1941 held 601 million yen of insurance-in-force, or 10 per cent that of Nippon Life. Bungei Kado, the president of Aikoku Life, was elected president of the LICA and was responsible for promoting reorganization. Aikoku Life, it seems, had no option but to transfer all contracts to Nippon Life because Nippon Life was not willing to merge.[19] In any case, this transfer was undoubtedly very profitable for Nippon Life because Aikoku Life had plenty of good real estate and assets.[20]

Cooperation in the war effort meant not only holding more national bonds but also holding shares and bonds of national policy concerns in Japan, Manchuria, and China and of important munitions companies. Meiji Life and Nippon Life held large quantities of such shares and bonds. The ratio of shares in heavy and chemical industries, including machinery, for example, increased; in the case of Meiji Life, it rose from 16.1 per cent in 1936 to 37.4 per cent in 1941 (see Tables 8.5 and 8.6).[21] Most of them became valueless after Japan's defeat in 1945, and life insurers had to make a new start as mutual companies.

Table 8.6. *Bonds and stocks by industry, 1941*

Industry	Bonds				Stocks			
	Nippon		Meiji		Nippon		Meiji	
	(¥1,000)	(%)	(¥1,000)	(%)	(¥1,000)	(%)	(¥1,000)	(%)
Heavy and chemical	36,079	21.6	27,086	18.1	65,768	52.0	39,871	22.8
Manufacturing	9,612	5.8	14,529	9.7	19,712	15.6	25,575	14.6
Electric	34,078	20.4	46,239	30.8	12,761	10.1	29,139	16.7
Fibre and textiles	9,742	5.8	3,306	2.2	9,704	7.7	10,000	5.7
Railway	45,952	27.5	25,508	17.0	7,047	5.6	8,564	4.8
Finance	23,278	13.9	17,143	11.4	3,772	3.0	19,406	11.1
Gas	—	—	1,008	0.7	1,277	1.0	7,256	4.2
Development	—	—	4,413	3.0	1,020	0.8	1,125	0.6
Distribution and service	7,026	4.2	—	—	200	0.2	—	—
Miscellaneous	1,264	0.8	10,716	7.1	5,413	4.1	33,886	19.4
Total	167,032	100.0	149,948	100.0	126,403	100.0	174,822	100.0

Sources: Nippon Life Insurance (ed.), *Nippon Seimei hyakunen shi*; Meiji Life Assurance (ed.), *Meiji Seimei Hoken 60nen shi*.

Conclusion

The life insurance industry developed as a private business from its first beginnings in the 1880s, and it retained its autonomy until the 1930s. When the hostilities in China broke out in 1937, the government requested the business world to support the government's war policy. The Japan Life Insurance Companies Association complied with this request, and underwrote war insurance without extra premiums. Life insurance companies, under pressure from the militarists, were thereafter unable to impose extra premiums and were even compelled to pay compensation for wartime death and injury without inspection. This was in marked contrast to what happened in the Russo-Japanese War, when the militarists agreed with insurance companies on wartime extra premiums. Events in 1937 reveal the despotism as well as the ignorance concerning insurance on the part of the militarists in the late 1930s.

The revision of the Insurance Business Law in 1939 was a severe blow to the autonomy of the insurance industry. The MOF applied stricter controls over the companies' fund management and promoted mergers and liquidations. After war broke out between Japan and the United States, the Life Insurance Control Association was established in 1942 in order to strengthen control. The establishment of the LICA dealt a fatal blow to the autonomy of life insurance companies, because it took control of fund management, insurance sales, product lines, and mergers or transfers of contracts. The case of Aikoku Life was a special one, as it was dissolved after the transfer. The company itself had grown through having other small companies transferred to it, and reportedly it was the only case of the transfer of contracts of a well-performing company.

Many large companies, such as Nippon Life and Meiji Life, took advantage of the wartime controls and grew rapidly. They were protected against severe competition from small companies by governmental restrictions, which enabled cheap tariffs. The vital factor in winning against the competition was the scale of the sales network rather than the premium rates. The promotion of mergers by the MOF also turned to their advantage, as has been pointed out earlier. Both individual company histories and the history of the industry report that the industry lost its autonomy under wartime control. This long-term assessment made after the war ended is correct, because life insurance companies suffered such severe damage that they had to make new starts as mutual concerns after the Pacific War, but it should also be remembered that they gained great advantages from the wartime control.

The legacy of the industry's two dimensions mentioned in the introduction can be seen in this account. Large companies reflect the modern dimension: they had a sound management basis, hired many actuaries and medical examiners, and had the ability to design attractive products, build up large, well-organized sales networks, offer large and good-performance contracts to their upper-class customers, and consequently realize sizeable profits. They could to some extent refuse government control because of the size of their assets. In contrast, the small companies in a way reflect the traditional dimension, even though they were far more sophisticated than the pseudo insurance operators of the Meiji era. Their main target was the general populace, whose income was only a little higher than that of the buyers of postal insurance. These companies managed to grow in the 1920s and 1930s because this portion of the population increased steadily during this period.

NOTES

1. According to this method, extra money is paid up front by the insured, in the form of a higher expense loading. Subsequent premium payments are reduced for a given period to make up for the heavier payment made earlier.
2. Chiyoda Life Insurance (ed.), *Gojunen shi* [A fifty-year history] (Tokyo: Chiyoda Life Insurance, 1955).
3. In Japan the population drift from villages to cities, and from self-management to employees, began during the First World War. The urban white-collar class grew in the 1920s, and this tendency became predominant in 1935 and after. See Makiko Nakamura, *Hito no ido to kindaika* [Social mobility in modern Japan] (Tokyo: Yushindo Kobunsha, 1999), 133–43.
4. Chiyoda Life Insurance, *Gojunen shi*, 91–112.
5. Hoken Ginko Jiho Sha (ed.), *Honpo seimei hoken gyoshi* [The history of life insurance in Japan] (Tokyo: Hoken Ginko Jiho Sha, 1933); Hoken Kenkyu Sho (ed.), *Nihon hoken gyoshi* [The history of insurance in Japan] (Tokyo: Hoken Kenkyu Sho, 1980), 27–8.
6. Chiyoda Life Insurance, *Gojunen shi*, 91–112.
7. Nippon Life Insurance (ed.), *Nippon seimei hyakunen shi* [A hundred-year history of Nippon Life Insurance] (Osaka: Nippon Life Insurance, 1992), 497.
8. JBHI (ed.), *Meiji Seimei hyakunen shi* [A hundred-year history of Meiji Life Insurance] (Tokyo: Meiji Life Insurance, 1981), 106–9.
9. Kenji Usami, *Seimei hokengyo 100nen shiron* [A historical inquiry into 100 years of life insurance] (Tokyo: Yuhikaku, 1984), 136.
10. Nippon Life Insurance, *Nippon seimei hyakunen shi*, 564.
11. Government bonds held by banks amounted to over 20 per cent of deposits in 1937. This rose to 27 per cent in 1940 and to 38 per cent in 1944. Those held by life insurance companies were 11, 19, and 35 per cent, respectively. It is obvious that life insurance contributed marginally to promoting the acceptance of bonds.

12. Kyoei Life Insurance (ed.), *Kyoei Seimei shi-ko* [History of Kyoei Life Insurance] (Tokyo: Kyoei Life Insurance, 1963), 20–31.
13. Nippon Life Insurance, *Nippon seimei hyakunen shi*, 696.
14. Daiichi Mutual also held a 'high-dividend, high-premium' policy in the 1920s. It is not clear why the company showed a comparably good performance in the late 1930s. A distinguishing feature of Daiichi Mutual's contracts was that average insurance money was at a high level. The average of new business of Daiichi Mutual was always the highest in the industry—about 1.57 times that of Nippon Life and 1.25 times that of Meiji Life in 1937. This suggests that the majority of customers were probably from the urban upper class, whose livelihood was somewhat more stable than that of the general populace. See Daiichi Life Insurance (ed.), *Daiichi Seimei nanajunen shi* [Seventy-year history of Daiichi Life] (Tokyo: Daiichi Life Insurance, 1972), 71–91.
15. The company states that it was more or less due to a technical reason that it replaced the old product. The author assumes that the new product in the contribution plan was considered capable of meeting a variety of needs. See Nippon Life Insurance, *Nippon seimei hyakunen shi*, 684–6.
16. Usami, *Seimeihokengyo 100nen shiron*, 188.
17. Kyoei Life Insurance, *Kyoei Seimei Shi-ko*, 20–31.
18. JBHI, *Meiji seimei hyakunenshi*, 134–7.
19. Nippon Life Insurance, *Nippon seimei hyakunen shi*, 720–40.
20. Nippon Life Insurance, *Nippon seimei hyakunen shi*, 736–8.
21. Meiji Life Assurance (ed.), *Meiji Seimei Hoken 60 nen shi* [Sixty-year history of Meiji Life Assurance] (Tokyo: Meiji Life Assurance, 1942), 272.

9

Growth Stocks for Middle-class Investors: Merrill Lynch & Co., 1914–41

EDWIN J. PERKINS

Introduction

One of the major consequences of the First World War was that New York surpassed London as the world's leading financial centre. Despite challenges from Tokyo in the late 1980s, New York has retained its dominant position in world capital markets.[1] Today, the combined market value of the corporate shares listed on the New York Stock Exchange and its main competitor, Nasdaq, top the world's equity markets by a large margin.[2]

Here, at the dawn of the twenty-first century, Americans have a higher participation rate in equity markets than the citizens of any other nation. Approximately two-thirds of US households currently own common stock either through direct investment or indirectly through mutual funds.[3] In the last quarter of the twentieth century, the managers of private pension plans, which are typically designed for a broad range of employees from top executives to assembly line workers, have increasingly focused on the acquisition of equities rather than bonds for their portfolios. Over 40 per cent of the net worth of American households is represented by common stocks. Meanwhile, less than 10 per cent of German households and 15 per cent of French households own stocks directly or indirectly. For Britain, the participation rates are higher than on the continent, but common stocks nonetheless constitute a much lower percentage of household net worth than in the United States.[4] For Japan, stocks accounted for only 6 per cent of the typical household's financial assets in the late 1990s.[5]

Among the important factors accounting for the success of American equity markets over the course of the twentieth century was an emphasis, first, on growth stocks as prudent vehicles for long-term investment and, second, on the solicitation of middle-class households as participants in the equity markets. The brokerage firm most closely associated with broadening the base of stock ownership was Merrill Lynch & Co. Headquartered in New York, the firm currently has hundreds of offices across the United States and around the globe, including Japan. During the 1990s Merrill Lynch was the largest underwriter of stock and bond issues in the global securities markets.[6]

This firm's emphasis on growth stocks and the solicitation of middle-class households had its origins in the interwar period. Charles Merrill, the founder, was an advocate of these dual strategies from the date he opened a small office in the Wall Street district in 1914.[7] He and partner Edmund Lynch applied these principles with great success during the boom years of the 1920s. The firm's progress was interrupted by the Great Depression; the two senior partners went into semiretirement during the 1930s, and they were not actively involved in the securities markets. In the early 1940s Merrill was coaxed back into a management position, and his innovative investment ideas and marketing concepts were reinstituted. In this instance, his strategies were perpetuated.

Investment in Stocks Prior to the First World War

Prior to the First World War the percentage of US households owning securities of all types was quite small.[8] Investors in securities were typically members of the upper class—roughly, the top 5 to 10 per cent of wealthholders. The primary objective of investors was to generate a steady income from their financial assets. Owning securities was viewed as a sound strategy for maintaining affluent lifestyles and preserving an inheritance. In contrast, few middle-class households owned securities of any variety. Instead, middle-income households, in addition to building equity in their homes, invested primarily in savings accounts at deposit banks, where they earned minimal interest rates.

A second vehicle for long-term saving, which became increasing popular in the early twentieth century for households in all income groups, was life insurance.[9] Most life insurance contracts in the first half of the twentieth century were 'whole-life policies' that combined in one convenient premium two related, but independent, financial services. One portion of the premium paid for term insurance; it provided a lump sum payment to beneficiaries upon the death of the insured. The second portion of the premium represented savings that increased the cash value of a given policy over time, invariably at a modest interest rate. The cash surrender value of the policy could be used to fund retirement if the insured lived to a ripe old age and opted for an annuity.

Common stock ownership as a path to upward mobility was not a viable option for the vast majority of American households prior to the 1920s. Neither the leading investment banking firms on Wall Street nor the tens of thousands of commercial banks scattered across the United States made any serious effort to encourage their customers to purchase common stocks.[10] Corporate securities were associated with the savings strategies of the already wealthy, and therefore not pertinent to the lives of the aspiring middle classes.

In the nineteenth century, what today we call growth stocks were likewise not popular investment vehicles. Indeed, the concept itself had not yet emerged; the two words—growth and securities—were rarely, if ever, linked in discussions of investment options. At the turn of the last century, the types of securities regularly available in US financial markets fell overwhelmingly into four main categories: fixed-income bonds issued by governments and railroads were the two largest categories; stocks issued by railroads plus a few industrial and service firms were two smaller categories. The powerful investment banking houses on Wall Street, such as J.P. Morgan and Kuhn Loeb, overwhelmingly recommended to their clients, whether financial institutions like insurance companies or wealthy individuals, the purchase of bonds with fixed interest rates and distant maturity dates. Avoiding the loss of capital was a major concern in this era, and the effects of inflation were ignored.[11] Occasionally, the leading investment banking firms sponsored an issue of preferred stock, but these securities, like bonds, had limited appreciation potential.[12]

When a few atypical customers of the mainstream investment banking houses insisted on diversifying their portfolios by adding equities, conservative advisors invariably recommended the common stocks of railroads and industrial corporations with long-standing records of steady dividend payments. Since the volume of financial information available to the public for careful analysis was usually scant, the most reliable method of judging the suitability of any common stock for investment was with reference to its past dividend record. Most corporations listed on the New York Stock Exchange paid out a high percentage of their annual earnings in dividends. As a result, the yields on common stocks were often in the range of 7–12 per cent.

But where there was the opportunity to earn higher returns that exceeded the modest yields available on bonds and saving accounts, there was also the element of added risk. During a business contraction, a corporation might reduce, or temporarily suspend, dividend payments on its common stock. Dividends were not contractual obligations. Because of uncertainties about possible interruptions in dividend payments, investment advisors counselled that common stocks were unsuitable for prudent investors. Indeed, the consensus among professionals who offered financial advice was that common stocks as a broad class of securities were inherently speculative and therefore dangerous. Equities might meet the requirements of active traders seeking instant wealth, but they did not qualify as sensible vehicles for prudent investors.[13]

The important point here is that the majority of investors, decades ago, did not anticipate the realization of sizable long-term capital gains on their investments in corporate securities. They aimed for a secure fixed income. Any appreciation in an investment portfolio was always a welcome bene-fit, of course, but achieving that goal was rarely an important considera-tion. Once investors had decided to add equities to their portfolios, the corporation's dividend record was the most important consideration in the selection process. The potential for price appreciation was invariably a sec-ondary factor when investment experts discussed portfolio strategies with their wealthy clients.

The only people who regularly bought and sold the common stocks of companies with erratic earnings and irregular dividend payments were participants who were pejoratively labelled 'speculators' in Wall Street cir-cles. They were traders with short-term objectives or perhaps even an intermediate horizon. They maintained accounts with brokerage firms that specialized in providing transactions services. Brokerage firms were typ-ically small, independent enterprises in the nation's large and mid-sized cities. They handled routine transactions in secondary markets for modest fees. Some brokerage houses also acted as dealers in unlisted securities.

This group was atypical because these investors were, in fact, aggress-ively seeking capital gains. Many people with active brokerage accounts were from the middle class, mostly the upper middle class; they had dreams of acquiring greater wealth in a short period of time. This category of investors was willing to accept the risk of interrupted dividend pay-ments and capital losses. Many traders hoped that widespread rumours of improving corporate profitability, whether based on fact or fiction, would give a sharp boost to the prices of the common stocks they owned; alter-natively, they hoped the circulation of unfavourable rumours would depress the stocks in which they held short positions. Many securities traders also dealt in the derivative markets: puts, options, and other types of risky futures contracts. They traded a wide range of corporate stocks, including smaller issues not listed on the organized exchanges. Some specu-lators became shrewd traders; a few were able to realize their ambitions and accumulate enough wealth to move up the economic ladder and join the upper crust. The US upper class was always fluid, and any family with sufficient financial resources could usually gain social acceptance within one or two generations.

Although exceptions to almost any broad generalization can usually be cited, it seems safe to conclude that the overwhelming majority of investors did not accumulate large blocks of common stocks and then hold their positions for years in anticipation of realizing substantial long-term capital gains. That style of investing was exceedingly uncommon, even if we include the ranks of investment professionals and other insiders on Wall Street itself. Even the senior partners in the leading investment banking firms tended to avoid significant long-term commitments to equities. Not hypocrites, they listened to their own advice and adhered to its broad principles of risk avoidance.

To summarize quickly before going forward, investors in securities in the early twentieth century were normally either very conservative, holding bonds plus a few preferred stocks, or they were speculative traders, holding securities or derivatives with the aim of realizing quick gains in periods measured in weeks or months. Between these two polar positions, there was little compromise, and little blending of investment strategies. Diversification, meaning the inclusion of various types of stocks and bonds in a given portfolio, was not a widely accepted investment concept.

What we would label as growth companies today were, in the late nineteenth and early twentieth centuries, almost exclusively privately held corporations. The initial involvement of these entrepreneurial firms in the capital markets was usually as the issuer of long-term bonds, or occasionally a mixture of bonds and preferred stock; the latter had a fixed dividend rate. Only after a corporation had reached a secure competitive position with little fear of earnings reverses were its owner-managers encouraged by the leading investment bankers to offer common stock for sale to the general public. Indeed, the most prominent investment banking firms on Wall Street were normally unwilling to sponsor any issue of common stock unless they were reasonably confident the corporation could sustain a healthy dividend. This narrow outlook meant that the common stocks listed on the New York Stock Exchange as late as 1910 were primarily the securities of large corporate enterprises in stable economic sectors— mainly the railroads and concentrated industries not threatened by serious competitive forces.

Hindrance to Widespread Middle-class Investment in Stocks

In a long career on Wall Street, which included a detour in the 1930s, Charles Merrill sought to bridge the chasm between stuffy conservatism and rampant speculation. He was an early promoter of the common stocks of corporations that seemed to possess better than average potential for earnings growth. He urged customers to add to their portfolios the common stocks of medium-sized corporations with increasing sales volume and detailed plans for continued expansion. Unlike most Wall Street experts, he believed investors should accumulate a balanced and diversified portfolio of securities. He thought there was a place among those investments for common stocks that had the potential to produce sizable capital gains over periods of five to ten years. The potential advantages of common stocks for more adventurous investors were actually twofold. First, the rising annual dividends of successful corporations could enhance the stockholder's income stream over time. Second, by taking sensible risks, long-term investors could steadily build added wealth rather than being merely satisfied with the maintenance of their principal.

Also contrary to the prevailing view on Wall Street, Merrill was an ardent believer in the radical concept that investment firms should attempt to solicit customers from the ranks of middle-income households. Numerous constituencies raised serious objections to middle-class involvement in the securities markets. Some voices concentrated on consumer protection issues. Most public commentators warned citizens about the dangers of investing in the stock market. Critics tended to equate common stocks with the purchase of lottery tickets and other forms of gambling. Only extraordinarily lucky investors allegedly profited in the stock market; the majority lost money; and in the very worst cases, their life savings might be severely diminished. Stock prices were volatile, critics warned, and subject to price manipulation by insiders on the trading floor of the exchanges. Under these unsafe circumstances, middle-class households were advised to steer clear of the erratic stock market.

Most brokerage firms in the early twentieth century were not keenly interested in the mass solicitation of middle-class households, and for very practical reasons. Individuals with moderate incomes typically opened small accounts; the potential for generating substantial commissions on the irregular trades of small accounts was severely limited. Brokerage firms did not have effective cost accounting systems to measure with precision the profitability of various types of customer accounts, but the managers of brokerage firms knew intuitively that the majority of small accounts probably cost more to administer than the commission revenues they generated.

A third factor that discouraged the involvement of middle-class households were the rigid rules governing members of the New York Stock Exchange and other organized exchanges with respect to advertising. Following the example set by professional organizations of physicians, dentists, accountants, and lawyers, the NYSE discouraged advertising by member firms by severely limiting the content. The exchanges permitted bare-bones announcements that listed the name of the firm, its street address, and the scope of its specialized services, but little else. Any advertising copy that went beyond that minimal standard was labelled 'unprofessional' and 'unethical', and violators could lose access to the trading floor of the securities exchanges.[14]

In this era the relationship between a financial services firm and its existing customers was considered inviolate. Advertisements which might induce an investor to switch from one firm to another were considered a breach of etiquette, a form of 'unfair' or 'underhanded' competition. The powerful firms that provided the leadership of the NYSE valued the maintenance of the status quo, and they erected organizational roadblocks to prevent upstart firms from encroaching on their territory. One of the inherent assumptions, pervasive on Wall Street, was that the total number of customers was largely fixed, since investors were presumably restricted to upper-class households, which were, by definition, a narrow group. The prevailing logic was that advertising tended to disrupt an essentially zero-sum game, and thus it was unwelcome in respectable circles.

Early Business Experience of Charles Merrill and Edmund Lynch

Charles Merrill was born in northern Florida in 1885. His father was a physician who practised medicine in a resort town catering to winter tourists. After high school, Merrill attended Amherst College and the University of Michigan, but he left college after three years, never earning an undergraduate degree. He moved to New York City in 1907 seeking fame and fortune and eventually landed a position in the financial services sector.[15] At George Burr & Co., a small firm on the fringes of Wall Street, Merrill headed the newly established bond department. Merrill hired Edmund Lynch, another ambitious young man about his age, as a securities salesperson.

The willingness to adopt unorthodox promotional techniques was one of the hallmarks of Merrill's half-century on Wall Street. Because his employer was not a formal member of the NYSE, Merrill was granted a fair amount of leeway in formulating marketing strategies. He was introduced to the power of advertising by Rudolph Guenther, the representative of an unconventional agency that catered to the financial services sector. At Guenther's urging, Merrill experimented with direct mail solicitations and newspaper ads, and the responses were very encouraging. Merrill saw nothing inherently wrong with the active solicitation of potential investors, so long as the information provided was accurate and included no misleading statements about the potential risks and rewards of various securities.[16] Since these bond issues, which were normally handled on a best efforts basis, added up to a relatively modest sum by Wall Street standards, usually under $1 million, the firm solicited not only wealthy investors, but also less affluent families from the upper middle class.

While still employed at George Burr & Co., Merrill published a maga-zine article in which he enunciated a series of basic principles that guided his career for the next half-century.[17] Addressing the needs of 'Mr. Average Investor', the author stressed the importance of taking into consideration an individual's overall circumstances before recommending any type of investment strategy. For retirees, who typically sought a steady income in old age, the preservation of capital deserved top priority; savings accounts, highly rated bonds, and perhaps a sprinkling of quality preferred stocks were therefore appropriate. For younger households, Merrill argued, a diversified portfolio of financial assets that included common stocks as well as a mixture of bank savings and life insurance constituted a sensible investment plan. Decades later, in the 1940s, these principles became the basis for the 'Know Your Customer' rule that Merrill Lynch & Co. imposed on thousands of its brokers and sales representatives.

In the same magazine article Merrill advocated the solicitation and maintenance of a broad customer base for firms in the brokerage field. He thought of breadth both in terms of geographical dispersion and house-hold income. 'Having thousands of customers scattered throughout the United States is infinitely preferable', he wrote, 'to being dependent upon the fluctuating buying power of a small and perhaps on the whole wealth-ier group of investors in any one section'. His proclamations about the advantages of possessing branch offices in many locales and serving thou-sands of middle-class customers were disregarded at the time, but they became a reality a quarter century later.

During his four years with George Burr & Co., Merrill had the opportun-ity to issue a limited volume of securities for chain stores in the retail sec-tor of the US economy. His exposure to the innovative entrepreneurs driving forward this commercial sector made an enormous impression—and the impression was lasting; in due course the business strategies of these innovators were imitated by Merrill himself. Regional chains of gro-cery stores, led by A&P (Atlantic & Pacific Tea Co.), emerged in the last quarter of the nineteenth century.[18] By the turn of the century, other retail-ers had climbed onto the bandwagon, among them 'variety' stores and 'five-and-dime' stores that sold inexpensive but practical merchandise to all classes of customers. The chains relied on economies of scale and scope to lower costs in both the acquisition and the distribution of goods, and they passed on the bulk of the savings to customers through lower prices.[19]

Small, independent retailers, with higher prices and lower volume, were threatened by this innovative retail concept, and they mobilized to halt the spread of chain stores through political action. The independents spon-sored legislation at the state level that placed escalating taxes on the mul-tiple outlets of retail chains; at the national level they lobbied for rules and regulations that prohibited chains from engaging in vigorous price com-petition. These political roadblocks slowed the expansion of chains in some regions, but over time, quality goods at lower prices proved popular with consumers and voters, and the restrictive laws were eventually modified or eliminated.

The equities of chain stores were, in retrospect, among the first identifiable group of twentieth-century growth stocks in the financial marketplace. Unlike railroads and most manufacturing firms, the initial startup costs for entry into retailing were not beyond the means of millions of ambitious citizens in thousands of locations, both urban and rural. Chain store entrepreneurs usually began with a single retail outlet and gradually expanded the number of locations. The prosperous firms evolved from proprietorships or partnerships into corporations. The major restraint on their rate of expansion in regional markets was typically financial—the lack of access to long-term capital to open additional store sites.

The first chain store that Merrill assisted in raising capital in the New York market was S.S. Kresge & Co. The principal owner, Sebastian Kresge, had opened his first variety store in Detroit, Michigan, and by 1912, the chain operated over 60 stores in the Midwest. In cooperation with Hallgarten & Co., a second-tier investment firm on Wall Street, Merrill arranged for George Burr & Co. to issue $2 million in preferred stock, plus 10,000 shares of common stock. The chain planned to use the proceeds of the underwriting to open an additional thirteen stores in 1913. Sebastian Kresge gave the underwriters the opportunity to acquire shares of the common stock before any were offered to the general public, a common practice in this era, and Merrill personally subscribed to 1,000 shares. The corporation continued to expand, and the price of its common stock rose in tandem. Merrill profited handsomely from this early investment in the retail sector.

In January 1914 Charles Merrill opened his own small office on Wall Street. He recruited Edmund Lynch as a partner a few months later, and the firm of Merrill, Lynch & Co. was created. The outbreak of the First World War in the late summer of 1914 led to the temporary closure of the New York Stock Exchange and nearly bankrupted the partnership in its first year of operations. The two principals cut expenses to the bone, and luckily they survived.

When the NYSE removed all restraints on trading in February 1915, Merrill pursued an underwriting deal with John McCrory, the founder and principal owner of the McCrory chain of five-and-dime stores. In this instance, Merrill Lynch cooperated with an investment firm in Chicago that arranged for the placement of $725,000 in mortgage bonds on the chain's real estate holdings. Merrill Lynch & Co. assumed responsibility for selling $1.25 million of 7 per cent cumulative preferred stock. In payment for their services, the partners received no cash; instead, they received as compensation about 20 per cent of the chain's outstanding common stock. When McCrory's stock price rose steadily over the next decade, the partners realized substantial capital gains.

In 1916 the partnership had its first opportunity to provide underwriting services for the retail grocery sector. The partners joined a syndicate in sponsoring an issue of securities for the Acme Tea Co., which was headquartered in Philadelphia and operated more than 400 grocery stores in eighty towns and cities along the East Coast. In a second major transaction, the firm helped to finance a $10 million merger of two major grocery chains in the New York area—Jones Brothers Tea Co. and Grand Union Tea Co. A decade later, the grocery sector became the primary focus of Charles Merrill's interests, so these early deals are noteworthy.

Following the American entry into the First World War in 1917, both Charles Merrill and Edmund Lynch joined the US Army. They turned the management of the firm over to trusted subordinates. Neither partner ever left American shores for the front lines in Europe, however. Merrill became a flight instructor for airplane pilots in the Army Air Corps, and Lynch trained on horseback for the cavalry. After the Armistice in 1918, they returned to New York and immediately resumed their financial careers.

In the 1920s Merrill Lynch strengthened its ties to the expanding retail sector. In addition to raising additional capital for the Kresge and McCrory chains, the firm became an underwriter for J.C. Penney & Co. The Penney chain of variety stores was among the nation's oldest, dating back to the late nineteenth century, and it ranked as one of the most successful in terms of its geographic spread and profitability. Merrill Lynch & Co. subsequently underwrote securities for numerous national and regional chains of specialty stores that offered a broad range of consumer goods— including shoes, drugs and cosmetics, ready-to-wear clothing, and automobile supplies. The popularity of the automobile gave millions of American households easy access to the mushrooming outlets of chain stores, which featured standard goods at competitive prices. Generally speaking, Merrill had a penchant for issuing senior securities, whether bonds or preferred stock, with convertibility features or with warrants attached. These 'sweeteners' permitted investors in senior securities to acquire the company's common stock at favourable prices in a rising market. With these extra inducements, all parties contributing to a firm's capitalization would share in the financial benefits if management was able to generate healthy sales and profits. Among the main benefactors of these sweeteners was the partnership itself. Over the years, Merrill Lynch accumulated thousands of shares of the common stock of its underwriting clients, and it held a substantial portion of these financial assets as long-term investments. When their corporate clients expanded their sales and profits, the partners' net worth increased correspondingly. Together, Merrill and Lynch put their faith in the common stocks of growth companies long before that descriptive terminology had entered the everyday language of Wall Street.

As the firm's tenth anniversary approached in January 1924, Merrill drafted a broad statement that summarized the partnership's accomplishments.[20] Always a strong believer in the value of publicity, unlike the vast majority of his contemporaries on Wall Street, Merrill mailed the upbeat message to every customer, and he arranged for its release to the business press. 'During the last ten years we have sponsored, issued, wholesaled, or retailed many millions of securities', he wrote; 'our business is to serve all classes of security buyers'. Nonetheless, he observed: 'The great American fortunes had been made by shareholders and not by bondholders'. Merrill continued: 'For our part we have invested a certain definite percentage of our own money in all the concerns financed by us. By far, the larger part of our present resources has come through a faithful adherence to this policy.' In other words, the partners put into practice what they had been consistently preaching to their retail customers. Merrill believed in the future of the enterprises that he financed, and by maintaining a substantial ownership position, his firm was functioning very much like modern merchant bankers.

Merrill Lynch offered its customers a fresh approach to investing in securities. The partners recommended a middle-of-the-road strategy, neither highly speculative nor extremely conservative. The partners asserted that speculative trading was no longer the only path to enhanced wealth; long-term investments in growth stocks was an alternative strategy for accomplishing that same ambitious goal. The process took longer, years rather than months, but the path to greater riches was safer and surer. Charles Merrill and Edmund Lynch, now multimillionaires, were living proof of the wisdom of their nontraditional advice. The partners had become exceedingly wealthy by investing in the equities of their underwriting clients in the expanding chain store sector of the US economy.

Two of the partnership's investments deserve more detailed attention. In the early 1920s the partners went beyond their role as minority shareholders in a prosperous enterprise and became the principal owners of a major firm in the motion picture industry. They assumed control of Pathe Exchange, the American subsidiary of the pioneering French motion picture producer and distributor.[21] In the silent era, many of the films shown in the United States originated in Europe. After its imported films had proven popular with American audiences, Pathe established complementary production facilities in the United States. Pathe's innovative newsreel format was particularly successful, and it was widely distributed to theatres across the nation.

The outbreak of the First World War disrupted movie production in France, and, in an effort to sustain the company's operations overseas, Pathe decided to add Charles Merrill and Edmund Lynch to the board of directors of its American subsidiary. When the war ended, Merrill Lynch & Co. had the opportunity to assume ownership of the company's

American assets, including its production and distribution facilities. Lynch spent three months in Paris ironing out the details of the sale. When he returned, Lynch became the de facto CEO of Pathe Exchange. He curtailed film production, except for the trademark newsreels, and concentrated on the distribution end of the movie business. Whereas most of the industry's production facilities had moved to southern California by 1920, all the major studios kept their national distribution networks headquartered in New York.

The partners' investment in Pathe Exchange was highly profitable. The motion picture industry was, like retail chain stores, in a rapid growth phase in the 1920s. Theatres, large and small, sprang up almost everywhere in the United States. Even farmers in remote rural areas rode in horse-drawn wagons or in their new Ford Model-T automobiles to the nearest small town or village for weekend exhibitions. By 1925 most citizens in urban areas attended the movies at least once a week.

In the middle of the decade the trend toward vertical integration and horizontal consolidation in the motion picture sector seemed irreversible, and Merrill Lynch decided to sell Pathe Exchange to the highest bidder. The partners concluded that, to remain competitive, they would need to invest an additional $150 million to enter the exhibition end of the business. Raising that enormous sum would require them to share managerial control with outsiders, and it would dictate that they exit the investment banking field and devote all of their time and energies to motion pictures. Instead, the partners sold Pathe Exchange to Joseph Kennedy, the future head of the Securities and Exchange Commission and the father of President John F. Kennedy.

The partners' second major transaction in the 1920s was closely related to the chain store sector with which the firm had been so closely linked, and this investment proved more lasting. The partners used the proceeds from the sale of Pathe Exchange to acquire a controlling share of the common stock of Safeway Stores, a grocery chain with West Coast origins. Through a series of mergers and acquisitions orchestrated by Charles Merrill in the late 1920s, Safeway became the leader in the western states and one of the nation's top five grocery chains.

In a broad statement addressed to employees, customers, and the investing public in January 1929, Merrill reflected on his experiences with the chain stores. 'I believe the popularity of chain store securities is due to the fact that the public in general believes that chain stores will be the main factor in solving the problem of distribution'. He continued: 'I can say with honesty and sincerity that the executives of the large chain stores rank among the highest, if not the highest, as to downright character. The men behind the big chain stores, . . . without a single exception, as far as I know, began life under modest circumstances'. With respect to his firm's close association with Safeway Stores, Merrill was direct and forthright: 'As we

are faithful to this trust, and alive to the responsibilities to the stockholders and to the consuming public, we will continue to grow and prosper.'[22]

Semiretirement

Beginning in early 1928 and continuing into 1929, Merrill became convinced that common stock prices had risen to unsustainable heights and
that the stock market was primed for a major correction.[23] In a form letter
addressed to customers with active accounts in March 1928, Merrill recommended that investors exercise extreme caution before making any additional commitments to common stocks. He was particularly worried about
customers who had purchased stocks on margin with borrowed funds.
'We do not urge that you sell securities indiscriminately, but we do advise,
in no uncertain terms, that you . . . lighten your obligations, or better still,
pay them off entirely'.[24] Customers who listened carefully to this message
fared much better than unwary investors over the next three or four turbulent years.

Because of Merrill's foresight in predicting the huge decline in security
prices, the partners emerged relatively unscathed by the crash in October
1929 and its aftermath. The firm had liquidated much of its portfolio,
including the common stock of many of the chain stores it had financed
over the last decade. The only exceptions to this mass liquidation were the
shares of Safeway Stores plus a few other grocery chains also located on
the West Coast.

Given the magnitude of the decline in the stock market and because of
other personal considerations, the two senior partners decided to withdraw from active participation in the financial markets in 1930. They transferred their six small retail outlets to E.A. Pierce & Co., one of the leading
chains of regional brokerage offices, and they invested a total of $3.8 mil-
lion in fresh capital in that firm. Charles Merrill and Edmund Lynch signed
a partnership agreement with E.A. Pierce with a ten-year expiration date.
They became passive, inactive partners in the brokerage house. Meanwhile,
Merrill Lynch & Co. was not dissolved but functioned with a skeleton staff
throughout the 1930s. Like most of its investment banking peers on Wall
Street, the firm did little business over the next decade because of the
depressed economy. Lynch retired to his palatial estate on Long Island.
Merrill chose semiretirement. He devoted up to half his boundless energ-
ies to monitoring closely his huge investment in Safeway Stores. In short,
Merrill left the securities field and shifted his interests to a totally different
business sector. He was now involved in the delivery of foodstuffs to a

mass market through a network of outlets in thousands of scattered locations.

In order to advance the narrative, we must skip lightly over Merrill's decade of involvement with Safeway Stores. He never held a management position nor did he serve as chair of the board of directors, but he held a controlling interest in the company. He consulted at length with Safeway officials on every major strategic decision. Because groceries supplied the singular goods that consumers literally could not live without, Safeway and most of its peers, large and small, remained profitable throughout the depression years. Safeway halted its programme of geographical expansion in the early 1930s, but it never retrenched. The company was either the second or the third largest grocery chain in the nation during the 1930s. Merrill gained a great deal of satisfaction from his Safeway years, and he subsequently applied many of the lessons he had learned from the mass marketing of foodstuffs to the brokerage field.

Before moving forward, we should also cite briefly the reform movement at the federal level that transformed the securities sector in the mid-1930s. Congress enacted a series of laws that increased the transparency of securities markets, and it created a new regulatory agency, the Securities and Exchange Commission, to exercise oversight and to enforce the rules and regulations.[25] Merrill was not active in the reform movement, although he agreed with its thrust. E.A. Pierce was quite active, however; he was one of the few Wall Street figures to endorse the proposed legislation in candid testimony before congressional committees. Most of the representatives of Wall Street firms were adamantly opposed to any change in the securities laws despite the ravages of the Great Depression.

A third topic that we must mention in this context was the unexpected death of Edmund Lynch, at age fifty-two, in 1938. Even in absentia, Lynch's name remained on the masthead, however, since Charles Merrill absolutely insisted on its inclusion in all future partnership agreements.

Quitting Semiretirement

In the fall of 1939, Merrill's partnership agreement with E.A. Pierce was about to expire, and discussions about its renewal or its abandonment came to the fore. Pierce's chain of brokerage offices had been unprofitable since the mid-1930s. Trading volume on the New York Stock Exchange had fallen dramatically and irreversibly after the recession of 1937. The brokerage firm's capital base had been severely weakened, and its dissolution seemed highly probable. Then, to the great surprise of almost everyone in the financial services sector, Charles Merrill played the role of white knight; he rode to the rescue and saved the struggling enterprise.

The person most responsible for convincing Merrill to return for a second career on Wall Street was Winthrop Smith.[26] A junior partner in Merrill, Lynch & Co. in the late 1920s, Smith had transferred to E.A. Pierce & Co. in the realignment of 1930. Thereafter, he became manager of the chain's Chicago branch. With the probable breakup of the Pierce firm on the horizon, Smith arranged a series of meetings with Merrill starting in October 1939. He gathered a cache of financial data for careful analysis. Based on the implementation of various cost control measures, Smith projected a return to profitability within a year or two even under the most dire circumstances. Merrill expressed a keen interest in Smith's proposal. Before agreeing to proceed, Merrill sought the advice of Ted Braun, a management consultant in Los Angeles with close ties to Safeway Stores.[27] Together, Merrill, Smith, and Braun developed a strategic plan that, in time, revolutionized the entire US brokerage sector.

Merrill agreed to a merger that combined Merrill Lynch & Co. with E.A. Pierce & Co. and, equally important, he consented to return to Wall Street as directing partner (CEO) of the enterprise. To keep the firm afloat, he provided $4.5 million in fresh capital; that investment constituted the firm's entire capitalization during the first year of operations. A year later, the partners negotiated a merger with another regional brokerage chain— Fenner & Beane. By the end of 1941, Merrill Lynch, Pierce, Fenner & Beane was a nationwide firm with branches in over ninety cities. No competitive brokerage firm had a similar organizational structure in terms of its scale and scope.

Merrill transferred the multitude of managerial skills he had honed over three decades—two decades in financial services and one decade in mass retailing—to the new enterprise. Indeed, the revitalized Merrill Lynch resembled in many ways the mass merchandising chains that the directing partner already knew so well. Brokerage represented the retail end of the capital markets, thus the emergence of a national chain of brokerage offices was a logical progression within the financial services sector. Frequently a controversial maverick during his first career on Wall Street because of his positive attitude toward advertising and sales promotion, Merrill aimed to create a brokerage firm unlike any of its predecessors, either in the United States or abroad. His goal was to provide superior service for all types of investors, but the main focus was uniquely and innovatively on the solicitation of millions of upper-middle-class households, and especially those residing in hundreds of localities beyond the metropolitan area of New York City.

In this visionary campaign, Merrill hoped to persuade tens of thousands of prudent savers to divert a portion of their financial assets away from bank accounts and whole-life insurance policies, which delivered modest returns, and into the common stocks of well-managed corporations with outstanding growth prospects. Many investments in this category qualified as 'blue-chip' stocks, with dividend yields in the range of 4–7 per cent. With these growth stocks investors could generate a competitive income and, as a bonus, they could look forward to the possibility of future capital gains.

At a meeting of branch managers representing every office in the chain in April 1940, Merrill and his closest advisors, among them Smith and Braun, divulged the key features of the firm's new operating policies.[28] The most dramatic announcement concerned the new employee compensation policy: all brokers henceforth would earn fixed salaries. For decades, on Wall Street and elsewhere, brokers and other sales personnel in the brokerage field had been compensated strictly on a commission basis. As a consequence, brokers in the same office competed not only with outsiders for customers and commissions, but with each other as well. Ted Braun, the Los Angeles management consultant, convinced Merrill to alter the traditional relationship between stockbrokers and their customers. Braun believed a radically different employee compensation plan would benefit customers and bolster public confidence in the trustworthiness and reliability of Merrill Lynch brokers and the entire support staff. If the firm could generate more business over the next two or three years, Braun thought the salary system would, in time, boost the annual incomes of brokers; meanwhile the new compensation system made all the firm's employees' paychecks more predictable than in the past.

The fundamental problem all brokerage firms faced in promoting good customer relations, Braun argued, was linked to the twin issues of trust and confidence. Whenever a broker recommended a stock trade, whether to buy or sell, many customers, somewhere in the back of their minds, wondered whether the primary motivation for the proposed transaction was to enhance the performance of their investment portfolio or, alternatively, to increase the broker's commission income. Under any commission system, this conflict-of-interest was pervasive and unavoidable. The solution, Braun insisted, was to alter the firm's compensation package and thereby the whole nature of the relationship between customer and broker. Any broker paid a regular salary, rather than a commission for initiating a transaction, would have little incentive to recommend a trade that was not genuinely in the best interest of the customer. The irresponsible 'churning' of accounts to generate commissions, which happened at so many competing brokerage firms, would cease altogether at Merrill Lynch, Braun concluded. After contemplating the matter for several weeks, Merrill concurred. The firm adopted fixed salaries for all employees in 1940, and it retained that compensation system for the next three decades.

Merrill strengthened the research capabilities of the firm by hiring a group of talented security analysts. Prior to the New Deal reforms of the 1930s, the financial information made available by corporations to the general public for analysis was uneven and not always verifiable.[29] Auditing standards were irregular.[30] The new securities laws in the mid-1930s promoted greater uniformity and transparency, and that openness gave professionals the data necessary to offer more informed recommendations to investors. The firm's security analysts could now identify more accurately those corporations with the best growth prospects in terms of sales volume and profitability. Simultaneously, the firm improved its internal information and communications systems so that brokers and their customers received the most recent and most reliable reports about developments impacting on specific corporations and the wider business community.

To reach new customers, Merrill budgeted a substantial sum of money for advertising and sales promotion. Whereas he delegated authority over branch administration and most routine managerial tasks to other senior partners, Merrill assumed personal responsibility for the formulation and implementation of the advertising programme. He authorized informative advertisements in the local newspapers of all the cities where the firm had branch offices. At Braun's suggestion, Merrill also placed a series of advertisements in *Time*, a popular weekly news magazine; it was chosen because its circulation reached a cross-section of upper-middle-class households from coast to coast.

The long-standing taboo, which had discouraged even the mildest forms of promotional activities by mainstream Wall Street firms, had finally been lifted in response to the declining volume of transactions on the New York Stock Exchange. In the late 1930s the leadership of the exchange had commissioned a national opinion poll to assess public attitudes toward the securities business, and the results were thoroughly disheartening. The general public was extremely distrustful of everyone associated with the securities sector; the reputation of stockbrokers was dismal—on a par with used-car salespersons, or lower.[31]

In the light of that discouraging news, the NYSE began running a series of public relations advertisements that asked savers to reassess their negative thinking and to reconsider investments in stocks and bonds. The message that the NYSE wanted to convey was that the investment climate on Wall Street had improved. Since reaching the depths in the summer of 1932, equity prices had risen steadily and recovered much of the territory lost in the crash.[32] No longer at odds with the Wall Street establishment in 1940, Charles Merrill and the leadership of the NYSE were on the same page with respect to the merits of informative advertising. Moreover, the basis of their agreement reflected Merrill's positive outlook, which dated back more than a quarter century to his earliest years in the securities field. Merrill Lynch's promotional activities, which were designed to attract new investors, were thankfully welcomed by almost everyone associated with the securities field.

Sceptics on Wall Street believed Merrill's ideas about expanding the universe of investors to include more middle-class households were noble and idealistic, but impractical from a cost perspective. Few of his peers in the brokerage sector thought that commission revenues on routine stock transactions would ever rise to levels sufficient to justify the expense of soliciting and then maintaining the accounts of tens of thousands of small and medium-sized accounts. The firm's own analysis of its costs and revenues revealed two stark facts: first, that only about 15 per cent of its customer base generated sufficient commission revenues to produce profits; and, second, that most small and medium-sized accounts were relatively inactive and consistently unprofitable. On the face of it, any strategy aimed at signing up thousands of marginal, money-losing accounts seemed dubious, if not suicidal. Yet Merrill was undeterred. A maverick by nature, he was stimulated by the challenge of disproving the doubters and converting what the majority believed would be an impossible goal into reality.

Merrill was convinced that, from the mass of small accounts, thousands of active traders would eventually emerge, and they would generate the volume necessary to cover the added cost of expanding and maintaining a large customer base. By nurturing younger investors and building the value of their portfolios, he anticipated that many would, in time, initiate more frequent trades and thereby advance into the ranks of genuinely profitable accounts. His plan, if workable, was a classic 'win-win' situation; customers would benefit from the sound advice of their brokers, who relied on the firm's incomparable research department, and Merrill Lynch would, in turn, generate more volume and higher revenues. Having a huge pool of small and medium-sized accounts, with constant inflows of new customers, could be advantageous, despite the expense, under the right circumstances. If Merrill's judgement proved correct, and increases in volume exceeded expectations, the firm had the potential of becoming a profitable enterprise.

In response to the aggressive promotional programmes and the word-of-mouth recommendations of satisfied customers, the growth in new accounts came quickly despite the disruptions of the Second World War. The percentage increases were impressive: 35 per cent in 1940; 60 per cent in 1941; 35 per cent in 1942; 45 per cent in 1943; and 30 per cent in 1944.[33] During the war years, the number of active accounts climbed from less than 40,000 to more than 250,000. Profits soon followed. After losing a modest amount in 1940, the firm earned $459,000 in 1941. Two years later, Merrill Lynch & Co. reported $4.8 million in pretax income; high wartime tax rates reduced that figure by over 75 per cent to $1.1 million, but the final result was nonetheless a respectable 16 per cent return on the partners' capital.[34] In the postwar years, the partnership experienced a series of new highs in terms of trading volume and profitability.

Charles Merrill's Legacy

Charles Merrill had a vision of the future that his peers on Wall Street lacked in the interwar period. He believed middle-class households, with the application of the right promotional techniques, could be drawn to investments in common stocks. These securities would supplement and complement his customers' saving accounts with deposit banks and the slowly rising cash values of their life insurance policies. Merrill also believed that the word *prudence*, with reference to investments in securities, was a term that required redefinition. In the past, prudence meant capital preservation and low returns; for investors in securities, it translated into low-risk investments in bonds, with a sprinkling of high-quality preferred stocks. Merrill thought intelligent investing was a broad concept that should be expanded to include the potential for capital gains, and the common stocks of growth companies were sensible alternatives for investors with long-term horizons. Common stocks were also a sensible hedge against inflation over the long run.

Contrary to prevailing views, he knew that investments in the common stocks of successful corporations were not, over the long run, highly speculative gambles. Given the transparency of the capital markets after 1935 and the skills of trained security analysts, that negative attitude toward common stocks was old-fashioned and out-of-date. Merrill had made his fortune by investing in the common stock of growing companies, and he saw no reason why others could not follow the same path to greater riches. According to his reasoning, any prudent financial plan for investors who were middle age or younger should, of necessity, include growth stocks as a significant component of their financial assets.

Charles Merrill died in 1956 and was succeeded as directing partner by Winthrop Smith. Over the second-half of the twentieth century, Merrill's legacy endured. His prescient vision about the potential of people's capitalism became a reality in the United States. Eventually, many brokerage firms and investment houses took their cue from the innovative policies and broad strategies of Merrill Lynch & Co. The firm had proved convincingly that middle-income households were legitimate seedbeds for a renewable customer base that produced sufficient commission revenues to cover the high costs of maintaining thousands of small accounts.[35] These small accounts, which were opened at Merrill Lynch and subsequently at competing brokerage firms, turned the United States into a nation of common stock investors.

As Merrill had argued for decades, investments in growing companies in the most rapidly expanding sectors of the US economy benefited customers. These securities produced capital gains, reduced the tax burden, and increased the value of portfolios, large and small. The inclusion of growth stocks created balanced portfolios that were neither excessively conservative nor recklessly speculative. Merrill advocated the golden mean, and he aggressively publicized that concept throughout the nation.

Merrill's boldest ideas—ideas that had once seemed revolutionary, imprudent, and impractical—were eventually accepted by the leadership of the New York Stock Exchange, by competitive firms, and by a majority of the investing public. By the last quarter of the twentieth century, these fundamental principles were commonplace and had become the recognized norm in the United States for individuals, households, and pension funds of all varieties. And that march goes on today; at the dawn of the twenty-first century, those very same principles are rapidly spreading to financial services sectors around the globe.

NOTES

1. At one point in the late 1980s, the market value of shares listed on the Tokyo Stock Exchange exceeded the values on the New York Stock Exchange by 25 per cent. By 1999, however, US equity markets were almost four times larger than their counterparts in Japan.
2. For a discussion of the current status of financial markets, see Henry Kaufman, *On Money and Markets: A Wall Street Memoir* (New York, NY: McGraw Hill, 2000).
3. The Fidelity Co., one of the nation's leading mutual fund issuers, had over $600 billion under active management at the end of the twentieth century; the company held about 3 per cent of the equities listed on US exchanges.
4. The socialist orientation of many European governments from 1945 until the 1980s was a major factor in discouraging public and private investment in corporate equities.
5. Clay Chandler and Kathryn Tolbert, 'In Japan, Reviving an Ailing Economy', *Washington Post* (8 January 2000), 14.
6. Merrill Lynch & Co., *Annual Report-1999*.
7. Edwin Perkins, *Wall Street to Main Street: Charles Merrill and Middle Class Investors* (New York, NY and London: Cambridge University Press, 1999); Henry Hecht, *A Legacy of Leadership: Merrill Lynch, 1885–1985* (New York, NY: privately printed, 1985).
8. For an overview of the US security markets, see George David Smith and Richard Sylla, 'The Transformation of Financial Capitalism: An Essay on the History of American Capital Markets', *Financial Markets, Institutions & Instruments* 2/2 (May 1993), 1–62; Kenneth Snowden, 'American Stock Market Development and Performance, 1871–1929', *Explorations in Economic History* 24/4 (1987), 327–53; Charles Geisst, *Wall Street: A History* (New York, NY: Oxford University

Press, 1997); Ron Chernow, *The House of Morgan: An American Banking Dynasty and the Rise of Modern Finance* (New York, NY: Atlantic Monthly Press, 1990).

9. J. Owen Stalson, *Marketing Life Insurance: Its History in America* (Cambridge, Mass.: Harvard University Press, 1942).

10. Vincent Carosso, *Investment Banking in America: A History* (Cambridge, Mass.: Harvard University Press, 1970).

11. In the late nineteenth century, prices generally fell at a steady rate so that the real return on interest and dividends exceeded the nominal rate. After 1896 and into the twentieth century, the price level was fairly constant.

12. Some preferred stocks had privileges that allowed the holder to convert to common stocks and obtain the benefit of higher returns.

13. Until the middle of the twentieth century, most regulated life insurance companies were not allowed to invest any of their accumulated funds in common stocks because of the risk factor.

14. The London Stock Exchange also had strict limits on advertising. See Ranald Michie, *The London Stock Exchange: A History* (Oxford: Oxford University Press, 1999) and *The London and New York Stock Exchanges, 1850–1914* (London: Allen & Unwin, 1987).

15. Stanley Chapman reveals how many of London's most successful investment bankers were originally outsiders who arrived from provincial cities in Great Britain and from continental Europe. See his *The Rise of Merchant Banking* (London: George Allen & Unwin, 1984).

16. For additional information on the power of advertising in the financial services sector, see Richard Wyckoff, *Wall Street Ventures and Adventures through Forty Years* (New York, NY: Harper, 1931), 96–7.

17. *Leslie's Illustrated Weekly*, November 1911.

18. Godfrey Lebhar, *Chain Stores in America, 1859–1962* (New York, NY: Chain Store Publishing Corporation, 1963); Richard Tedlow, *New and Improved: The Story of Mass Marketing in America* (New York, NY: Basic Books, 1990).

19. Allan Raucher, 'Dime Store Chains: The Making of Organization Men, 1880–1940', *Business History Review* 65/1 (1991), 130–63; Sandra Vance and Roy Scott, 'Butler Brothers and the Rise and Decline of the Ben Franklin Variety Stores: A Study in Retail Franchising', *Essays in Economic and Business History* 11 (1993), 258–71.

20. Statement in ML Files.

21. Martin Norden, 'The Pathe Freres Company during the Trust Era', *Journal of the University Film Association* 33/3 (1981), 15–32; Benjamin Hampton, *History of the American Film Industry: From Its Beginnings to 1931* (New York, NY: Dover, 1931).

22. Memorandum drafted by Merrill, 3 January 1929, in ML Files.

23. Robert Sobel, *The Great Bull Market: Wall Street in the 1920s* (New York, NY: W.W. Norton, 1968); Gene Smiley and Richard Keehn, 'Margin Purchases, Brokers' Loans, and the Bull Market of the Twenties', *Business and Economic History*, 2nd ser. 17 (1988), 129–42.

24. Merrill letter, 31 March 1928, ML Files.

25. Joel Seligman, *The Transformation of Wall Street: A History of the Securities and Exchange Commission and Modern Corporate Finance* (Boston, Mass.: Houghton Mifflin, 1982); Ralph De Bedts, *The New Deal's SEC: The Formative Years* (New York,

NY: Columbia University Press, 1964); Michael Parrish, *Securities Regulation and the New Deal* (New Haven, Conn.: Yale University Press, 1970).

26. For an illuminating sketch of Smith's career, see chapter four, 'Winthrop Smith, A Breed Apart', in David Heenan and Warren Bennis, *Co-Leaders: The Power of Great Partnerships* (New York, NY: John Wiley & Sons, 1999).

27. 'Theodore Braun: A Biographical Sketch' (Public Relations Office, Braun & Co., Los Angeles, Cal.).

28. The firm made a transcript of the entire meeting and distributed it to the managers in attendance; see 'Conference of Branch Managers', April 1940, in ML Files.

29. James Burk, *Values in the Marketplace: The American Stock Market under Federal Securities Law* (Berlin and New York, NY: Walter de Gruyter, 1988).

30. Paul Miranti, *Accountancy Comes of Age: The Development of an American Profession, 1886–1940* (Chapel Hill, NC: University of North Carolina Press, 1990).

31. 'What Does the Public Know about the Stock Exchange? Roper Survey Reveals Extent of Misconceptions and Misinformation about the Services of the Exchange', *Exchange Magazine* (January 1940).

32. From a low of $41 in 1932, the Dow Jones Industrial Average had climbed to $154 at the end of 1938, representing an average annual increase of 20 per cent over a seven-year period. The 1938 closing figure for the DJIA equalled its close in 1927, just prior to the final phase of the bull market. The index dropped as low as 92 in 1942, but it had gained an additional 100 points by the end of 1945.

33. Merrill Lynch & Co., *Annual Reports*, 1940–5.

34. These figures are found in the firm's annual reports, 1940–5.

35. Joseph Nocera, *A Piece of the Action: How the Middle Class Joined the Money Class* (New York, NY: Simon & Schuster, 1994).

10

Securities Markets and a Securities Company in Interwar Japan: The Case of Yamaichi

MAKOTO KASUYA

Introduction

The Japanese government first introduced a banking system and a stock exchange system after the Meiji Restoration. While the establishment and operation of both these systems contributed significantly to Japan's subsequent economic development, most historical studies have tended to focus on the development of the banking system (including many publications in English),[1] with little attention having been paid to the stock exchange system. The Japanese banking system, known now as the 'main bank system', is thought to have played a major role in Japan's postwar high economic growth.[2] But even before this, the contribution to financing by capital, reserves, and corporate bonds was high before the outbreak of the Japanese–Chinese War in 1937,[3] such that Japanese securities markets also played an important role in the development of the economy before it was transformed into a wartime planned economy in the late 1930s.

This chapter aims to analyse the conduct of securities companies in interwar Japan. With the development of the electric power and electric railroad industries in the 1920s, companies in these industries began to issue large amounts of corporate bonds. As a result, the underwriting of bonds emerged as a rapid growth area, and many financial institutions rushed into the business. Stock issues also increased during this period, with stock market booms occurring in the second-half of the 1910s and in the mid-1930s, although these were matched by significant stock market crashes in 1920 and 1929/30. The period also saw the Japanese government introduce numerous financial regulations, mainly in reaction to the occurrence of financial crises.

How did Japanese securities companies cope with this business environment? How, for example, did they compete with one another? How, also, did securities houses compete against and cooperate with other kinds of financial firms? This chapter aims to shed more light on such questions and, in particular, to examine the complex relationships at that time between securities companies and other financial institutions such as banks, trust companies, and insurance companies. Thus, for example, securities companies competed with banks in underwriting bonds, but at the same time they often had banks buy bonds that they themselves had underwritten.

In looking to address these broad questions, this chapter focuses on the particular example of Yamaichi Securities.[4] Yamaichi provides a good model of the development of the securities business in Japan, as it was one of the largest securities firms of the period and dealt in both stocks and bonds in the early 1920s.

From a Broker to a Dealer

Development of Securities Markets during and after the First World War

Economic conditions

In the period following the outbreak of the First World War, the Japanese economy prospered. During this period stock prices soared, and the amount of issued stocks multiplied many times over. But with the crisis of March 1920 the boom period of the previous decade ended. The stock price index fell from 247 in February 1920 to 120 in June 1920, and then fluctuated between 100 and 120 over most of the rest of the decade until the Great Depression (see Fig. 10.1). The period therefore witnessed a significant drop in the issue of shares. Not all industries experienced a depression, however. The electric power industry, in particular, grew rapidly over the 1920s. Urban populations increased significantly, and with them came rapid expansion of electric railways and demand for electricity. While companies in these expanding industries needed to raise funds, the stock market climate was not good for this purpose. For this reason, and because the interest rate remained low as a result of the overall bad business conditions, these firms sought to raise funds through the large-scale issuance of bonds. As a consequence, the bond market in Japan grew very rapidly over the 1920s.

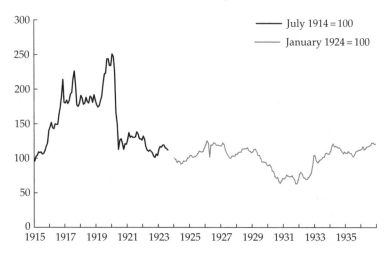

Fig. 10.1. *The stock price index*

Sources: The Bank of Japan (ed.), *Honpo keizai tokei* [Economic statistics of Japan] (Tokyo: The Bank of Japan), annual editions.

In March 1927 the central bank in colonial Taiwan, the Bank of Taiwan, which had obtained large amounts of its funds on the interbank market, went bankrupt, sparking a tremendous run on banks throughout Japan. In response, the Bank of Japan supplied emergency loans on a large scale, while the government declared a three-week moratorium on all outstanding liabilities. Through these measures, the authorities were able to end the Financial Panic of 1927. But with the closure of the Bank of Taiwan, which had been the largest single borrower of the time, the at-call money market shrank significantly.

The introduction of the Banking Law of 1927 did not clearly provide for the separation of banking business and securities business. But while the Ministry of Finance prohibited securities houses from carrying out banking business, it did allow banks to carry out securities business.

Stock markets

Prior to the Second World War, commercial codes in Japan allowed the issue of part-paid stocks, so that stocks had only to be at least one-fourth paid up at the time companies were established. Part-paid stocks were listed on stock exchanges and were traded widely. Only when it was decided at a general meeting of shareholders that shareholders should pay some of the remaining sum on their part-paid stocks, were they required to do so. But, if a shareholder failed to provide the necessary payment, that person's shares were sold at auction. Only companies whose shares were paid in full were permitted to issue new ones.

Before the Great Depression, when entrepreneurs intended to form a company, they drew up prospectuses and gathered shareholders, normally through personal connections. Banks and securities companies did not usually take part in this establishment process. Moreover, because banks, especially big banks, regarded stocks as risky, they rarely held stocks. In those cases in which companies issued shares to increase their capital, they would ordinarily use rights issues, although banks and securities firms did not usually participate in this process either. In the boom period of the 1910s, however, when stock prices were high, stocks could be offered to the public at a premium. In most cases securities companies formed syndicates to underwrite shares, or played the role of subscription agents, a role banks did not normally play. In this way, securities companies began to participate in the public subscriptions of stocks from around 1910. This type of business developed most rapidly during the boom that occurred in the latter half of the 1910s, although it shrank again in the 1920s following the boom's collapse.

The Tokyo Stock Exchange (TSE) and the Osaka Stock Exchange were established in 1878 as joint-stock companies, membership in which was subject to the regulations of the Stock Exchange Law that was introduced in the same year. Under this law (which would later be revised), corporations were not permitted to become exchange members, and members were forbidden to operate branch agencies. In contrast, nonmember houses were not subject to any government regulations until as late as 1938. Stock exchange members dealt on the exchanges for their customers as brokers, at the same time often trading on their own accounts as dealers. They also conducted both spot and forward transactions, with the forward transactions involving initially the buying (and later selling) of future stock-based contracts (without any actual transaction of stocks), by which they profited from the spread. As exchange members tended to concentrate on such forward transactions, the exchanges were widely considered too speculative by the public and were described at the time as merely 'authorized gambling places'.

In addition to exchange-based trading, stocks also changed hands in over-the-counter (OTC) markets. While the exact volume of these OTC transactions is unknown, it is widely believed to have been very large. Those securities firms that regarded OTC transactions as more important than exchange-based trading in future contracts developed customer bases slowly but steadily and, through the formation of syndicates, began to underwrite shares from around 1910.

Bond markets

There were four types of bonds in Japan before the Second World War: government (national) bonds; local bonds; bank debentures (which only certain banks were permitted to issue, such as the Japan Hypothec Bank, agro-industrial banks, the Hokkaido Takushoku Bank, the Industrial Bank of Japan (IBJ), and some other government-related banks); and corporate bonds. The issuance of the last-mentioned type of bonds grew most rapidly over the 1920s, particularly from the mid-1920s (see Fig. 10.2). With the rapid expansion of the electricity industry following the First World War, companies within this industry became the largest issuers of corporate bonds during the period, followed by railroad companies.[5]

The proportion of the total amount of corporate bonds and bank debentures in the market held by financial institutions began to increase over the second-half of the 1920s, rising from 30 per cent in 1925 to 45 per cent in 1930. Financial institutions thus became the main investors in these kinds of bonds over the period.

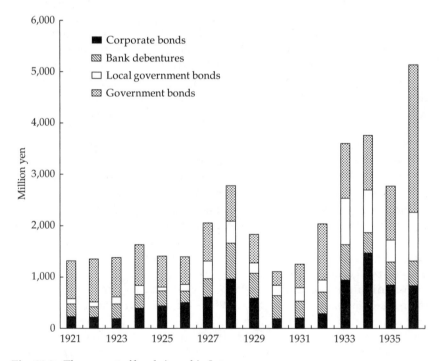

Fig. 10.2. *The amount of bonds issued in Japan*

Sources: Kaichi Shimura (ed.), *Nihon koshasai shijo shi* [History of Japanese bonds markets] (Tokyo: University of Tokyo Press, 1980); Ministry of Finance (ed.), *Kinyu jiko sankosho* [Reference book for financial statistics] (Tokyo: Naikaku Insatsukyoku), annual editions.

While banks were hesitant to underwrite shares, they were eager to underwrite bonds. Banks began to underwrite corporate bonds in the early 1900s, sometimes forming syndicates with other banks for this purpose. Under the Mortgage Debenture Trust Law (introduced in 1905), the government made it a principle to give only big banks and trust companies a licence to become a trustee of corporate bonds. Even though these large financial institutions were receiving licences and becoming trustees, most domestically issued bonds in the period before the Great Depression were unsecured, rather than secured, bonds. The bulk of first-class corporate bonds, both secured and unsecured, were underwritten by the IBJ and the large city banks. In the early 1900s the large banks began forming syndicates for the purpose of underwriting corporate bonds and the local bonds of large cities; in 1910 they began to form syndicates to underwrite national bonds.

As large banks underwrote national bonds and first-class corporate bonds, securities firms were mainly only able to sub-underwrite these bond issuances or receive subscriptions to them. But they were often able to underwrite second-class corporate bonds, local bonds issued by prefectures and small cities, and bank debentures.

Yamaichi's Activities[6]

Yamaichi's establishment

Yamaichi Goshi Kaisha[7] was established in April 1917 to take over the customers, employees, building, and trademark of the already established firm of Koike Goshi Kaisha. Kunizo Koike, the founder of Koike Goshi Kaisha, received a seat on the TSE in 1897 and opened his own brokering business. Although he sometimes engaged in speculative buying and selling of stocks, he mainly undertook arbitrage trades, and through these and a buildup of OTC transactions, he was able to engineer a steady increase in profits. It is likely that he formed close relationships with his clients in the course of such operations. His business prospering, in 1907 he moved to establish Koike Goshi Kaisha with an initial capital of one million yen. Some employees of Koike's earlier business became limited partners of the new company. Because Koike Goshi Kaisha could not gain TSE membership by law, Koike remained a member as an individual, a distinction observed as a formality if not in practice.

Koike strove to enlarge the bond business. He sub-underwrote national bonds and began fully underwriting corporate bonds in 1910. He both distributed these bonds and later facilitated their trading. Gradually the bond business expanded so as also to include new share underwriting and trading. He began to receive subscriptions of newly issued stocks in 1911 and began underwriting them in 1912. From that point on he was able to achieve a great expansion of these new stock activities. This placed Koike in the minority among his fellow TSE members, as many were apt to concentrate only on speculative trades on the Exchange.

Koike decided to close Koike Goshi Kaisha in 1916, though the actual withdrawal from the stock-brokering industry was not finalized until 1917. Following this, Koike concentrated most of his efforts on running the Koike Bank, formerly the Shoei Bank, which he had acquired in 1911 while also acting as a director of many other respectable corporations.

Nobukiyo Sugino, who had previously been a limited partner of Koike Goshi Kaisha, became president of the newly established Yamaichi Goshi Kaisha. The new entity was capitalized at one million yen, and Sugino was made a sole general partner. Other partners, of limited liabilities, were Koike's ex-partners or ex-employees. Koike himself became the largest investor in Yamaichi, but it is understood that he did not interfere in its management.[8] Sugino was granted a seat on the TSE as an individual, but this distinction was only nominal, like the earlier distinction between Koike and Koike Goshi Kaisha.

Yamaichi traded in many shares on, and outside, the TSE, and the volume of transactions soared as stock prices rose. The rapid increase in publicly issued shares in the late 1910s saw Yamaichi's activities as a subscription agent of stocks reach a very high level when it underwrote five companies' share issuances in 1919–20. Yamaichi's approach to the bond business largely followed the line taken by Koike Goshi Kaisha before it, in that it received subscriptions of foreign governments' bonds (that were floated only during the First World War), national bonds, bank debentures, and corporate bonds. Of the firm's total trading activities, however, the volume of share trade remained at a level approximately four times that of bond trade for two to three years after its establishment.[9] Yamaichi thus started business on a sound footing with healthy profits, leading to a rise in the company's capital to an estimated 1.5 million yen by 1919. The company's accumulated profits were transferred to the new capital, thus enabling bonus shares to be given to the initial partners and employees.

In February 1920 Sugino wrote in *The Bulletin of Yamaichi* to warn customers that stock prices were reaching their peak and, in line with this belief, the company simultaneously began to sell its stock holdings. The Crisis of 1920 followed only one month later, with share prices taking a steep dive. Thanks to the president's good judgement, Yamaichi was saved from serious loss and, in the period that followed, was able to gain an edge over other stockbrokers as the volume of its transactions became the largest on the TSE.

Development of the bond business

As share prices did not recover over the 1920s, and stock dealing, brokerage, underwriting, and subscribing activities all remained at low levels, the
stock business in the 1920s was not highly profitable. On the other hand,
Yamaichi's bond-related transactions increased significantly over the
period. This expansion can be attributed to three main factors. First, bond
prices gradually rose over the period. Second, the government undertook
what was called a 'Bonds Democratization Campaign' to promote the
absorption, especially by individuals, of the national bond issues that had
multiplied greatly during the First World War. In the context of this campaign, additional seats for the spot trading of bonds on the TSE were established in 1920. Sugino received one such seat, and from the beginning he
was the largest bond trader on the TSE. The third factor was the import and
export of bonds. Europeans, impoverished by the war, sold large amounts
of Japanese bonds that had been issued in the markets of London and
Paris, leading the prices of these bonds to fall and their yields to rise. These
foreign-currency denominated bonds were largely imported around
1919–20, but in the mid-1920s, as the yen became weak (particularly after
the Great Kanto Earthquake in 1923), they were exported from Japan.
Yamaichi added this international trade in bonds to its activities, as did a
few other securities houses.

As shown in Table 10.1, around the middle of the 1920s the amount of bonds
traded by Yamaichi was three or four times larger than that of stocks traded.
The ratio of bond trades to stock trades had changed dramatically, from 1 : 4
to 4 : 1, in the space of only a few years. This meant that by the mid-1920s the
company's revenue was mainly generated through its bond business.

The speed with which bond markets were growing saw many firms enter
the business. Tokushichi Nomura, a well-known stockbroker in Osaka,

Table 10.1. *The amount of Yamaichi transactions (¥1,000,000)*

	1924	1925
The amount of bonds bought and sold	440	654
The amount of bonds underwritten and sub-underwritten and the amount of bonds traded by Yamaichi acting as a subscription agent	111	165
The amount of stocks traded over the counter and on the spot market on the TSE[a]	73	151
The amount of stocks traded on the future market on the TSE[a, b]	76	136

[a] Transactions on the TSE were made in Sugino's name.
[b] The amount does not include resales or repurchases.

Source: Yamaichi Securities Co., Ltd., *Yamaichi Shoken shi*, 660–1.

founded the Osaka Nomura Bank in 1918 and transformed its bond division into Nomura Securities Co. (NSC) in 1926.[10] The Fujimoto Bill Broker Bank (Fujimoto) was originally a bill discount house, but it had strengthened its bond business since the 1910s.[11] In 1920 the IBJ founded Nikko Securities Co., initially in order to sell IBJ's debentures through it, although it also dealt in other kinds of bonds. Gen'ichi Toyama, who in 1918 established Kawashimaya to deal in stocks, was also granted a seat on the TSE, and in the 1920s Kawashimaya began to expand into the bond business. Furthermore, despite being a bank, the Koike Bank did not accept deposits from the public, and instead concentrated on its main business, that of underwriting bonds.

Intense competition between these companies led to a significant change in the way the bond business was conducted in three key respects. First, these bond trading houses established branches despite the fact that TSE members were prohibited from doing so by law. The large bond houses opened branch offices in cities such as Tokyo, Osaka, Nagoya, Kyoto, and Kobe, and also in smaller cities such as Hiroshima and Okayama.[12] These branch officers not only sold bonds but also maintained direct contacts with regionally based companies (for example, electric power companies and railroad companies), in order to further encourage the issuance of securities.

Because Sugino was a TSE member, the branches he established were those of Yamaichi Goshi Kaisha, not those of the individual stockbroker named Sugino. In 1919 he opened the first branch office in Yokohama, where many foreign banks were located. In 1923 he set up a second one in Nagoya, where he had once been employed as a bank manager. As these offices were located in the eastern part of Japan, it was also necessary to establish offices in western districts where bond markets were experiencing rapid growth. For this reason branches were established in Osaka, Kyoto, Kobe, Okayama, Hiroshima, and Fukuoka in subsequent years.[13]

Sugino regulated both the ask and bid price on each kind of security across all branch offices, with the aim of increasing the number of clients and the volume of trade across the provinces in the long run by offering relatively low prices.[14] Indeed, he established the branch offices specifically so that he could increase the number of individual customers. However, under this regulated price system it was not easy for individual branch managers to make a profit because of the low demand, and for this reason the branches did not become profit centres for Sugino, as they had been for other companies with branch offices. The hard truth was that transactions with individuals through the newly opened offices did not grow as fast as had been expected.

Second, as bond houses grew larger and began branching out, they also needed to improve their organization structures and find more talented workers. Fujimoto had already established its formal company structures and internal bylaws in the 1910s; NSC, too, had them at its establishment, while Gen'ichi Toyama drew them up in 1923. Yamaichi, however, only formalized them for the first time in 1938,[15] despite the number of Yamaichi employees in 1926 being as high as 213 (NSC, for example, employed only 84). In contrast to the securities houses, banks had been operating a branch system since the nineteenth century, and the large banks also had well-established and detailed rules. Because NSC and Fujimoto had their origins as banks, they were naturally better able to set up such structures. Stockbrokers, however, being forbidden to open branches, operated without such formalized stipulations.

Bond houses maintained research sections whose job was to produce and issue pamphlets and journals to help sell more securities. While securities firms had been publishing price lists of bonds and stocks for customers since around 1890, researchers and managers increasingly began to provide in their firms' periodicals comments on current topics and estimations of both economic conditions and the trend of securities prices. Yamaichi produced more kinds of publications than any of its competitors.

Securities firms also gradually began to employ university graduates to strengthen their research capacity or their management in general. Banks began to hire graduates as early as the 1890s, but stockbrokers were late in doing so, both because securities firms were thought of as speculative ventures and because salaries for university graduates were very high. Kunizo Koike and Tokushichi Nomura, however, began to hire graduates from around 1910, with other bond houses gradually following suit.

The third major change to the way the securities business was conducted was that, from around the beginning of the 1920s, it became necessary for securities firms to hold bonds on their own accounts. Securities firms had been acting only as subscription agents for several issues. Even if they underwrote or sub-underwrote bonds, they usually would find buyers in advance and receive prior subscriptions to almost the same value as what they had underwritten. Thus it was hardly necessary to own bonds or to raise funds in their own right. When it did become necessary, they would sell bonds to one another or on the exchanges. Sugino described this way of business as the 'brokers' style'.[16] According to him, however, 'competition became so bitter that an actual schedule of issues and the order of issue prices among peers disappeared', with the result that securities firms were forced to abandon 'brokers' style' practices. They began to underwrite many more bonds than they could receive subscriptions to before their issuance. As a result, they had to hold large amounts of surplus bonds on their own accounts while they found buyers for them. In the new environment, securities firms had to adopt this business practice in order to continue underwriting and sub-underwriting contracts. Sugino called this new way the 'dealers' style'.

As Yamaichi adopted the dealers' style practices, the amount of outstanding securities held by the firm increased from ¥6.8 million on 30 November

1923 to ¥15.8 million on 30 November 1925. Because Yamaichi was capitalized at only ¥1.5 million and the amount of reserves was about ¥1 million,
the company thus had to obtain loans. The firm's outstanding loans
increased from ¥5.4 million on 30 November 1923 to ¥14.1 million on
30 November 1925. In addition to these borrowings, the outstanding amount
of bills payable that Yamaichi had issued was ¥2.2 million on 30 November
1925.[17] Yamaichi borrowed money from the Mitsubishi Bank, the Mitsui
Bank, the Daiichi Bank, and various other financial institutions.[18] These
three principal lenders were all first-class banks in Japan, indicating that
Yamaichi had the confidence of the big banks. Moreover, because the name
Yamane Bill Broker appears on a Yamaichi lenders' list in 1925, we can conclude that Yamaichi also had access to the at-call money market at that time.
Yamaichi was the only securities firm to raise funds on the Tokyo at-call
money market in 1927. The outstanding amount of funds received by the
company was ¥48 million by the end of November 1927; this represented
37 per cent of the total outstanding amount on the market.[19] With the total volume of transactions in the money market shrinking after the Financial Panic
of 1927, Yamaichi's involvement in the money market grew considerably.

In 1925, twenty-nine bond issues were recorded on the list kept in the
boshu-bu (placement section). These included three issues of national bonds,
two of local government bonds, eight of bank debentures, and sixteen of
corporate bonds. In ten of these cases Yamaichi placed half or more than
half of the total number of bonds on issue, and in two of these it placed *all*
of the issued bonds: the three-million-yen fortieth debenture of the Chosen
Shokusan Bank (which was an agro-industrial bank in colonial Korea), and
the one-million-yen fiftieth debenture of the Kanagawa Agro-Industrial
Bank.[20] The former was solely underwritten by the Mitsubishi Bank, which
received some of the underwriting commission when it moved these bonds
from the Chosen Shokusan Bank to Yamaichi. The Mitsubishi Bank, which
used its strong credibility to advantage in its underwriting activities, had a
close relationship with Yamaichi. The other issuance may have been placed
privately by Yamaichi, as the issuance was not advertised in newspapers.
Records show, however, that the firm did not obtain a higher rate of profits
in that transaction, which may indicate that Yamaichi may have had to
return commissions to clients in order to promote the sales.

Among the eight other major issues in which Yamaichi was involved, the
¥10-million fourth bond of Oji Paper Manufacturing Co. was solely underwritten by the Mitsui Bank, while the ¥10-million third bond of Fuji Gas
Cotton Spinning Co. and the ¥3-million first bond of Kirin Brewery Co. were
both solely underwritten again by the Mitsubishi Bank. When big banks
underwrote a large amount of bonds alone, they became heavily dependent on the sales activities of the securities companies.[21] Yamaichi entirely
underwrote the ¥2-million first bond of Meguro-Kamata Electric Train Co.,
but it only sold ¥1.2 million bonds by itself. Thus Yamaichi not only sold bonds
directly to investors by itself but it also let other companies sub-underwrite

them (i.e. it was developing a capacity to operate also as an underwriter). It participated in underwriting syndicates in three of the other major issues. Lastly, the ¥3-million fiftieth debenture of the Tokyo Agro-Industrial Bank was sold through post offices, banks, and securities firms. Yamaichi traded in ¥2 million of these bonds, but without forming in this case an underwriting syndicate, so it seems that Yamaichi may have been allotted two million yen in bonds in advance, with the remainder to be floated publicly.

Expansion and contraction in 1928

Faced with these changing circumstances, Sugino felt it necessary to raise new capital to keep up with the growing market. Moreover, he realized how necessary it was to turn Yamaichi into a joint-stock company in order more easily to increase its capital. In 1926 he decided to dissolve Yamaichi Goshi Kaisha and to establish in its place Yamaichi Securities & Finance Co., Ltd. This new Yamaichi entity's authorized capital was ¥5 million, of which ¥3.5 million was paid in. Partners and employees of Yamaichi Goshi Kaisha were allotted shares in the new company, while clients and relatives as well were invited to invest in the new entity. A total of 50,000 stocks were issued, and at the opening of its operations there were 516 shareholders. Konosuke Koike, a son of Kunizo (who had died in 1925), held 7,500 stocks, while Sugino held 3,200 stocks. All of the new Yamaichi's eight directors and two of its five auditors were ex-partners of the former entity; Sugino was appointed president. In 1928 the new Yamaichi became a TSE member as a corporate body (as the ban on corporate membership had been lifted in 1922, although branches were still prohibited from ordering on the Exchange).

Soon after its reorganization, Yamaichi had to deal with the Financial Panic of 1927. The Panic predominantly affected the banking sector, however, so it did not significantly affect Yamaichi. After the Panic subsided, interest rates declined, bond prices climbed, and trade volumes and the amount of bonds issued on the market increased. The amount of domestic-ally issued bonds rose from ¥1,394 million in 1926 to ¥2,056 million in 1927, then on to ¥2,779 million by 1928. Over this period, Yamaichi's underwriting and sub-underwriting business also expanded at the same, or an even more rapid, pace. The volume of securities that Yamaichi's placement section dealt in rose from ¥403 million in the first-half of 1927 to ¥436 million in the next half, and then more than doubled to ¥915 million in the first-half of 1928.[22]

Table 10.2 shows where the placement section placed bonds between October 1927 and April 1928.[23] The main clients were the banks, with the big city banks the largest buyers of bank debentures and local government bonds, the smaller local banks the largest buyers of corporate bonds, and the special banks the largest purchasers of national bonds. As the city banks commonly let securities companies sub-underwrite corporate bonds that

Table 10.2. *The amount of Yamaichi bond sales (¥1,000)*

Sold to	National bonds	Local bonds	Bank debentures	Corporate bonds	Total
Government and local governments	—	3,911	417	10	4,338
Postal Life Insurance and Mutual aid societies	638	843	872	—	2,353
Foundations	—	2,538	759	323	3,619
Securities companies	—	200	1,221	5,392	6,813
Credit associations	—	686	2,009	445	3,140
Trust companies	276	1,022	880	6,839	9,017
Life insurance companies	128	1,572	2,042	6,599	10,341
Marine and fire insurance companies	—	110	100	130	340
Local banks	620	1,897	4,139	12,943	19,598
Savings banks	2,830	585	3,050	3,604	10,069
City banks	5,000	4,623	15,903	6,067	31,593
Special banks	7,801	3,200	1,305	55	12,361
Corporations	5	21	1,405	1,909	3,340
Individuals and others	453	791	4,434	7,707	13,386
Bond section of Yamaichi[a]	65	2,548	745	1,045	4,402
Placement section of Yamaichi[b]	—	1,328	21,404	16,494	39,226
Total	17,816	25,874	60,685	69,562	173,937

[a] The *kosai-bu* (bond section) might sell these bonds on the TSE.

[b] The *boshu-bu* (placement section) might hold bonds that Yamaichi could not sell during this period.

Note: Sales amount from October 1927 to April 1928.

Source: Boshubu saiken moshikomi kinyucho dai 3 go [Account book for application of bonds to the placement section, No. 3].

were underwritten by themselves, it was the local banks, rather than the city banks, that became the most important customers for corporate bonds. Moreover, although city banks rarely underwrote bank debentures, they were the largest purchasers. The proportion of individuals and others in the total was very low. Yamaichi sold bonds mainly to banks and other financial intermediaries, with ¥91 million worth of bonds (out of a total of ¥174 million bonds) being sold through its main Tokyo office, ¥20 million through its Osaka branch, and ¥8 million through its Nagoya branch.[24] Despite Sugino's ambition to sell bonds on a large scale to individual investors (one of the main reasons behind the opening of the provincial branches), he was largely unsuccessful in this aim. At the time, the proportion of corporate bonds bought up by financial institutions was rising, and Sugino was unable to buck this trend.

Conditions in the overall bond business remained good until July 1928, when a very large number of bonds were floated, leading to a rise in interest rates and a fall in bond prices.[25] At the time, Yamaichi was beholden to underwriting and sub-underwriting contracts in which the bonds were actually to be issued later. Given the downturn in conditions, Yamaichi either had to sell these bonds at a loss or to hold a large inventory of securities. As the volume of bonds that the company could sell at a loss was of course limited, it was forced to hold many securities. The balance of bonds and stocks held rose from ¥52 million on 31 May 1928 to ¥84 million on 30 November of that year. As Yamaichi had to borrow funds to carry these securities, the balance of its borrowings went up from ¥51 million to ¥81 million over the same period, with the semiannual interest payments it had to make at that time increasing from ¥2.3 million to ¥2.9 million. As a result the company registered a loss of ¥818,545 for the six months ending 30 November 1928. Moreover, book losses on bonds held were likely to be very large. Through this experience, Sugino came to realize the risk inherent in the 'dealers' style'. He admitted that he had been too confident of the company's ability and subsequently apologized to shareholders. In 1929 the volume of bonds underwritten or sub-underwritten by Yamaichi fell significantly and remained low throughout the period of the Great Depression, as can be seen in Table 10.3.

Other securities firms underwent very similar experiences. For example, at NSC the amount of securities held more than doubled, to ¥52 million by 30 June 1928 from ¥22 million at the end of 1927, then more than halved again to ¥21 million over the next six months, while the balance of borrowings increased from ¥54 million on 31 December 1927 to ¥79 million on 30 June 1928. NSC did not, however, record a loss at this time. It may have reduced its underwriting business earlier than Yamaichi or may not have been so deeply exposed to the business. Fujimoto held ¥53 million bonds

Table 10.3. *Yamaichi's underwriting business (¥1,000)*

	Local bonds	Bank debentures	Corporate bonds	
			Underwriting	Sub-underwriting
1928	51,301	158,484	62,036	167,950
1929	8,638	51,680	19,992	62,591
1930	14,933	24,316	3,052	10,200
1931	21,519	25,570	1,250	10,000
1932	6,011	35,200	8,300	24,250
1933	90,212	15,331	35,260	122,666
1934	72,026	43,534	41,940	261,132

Note: Most local bonds and bank debentures would have been underwritten.

Source: Yamaichi Securities Co., Ltd., *Yamaichi Shoken shi*, 721.

and shares at the end of 1928, though it had ¥27 million worth only a half a year earlier, while the amount of borrowings it had rose from ¥68 million to ¥108 million over the same period. Over the semiannual accounting period ending 30 June 1928, Fujimoto made a loss of ¥1.2 million; this came six months earlier than Yamaichi's loss.

The Mitsubishi Bank, along with the Daiichi Bank, the Daiichi Mutual Life Insurance Co., and other financial firms, supplied emergency loans to help bail out Yamaichi.[26] Because Mitsubishi Bank's managers regarded its securities as virtual reserve assets for the withdrawal of deposits, they needed the securities market to be one in which they could actually sell securities whenever they wanted. Hence they wanted to foster a securities market that would fulfil this condition,[27] and this may have been what prompted Mitsubishi Bank to rescue Yamaichi at this time.

Big banks like Mitsubishi Bank allowed securities companies like Yamaichi to sub-underwrite bonds so as to mitigate the risks inherent in underwriting. A big bank was unable to be sole underwriter of a large amount of bonds; it needed the assistance of securities firms' sub-underwriting. Now, if sub-underwriters were unable to sell securities and were facing bankruptcy, they would be unable to pay off their debts to the banks. Securities firms also raised funds on the short-term money market, and the big banks were suppliers of funds in this market. Therefore, the big banks had to supply additional emergency funds to those securities houses that faced insolvency, lest there be a financial panic. Through their experiences in the late 1920s, the large banks came to realize the consequence of their risk management practices, in that they were actually running large risks when they thought they could avoid risks by making securities firms sub-underwrite their bonds.

Growth and Limitations as a Sub-underwriter of Bonds

Structural Change within Bond Markets

The Great Depression, and recovery from it

In Japan the stock price index went down from 113 in March 1929 to 95 in September of that year. Commodity prices also began to decline in the autumn of 1929. The Great Depression began in the United States and spread to Japan. The Japanese economy fell into a deflationary period.

Following the abandonment of the gold standard by the United Kingdom in September 1931, the Japanese government, which had only adopted it in January 1930, also abandoned it in December 1931. Following this decision, the yen immediately depreciated against the US dollar from about ¥100 = $50 to about ¥100 = $30. This in turn led Japanese exports to increase, while imports, with the added factor of a rise in the customs tariffs, decreased. The Japanese government issued deficit-covering bonds and spent much of the funds on both the Manchurian Incident and the restoration of farming villages hit hardest by the Depression. Through these policies Japan was able to be the first country to recover from the Depression.

From around 1932 on, the government began gradually to take control of the country's financial markets. First of all, it brought in the Capital Flight Protection Act of 1932 and the Foreign Exchange Control Law of 1933, which acted to impose restrictions on the foreign exchange dealings of financial institutions. Second, the Convertible Bank Note Regulations were revised, and the fiduciary note issue ceiling was raised from ¥120 million to ¥1 billion, so that the amount of notes issued was not restricted by the amount of gold reserves held at the Bank of Japan. After the government introduced this de facto managed currency system in 1932, the central bank began to buy national bonds directly from the government and then sold them to financial institutions. In this way the influence of the authorities on financial markets grew increasingly stronger. The Bank of Japan reduced the official bank rate from 6.57 to 4.38 per cent in 1932, then to 3.65 per cent in 1933 and to 3.285 per cent in 1936. The postal savings rate was also lowered from 4.2 to 3 per cent. In the face of such conditions, banks were forced to lower the agreed rate on term deposits from 4.7 to 4.2 per cent in 1932, then to 3.7 per cent in 1933 and to 3.3 per cent in 1936, in a general process of alignment with the official discount rate.

When the Japanese–Chinese war broke out in July 1937, the Japanese economy shifted to a wartime controlled economy. In September 1937 the government introduced the Temporary Export and Import Commodities Measures Law and the Law for the Extraordinary Adjustments of Funds. The former regulated not only exports and imports but also the production, sale, and consumption of commodities, while the latter regulated money markets in order to restrict investments in peacetime industries and to promote investments in wartime industries. The National General Mobilization Act was enforced the following year, and this allowed the government to control the whole national economy.

The 'Campaign to Clean Up Corporate Bonds'

As the depression deepened, issues of corporate bonds decreased, with the volume falling from ¥963 million in 1928 to ¥191 million in 1930. Moreover, many companies failed to repay their debts, while some could not pay back the principal or the interest on their issued bonds. Still, the issuance of bonds began to grow again in 1933 as the Bank of Japan guided interest rates lower. The value of corporate bonds on issue in 1934 had jumped to ¥1,430 million. As investment in manufacturing industries remained low, most of the corporate bonds issued at this time were used as refunding bonds, in that companies were undertaking conversion operations to take advantage of the lower interest rate environment.

Big banks began to suspect that unhealthy bonds were being issued that would not easily be redeemed when business activities recovered. On this understanding, first-class banks, trust companies, and insurance companies in Tokyo came to an agreement on bond issuance. They declared in 1933 that they would give preference to secured bonds issued by firms that had established sinking funds,[28] and that they would only underwrite this kind of bond. In addition, they decided that banks should not advance any money on the security of a bond that they did not favour, while trust companies and insurance companies should buy only bonds to which they gave preference. As a representative of first-rate financial institutions in Tokyo, Toyotaro Yuki, president of the IBJ, asked securities firms to conduct their underwriting business in accordance with this agreement. Securities houses approved of the aims of the proposal.

Because first-class financial organizations intended to remove bad bonds from the market, their campaign to increase collateral-backed bonds and to make issuers of bonds establish sinking funds came to be referred to as the 'Campaign to Clean Up Corporate Bonds'. The government also acted in support of this campaign, revising in 1933 the Mortgage Debenture Trust Law so as to permit the issue of open-ended mortgage bonds. This revision made it easier for companies to issue bonds backed by their corporate collateral. As a result of the Campaign the proportion of issued secured corporate bonds out of the total amount of corporate bonds rose from 12 per cent in 1930 to 42 per cent in 1935. If the government-related South Manchuria Railway Co. and the Toyo Takushoku Co. had not continued to issue large amounts of unsecured bonds at the time, the total proportion of secured bonds would have been much higher.

Diffusion of these collateral bonds caused a particular problem for securities firms. Companies were required to designate trustees to issue them, and to become a trustee one needed to be licensed. The government, however, gave licences only to large banks and large trust companies (as mentioned earlier). A trustee normally underwrote bonds alone or formed an underwriting syndicate, and big banks did not usually allow securities firms to join a syndicate. Thus it became difficult for securities firms to underwrite bonds under the new arrangements.

In the 1930s large banks became increasingly cooperative, often forming underwriting syndicates, while during the 1920s they most often solely underwrote. The agreement on secured bonds might be considered an out-come of this new cooperation. Because the amount of bonds issued by each issuing company increased during the period of economic recovery from the Depression, it became difficult even for large banks to underwrite bonds alone. Still, if the banks made securities firms sub-underwrite some of the bonds that they underwrote, they were exposed to greater risk, as was shown in the crises of bond houses in 1928, and this may have been one reason why syndicates were formed. Further, it is believed that severe competition for underwriting in the 1920s often made the terms of under-writing contracts unfavourable for the underwriters. This environment encouraged many underwriters to underwrite securities without strict screening for the risks involved. Thus, syndicates were seen as necessary to avoid such cutthroat competition.

Securities firms usually had no choice other than to sub-underwrite cor-porate bonds.[29] They also were forced to underwrite bank debentures and local government bonds that were usually unsecured. These pressures led securities firms to begin to underwrite bonds cooperatively. In March 1931 the five principal securities companies (Yamaichi, Koike Securities Co.,[30] NSC, Nikko Securities Co., and Fujimoto) established an association in order to avoid competition against one another in the business of under-writing local government bonds. This collaboration was also extended to the underwriting of corporate bonds. In this way the average number of sub-underwrites on each corporate bond issue increased over the 1930s, and the five securities firms within the association participated in the sub-underwriting of most of the corporate bonds at the time.[31]

Yamaichi's Bond Business

The decline in bond business during the depression

After the Financial Panic of 1927 the import of foreign-currency denomi-nated bonds increased because interest rates in the United States rose while the prices of Japanese bonds fell. Through their branches in the United States, big Japanese banks bought these bonds because of their high yields, while securities companies imported them to sell to clients in Japan. As prices of Japanese bonds declined in foreign markets further after the out-break of the Manchurian Incident, the import of bonds continued. A *gaikoku-bu* (foreign affairs section) in Yamaichi was set up in the second-half of 1929. The amount of bonds dealt in by the section was ¥61 million in 1930 and ¥22 million in 1931, respectively, while in 1929 it was only ¥9 million. Although it is not certain that these figures include the volume of foreign-currency dominated bonds sold domestically, it is certain that the import of such bonds expanded very fast over the period. But then in December 1931 the export of gold was forbidden, and in July 1932 the Capital Flight Protection Act was introduced. As a result, Yamaichi found it very difficult to continue to import bonds, with the amount of bonds traded by its *gaikoku-bu* falling sharply to a mere ¥7 million in 1932 and down further to ¥3 million in 1933.

While Yamaichi's bond business declined with the drop in total bond issuance in Japan during the Depression, its bill transactions grew over the period. If a company wanted to raise funds, it could not issue bonds at once. Rather, it had to procure the necessary funds by some other means before it was able to issue bonds. If banks planned to underwrite the bonds, they could simply lend the amount required to the company. But if securities companies were unable to lend such funds, they could not underwrite the securities. Therefore, in order to overcome this funding problem, underwriting securities firms first asked the company to issue notes (bills), which the securities firms would then sell. In this way, the bill business was, in practice, closely related to the underwriting business. With the poor financial conditions during the Depression, companies issued notes while they waited for a good opportunity to issue bonds. Although Yamaichi had dealt in bills since the 1920s, it only began to report the volume of its note transactions from 1931. As that figure was ¥123 million, and the figure declined significantly to ¥43 million in the following year, the growth of the bill trade during the Depression can be assumed.

Yamaichi usually sold two-month bills to local banks, trust companies, and other financial organizations. For this reason the composition of the buyers of bills was almost the same as that of buyers of corporate bonds, with the main exception being life insurance companies, which did not purchase notes to the same degree as corporate bonds because they preferred longer term investments.

Among the other securities companies, the volume of bills dealt in by NSC fell from ¥176 million in 1931 to ¥72 million in 1932.[32] The degree of decline was similar to Yamaichi's. Although NSC traded in more bills than Yamaichi, it, like Yamaichi, regarded the bill business as supplementary to the underwriting business.

Acquisition of the Chiyoda Trust Company

Yamaichi's bond business, including its dealings, brokerage, and underwriting activities, developed rapidly along with the Japanese economic recovery after 1933. Thus, for example, in 1932 a special committee for underwriting was formed within the firm, whose purpose was to increase underwriting contracts, promote bond sales, and screen issuers. Yamaichi principally underwrote agro-industrial banks' debentures and corporate bonds issued by electric power companies or railway companies in the provinces. It sub-underwrote first-class corporate bonds that were under-written by large banks and large trust companies. As for corporate bonds, the amount of underwriting undertaken did not increase as much as sub-underwriting, as can be seen in Table 10.3.

This pattern was common to all securities firms, with the only exception being NSC. The amount of corporate bonds underwritten by Yamaichi was almost equal to that by NSC in the 1920s, as shown in Table 10.4. Yet after the Depression NSC's underwriting business grew much more rapidly than Yamaichi's. The difference between the two companies was in their respective success as sole underwriters. Most of the solely underwritten bonds listed in Table 10.4 can be identified, and identified bonds can be classified by collateral. The result is shown in Table 10.5, which shows that NSC was able to solely underwrite a large amount of secured bonds, while Yamaichi was hardly able to do any. When the issuance of collateral-backed bonds began in earnest in the 1930s, NSC was able to cope well

Table 10.4. *Amount of bonds underwritten by securities companies (¥1,000)*

	NSC		Yamaichi		Others	
	A	B	A	B	A	B
1927–9	23,300	76,567	24,050	64,903	22,600	10,214
1933–5	101,110	125,378	21,000	95,804	25,000	51,798

Note: A is the amount of bonds underwritten solely by each company. B is the amount of bonds underwritten by each company within syndicates. The amount of bonds underwritten by one company in each issue is the amount of the issue divided by the number of underwriting members. B is calculated by adding up all the amounts of each issue for each securities company.

Source: Kaichi Shimura, *Nihon shihon shijo bunseki*, 328.

Table 10.5. *Amount of bonds underwritten solely by NSC and Yamaichi (¥1,000)*

	NSC		Yamaichi	
	Secured	Unsecured	Secured	Unsecured
1927–9	6,650	150	—	22,050
1933–5	57,900	42,400	500	15,000

Note: The amount of identifiable solely underwritten bonds is extracted from Table 10.4.

Sources: Kaichi Shimura, *Nihon shihon shijo bunseki*, 328–9; the IBJ, *Shasai ichiran* [List of corporate bonds] (Tokyo: IBJ, 1970).

with the new environment, and for this reason it moved decisively ahead of Yamaichi.

As mentioned earlier, NSC was spun off from the Nomura Bank in 1925; it was, therefore, able to maintain a very intimate relationship with the Nomura Bank, which had already been granted a licence to become a trustee of corporate bonds in 1918. When a company wanted to issue secured bonds, a securities firm might ask the bank to be a trustee and to underwrite the bonds. In return, the bank was supposed to request the securities firm to underwrite bonds in the case where a company wanted to appoint the bank as a trustee (because of its relationship as an important customer of the bank). Now, while organizations other than the Nomura Bank became trustees of bonds underwritten by NSC, it is clear that NSC enjoyed a competitive edge because of its relation with the Nomura Bank.[33]

Yamaichi had to do something to remain competitive with NSC. The solution, it was thought, was the acquisition in April 1934 of a 43 per cent stake in Chiyoda Trust Company (where Sugino was installed as president). But the Chiyoda Trust Co.'s performance had been poor, so it had not been licensed as a trustee by the authorities. When it was acquired by Yamaichi, it was widely believed that the firm's profitability would have to be improved before the government would grant it a trustee's licence.[34] Despite this widely held opinion, Sugino applied to the Ministry of Finance for a licence soon after his appointment as president. His application was turned down. Reacting to this rejection, Sugino in December 1934 changed the newly acquired company's business from trust to investment (and changed its name to Chiyoda Securities Investment Company). Nevertheless, Yamaichi's new strategy to deal with the restrictions imposed on it by the 'Campaign to Clean Up Corporate Bonds' was undermined by the government regulations of the times.

Failure as a Stock Dealer

The Boom in the Stock Market Around the Middle of the 1930s

With the general recovery of share prices around the mid-1930s the volume of shares traded and the amount of shares issued increased. At the same time, the process involved in establishing companies also began to change. For example, the number of subsidiaries and joint ventures of large corporations as a proportion of all newly established companies rose, thus reducing the role of promoters from what it had been in the 1910s. In most cases, however, some part of the initial stock offerings in these newly founded companies were sold to the public. In these instances, securities companies underwrote these shares or received their subscriptions as agents.

In addition to public subscriptions, secondary offerings also increased after the Depression. These involved large shareholders selling their own holdings to the public at a premium. Zaibatsu, large business groups of companies (in some of which families had controlling stakes), sold stocks in this fashion because they had been accused of monopolizing profits during the Depression. The proceeds of these sales were used in large part to invest in heavy chemical industries. Other large shareholders of the time engaged in similar sales to enable further investment in the companies under their influence that were increasing their capital at a rapid pace. Securities companies also took part in these offerings, though zaibatsu sold many of their stocks directly to life insurance companies.

Corporations and insurance companies emerged as large shareholders, while the proportion of stocks held by individuals declined between 1919 and 1936, leading to the gradual institutionalization of stockholders.[35] In October 1930 several life insurance companies founded the Seiho Securities Company (Stock Holding Company of Life Insurance) to support the stock market. The amount of policy reserves held by life insurance companies increased rapidly in the 1930s, and the high yields on shares at the time made them popular reserve assets among life insurers. While Seiho Securities was dissolved in February 1933 on the back of rising stock prices, in its place a Second Seiho Securities was established in August 1935 in order to underwrite, buy, and sell securities. The influence of life insurance companies on the stock market was growing.

Neither NSC nor Fujimoto dealt in stocks before the Great Depression because they thought the shares business was too speculative. But when blue-chip stocks such as zaibatsu-affiliated companies' stocks were offered to the public, individuals who had stayed away from the stock market on account of its speculative aspects began to be interested in stocks. In addition, large financial institutions, which were NSC's and Fujimoto's main bond clients, were also expanding their holdings of stocks. These factors led Fujimoto to commence the share business in May 1934 and NSC in May 1938. Yamaichi now had two new competitors in this market.

Placement to Financial Institutions

In December 1935 Sugino, who had served as president of Yamaichi since the establishment of Yamaichi Goshi Kaisha, resigned his position to become president of the TSE. Osamu Ohta succeeded him as president at Yamaichi. Ohta graduated from the University of Tokyo and entered Koike Goshi Kaisha in 1916. He was promoted to a limited partner in 1919 and to a director in 1921. When the Yamaichi Securities & Finance Co. was established, he was elected a managing director. He was chiefly involved in the bond business and built up close connections with managers of large financial organizations, including Kiyoshi Seshita at the Mitsubishi Bank and Taizo Ishizaka at Daiichi Mutual Life Insurance Co. (DLI).[36]

Ohta dealt in futures on the TSE, whereas Sugino had focused on spot transactions. Ohta was different, however, from the traditional type of speculative dealer who aimed at earning only the spread between the buying and the selling price. He brought a new way of trading to the share business. He bought shares for future delivery on the TSE futures market, found buyers for these shares, and received their delivery. While there was nothing particularly new in this, where Ohta's originality lay was in the fact that he sold stocks to financial institutions such as life insurance companies on a large scale. He was able to do this on the basis of the close connections he had earlier formed with these companies when selling bonds. Obviously, he could buy stocks on the spot market in the same way, but the volume of trade on the spot market was much smaller than that on the futures market, and so the price would have been pushed up sharply if he had ordered a large sum of stocks in that market. In other words, he utilized the futures market in order to prevent volatile fluctuations of stock prices. Yamaichi was often exposed to price fluctuation risk in the interval between the time of purchase and the time of sale, as it did not always deal in stocks on a commission basis. As stock prices were generally rising at the time, and because Ohta usually began this type of transaction with a purchase, exposure to this risk did, in fact, also provide profits for Yamaichi.

Because the shares of Yamaichi Securities & Finance Co. had been fully paid by January 1934, it issued new stocks in December 1936 to raise the firm's total capitalization to ¥10 million. This new issue involved an allocation of 100,000 stocks, 50,000 of which were allotted to existing shareholders, and 50,000 of which were allocated to clients, directors, employees, and other related bodies. One result of this new allocation of shares was that DLI became the largest shareholder in Yamaichi with a 7.5 per cent stake (or 15,000 shares), a fact that helped foster a solid relationship between the two firms.

Around the beginning of 1937 Ohta began to pay close attention to the Kanegafuchi Cotton Spinning Company (KCS), which at the time was one of the largest cotton spinning companies in Japan. In December 1936 the authorized capital of KCS was ¥60 million, and the paid-in capital was ¥39,063,825 (837,447 shares out of a total of 1.2 million shares were only half paid). It is believed that Ohta somehow received information that KCS planned to make all its shares fully paid so as to increase its capital base.[37]

Since new stocks were normally allotted to shareholders at face value, and since KCS's equity price was higher than face value, Ohta predicted that the price of half-paid stocks would soon rise. Hence Ohta began to purchase mainly part-paid stocks in KCS. Yamaichi owned 3,071 fully paid stocks and 14,580 part-paid stocks in KCS in December 1936.[38] As he had expected, KCS directors soon announced that part-paid stocks should be partially paid in by a quarter of face value by March 1937, and this announcement saw the stock price rise. Ohta sold much of his holdings on to financial institutions. This operation attracted considerable attention among the stockbroker community at the time.[39]

The DLI had more actively invested in shares than the average life insurance company, and it also bought stocks in KCS from Yamaichi at this time. The outstanding number of KCS stocks held by the DLI was 3,000 fully paid stocks on 31 August 1935, 5,000 fully paid and 65,000 part-paid ones on 31 August 1936, and 125,000 part-paid on 31 August 1937.[40] The proportion of KCS stocks in DLI's total stock holdings rose from 1 per cent on 31 August 1935 to 18 per cent by 31 August 1937. Such concentration of investment on one issue was exceptional (from the viewpoint of risk diversification) within large life insurance companies of that time.

Ohta's tactics initially seemed to succeed. But with the onset of the Japanese–Chinese War in July 1937, and with KCS owning factories in China and operating a cotton spinning business (a peacetime industry) that would not gain favour during wartime, the price of KCS stocks fell sharply. The price of the part-paid stock peaked in July at ¥295, before falling to a low of ¥193 in August 1937. Both DLI and Yamaichi were left with latent losses on their KCS stocks, thus turning Ohta's scheme into a serious failure.

Ohta felt a great deal of responsibility for these losses, and he was anxious to make up for them somehow. When the Japanese army occupied Nanjing in December 1937, he forecasted stock prices would become bullish again. Once more he began to buy stocks in KCS, although this time cautious financial institutions chose not to purchase as many shares as they had before. But KCS's stock price did not climb as he had hoped, and Ohta became increasingly anxious. Finally he resorted to purchasing part-paid stocks in the TSE for future delivery, a speculative venture that was well known for its large price fluctuations. He even personally undertook these purchases on his own account, despite the fact that such activity was forbidden by Yamaichi; as president, he chose to break the prohibition. In the end, and in spite of his expectations, the price of the TSE part-paid stock declined. His speculation ended in failure. He was forced to resign as president in May 1938, and this was followed, in December 1938, with the first formal stipulation of the rules and bylaws of Yamaichi. The number of employees in November of that year was 564. In its business administration, Yamaichi was thus well behind NSC, which had formed rules and bylaws at its establishment in 1926, when the number of its staff had been only eighty-four.

Concluding Remarks

Yamaichi started its business as a stockbroker during the First World War. As the bond markets grew in the 1920s, Yamaichi strengthened its bond business. It sub-underwrote bonds underwritten by big banks and trust companies and sold them to financial institutions. It also competed directly with banks in underwriting bonds, underwriting mainly corporate bonds issued by electric power companies and electric railroad companies in the provinces, bank debentures, and local bonds. It also dealt in two-month bills for its clients to raise funds. It raised funds from first-class banks, and also directly on the at-call money market. Furthermore, it both imported and exported foreign-currency denominated bonds, so that, overall, it can be said that Yamaichi was able to connect the money market and capital market, and the domestic market and foreign market.

The climate of conducting business changed in the 1930s. First, the international flow of funds began to be controlled, such that Yamaichi's import and export of bonds ceased. Second, the issuance of bonds came under the strong influence of big banks and trust companies with the launch of the 'Campaign to Clean Up Corporate Bonds' which acted to force Yamaichi into sub-underwriting. Third, the stock boom of the mid-1930s was brought about by an easy money policy by monetary authorities after 1932. The process of establishing firms and increasing authorized and paid-in capital became increasingly controlled by the government after 1937, however, leaving Yamaichi to suffer heavy losses in its stock business in 1937 and 1938.

Unlike NSC, Yamaichi did not have the advantage of an affiliated trust company, hence its bond business lagged behind that of NSC. Furthermore, Yamaichi's managerial control was not as strict as NSC's.

NOTES

1. For more on Japanese banking, see Raymond W. Goldsmith, *The Financial Development of Japan, 1868–1977* (New Haven, Conn.: Yale University Press, 1983);

Norio Tamaki, *Japanese Banking: A History, 1859–1959* (Cambridge: Cambridge University Press, 1995); and William M. Tsutsui (ed.), *Banking in Japan, vol.1: The Evolution of Japanese Banking, 1868–1952* (London and New York, NY: Routledge, 1999).

2. Masahiko Aoki and Hugh Patrick (eds), *The Japanese Main Bank System: Its Relevance for Developing and Transforming Economies* (Oxford: Oxford University Press, 1994).

3. Juro Teranishi, 'Loan Syndication in War-Time Japan and the Origins of the Main Bank System', in Aoki and Patrick, *The Japanese Main Bank System*, 55.

4. Yamaichi Goshi Kaisha was established in 1916 and was transformed into the Yamaichi Securities & Finance Co. in 1926. For the sake of simplicity, these firms are referred to as Yamaichi when it is unnecessary to distinguish between them.

5. Because the rate of interest declined gradually and business demand for credit was not so great owing to the poor overall economic conditions, a large number of conversion operations were undertaken.

6. When no reference is made to other source materials, the descriptions of Yamaichi are based on Yamaichi Securities Co., *Yamaichi Shoken shi* [History of Yamaichi Securities Co., Ltd.] (Tokyo: Yamaichi Securities Co., Ltd., 1958).

7. A goshi kaisha is a partnership that has juridical personality and a stated amount of capital. It is composed of general partners with unlimited liabilities and limited partners.

8. Sugino declared in Yamaichi's promotion prospectus that Koike was only an investor, not an active partner.

9. Yamaichi Archive A8-5.

10. The name of the Osaka Nomura Bank was changed to the Nomura Bank in 1927, but hereafter, for the sake of simplicity, the name Nomura Bank is used in accounts of events before 1927, too.

11. The Fujimoto Bill Broker Bank was transformed into Fujimoto Bill Broker Securities in 1934.

12. NSC established a New York subbranch, and Fujimoto established an affiliate company in Dover, Delaware that had branches in New York, San Francisco, and Osaka. They exported securities to Japan and imported them from Japan.

13. Yamaichi acquired half of the issued stocks of Hamashin Securities Co. in Hamamatsu near Nagoya in 1923 and opened a branch in Niigata in northern Japan in 1926. It also opened a small branch office at Kyobashi in Tokyo.

14. Yamaichi Archive A8-5.

15. There were some 'sections' in Yamaichi before 1938, but they were customary ones, not stipulated.

16. Yamaichi Archive A8-5.

17. Yamaichi Archive B3-1.

18. Yamaichi Archive B4-2.

19. The Bank of Japan, *Kanto shinsai yori showa ninen kin'yu kyoko ni itaru waga zaikai* [The business world from the Great Kanto Earthquake to the Financial Panic of 1927], in the Bank of Japan (ed.), *Nihon kin'yu shi shiryo Showa-hen*, 24kan [Materials on monetary history in the Showa period, xxiv] (Tokyo: Printing Bureau, Ministry of Finance, 1969), 143.

20. Yamaichi Archive B4-2.

21. Seihin Ikeda, a managing director of Mitsui Bank, wanted the Bank to sell as many securities as possible by itself, but his plan was not fully realized. Shinji Ogura, *Senzenki Mitsui Ginko kigyo torihiki kankei shi no kenkyu* [Study of the history of Mitsui Bank's relationship with firms] (Tokyo: Senbundo, 1990), 274.

22. What the figures cover is unknown, but they may include the volume of securities underwritten and sub-underwritten by Yamaichi and the volume of securities traded by Yamaichi as a subscription agent. If Yamaichi underwrote ¥10 million of bonds and placed ¥8 million of bonds from them, the volume of transactions through this section would be ¥18 million. The amount relating to stocks may also be included in the figures for the section, but it would have been negligible in this period.

23. It is unknown whether or not Table 10.2 shows all bonds that the section sold during the period. Two national bonds, eighteen local government bonds, eighteen bank debentures, and seventeen corporate bonds are covered in Table 10.2.

24. The figures for the main office in Table 10.2 do not include the amount of bonds sold to the placement section and to the bond section.

25. The expectation that Japan would soon return to a gold standard also caused interest rates to rise at this time.

26. Sohachi Yamaoka, *Ohta Osamu den* [Life of Osamu Ohta] (Tokyo: Kasuga Publishing Co., 1939), 182.

27. The Mitsubishi Bank, *Mitsubishi Ginko shi* [History of the Mitsubishi Bank] (Tokyo: The Mitsubishi Bank, 1954), 204.

28. Kaichi Shimura, *Nihon shihon shijo bunseki* [Analysis of Japanese securities markets] (Tokyo: University of Tokyo Press, 1969), 297.

29. Securities companies often underwrote corporate bonds with trust companies.

30. Koike Securities Co. was established in 1930 and merged with Koike Bank in 1933.

31. Securities firms normally did not form sub-underwriting syndicates. They individually concluded a contract with the lead underwriter. Shimura, *Nihon shihon shijo bunseki*, 451.

32. Nomura Securities Co., *Nomura Shoken Kabushiki Kaisha junen shi* [Ten-year history of Nomura Securities] (Osaka: Nomura Securities Co., 1936), 100. In the ten-year period between 1926 and 1935, the peak year for NSC trade in bills was 1929.

33. Tokushichi Nomura took control of the Taisho Trust Co. in March 1933 and changed its name to Osaka Trust Company. Otogo Kataoka, who was president of NSC, was appointed president. Osaka Trust Co. changed its name to Nomura Trust Co. in 1938.

34. *Daiyamondo* [Diamond], 21 January 1934, 89.

35. Shimura, *Nihon shihon shijo bunseki*, 406–28.

36. Yamaoka, *Ohta Osamu den*, 115.

37. Reikichi Nanba, *Kabukai seikatsu rokuju nen* [My sixty years in the world of stocks] (Tokyo: Kawade Publishing, 1953), 186. Sohachi Yamaoka rejected this opinion; see Yamaoka, *Ohta Osamu den*, 211.

38. KCS, *Semiannual Report* for the accounting period ending 25 December 1936.

39. It is thought that Ohta sold famous shipping companies' stocks in the same way.

40. DLI, *Annual Reports* for 1935, 1936, and 1937.

INDEX